The Philippines

Nearly five million migrant workers from the Philippines are employed in over 190 countries and territories. They work as doctors and domestic helpers, engineers and entertainers, seamstresses and surveyors. It is through their collective labor that the Philippines has assumed a global presence.

The Philippines: Mobilities, Identities, Globalization seeks to understand how the Philippines has become the world's largest exporter of government-sponsored temporary contract labor and, in the process, has dramatically reshaped both the processes of globalization, and also our understanding of globalization as a concept.

James A. Tyner (Ph.D., University of Southern California) is Professor of Geography at Kent State University. His research interests include population geography, political geography, and Southeast Asia. He is the author of nine books, including *Made in the Philippines: Gendered Discourses and the Making of Migrants* (Routledge).

***Global Realities:* A Routledge Series**
Edited by **Charles C. Lemert**, *Wesleyan University*

The Series *Global Realities* offers concise accounts of how the nations and regions of the world are experiencing the effects of globalization. Richly descriptive yet theoretically informed, each volume shows how individual places are navigating the tension between age-old traditions and the new forces generated by globalization.

Books in the Series

Available:

Australia by Anthony Moran
Global Ireland by Tom Inglis
Global Hong Kong by Gary McDonogh and Cindy Wong
The Koreas by Charles K. Armstrong
The Netherlands by Frank J. Lechner
The Globalization of Israel by Uri Ram
Morocco by Shana Cohen and Larabi Jaidi
On Argentina and the Southern Cone by Alejandro Grimson and Gabriel Kessler
China and Globalization, Second Edition by Doug Guthrie

Forthcoming:

Iberian Worlds by Gary McDonogh
Military Legacies by James Tyner
Urbanizing A New Global South by AbdouMaliq Simone
Turkey by Alev Cinar
South Africa and the Long History of Globalization by Kevin R. Cox

The Philippines

Mobilities, Identities, Globalization

JAMES A. TYNER

Routledge
Taylor & Francis Group
NEW YORK AND LONDON

First published 2009
by Routledge
711 Third Avenue,
New York, NY 10017

Simultaneously published in the UK
by Routledge
2 Park Square, Milton Park, Abingdon,
Oxon OX14 4RN

Routledge is an imprint of the Taylor & Francis Group, an informa business

Typeset in 11/14pt Joanna by RefineCatch Limited, Bungay, Suffolk

Library of Congress Cataloging in Publication Data
Tyner, James A., 1966–
The Philippines : mobilities, identities, globalization / by James A. Tyner.
p. cm.
1. Alien labor—Philippines. 2. Contract labor—Philippines. 3. Globalization—Philippines.
4. Urban poor—Philippines—Manila. I. Title.
HD8716.5.T96 2008
331.6′2599—dc22

2008006967

ISBN10: 0–415–95806–7 (hbk)
ISBN10: 0–415–95807–5 (pbk)
ISBN10: 0–203–89241–0 (ebk)

ISBN13: 978–0–415–95806–6 (hbk)
ISBN13: 978–0–415–95807–3 (pbk)
ISBN13: 978–0–203–89241–1 (ebk)

Contents

To Belinda, Jessica, and Anica Lyn

Acknowledgments

My first visit to the Philippines came in 1993. For me, Manila seemed like a second home. There was much of the city to remind me of my own home, Los Angeles. To be sure, Manila resembled LA at a superficial level: The chaos and congestion, traffic and pollution. But underneath the obvious, I sensed something else. Manila, and the Philippines as a whole, is a fascinating, captivating place. And with my knowledge of its history and geography, my appreciation increased exponentially. For many families in the Philippines, international migration is a global reality. The causes and consequences are complex, and this book addresses these concerns.

At Routledge, thanks are extended first to my editor, Stephen Rutter, for his guidance, patience, advice, and vision in seeing this book through to completion. It is a much better work because of his efforts. Thanks also are extended to Charles Lemert, series editor, and to Dave McBride, who originally commissioned me to write this book. And lastly at Routledge, thanks are extended to Beatrice Schraa, who guided my book through the production process.

Heartfelt thanks are extended to the many colleagues who have helped me over the years: Stuart Aitken, Marla Asis, Adrian Bailey, Rochelle Ball, Graziano Battistella, Paul Boyle, Larry Brown, Dennis Conway, Michael Dear, Mona Domosh, Pierrette Hondagneu-Sotelo, Graeme Hugo, Philip Kelly, Lisa Law,

Kevin McHugh, Deirdra McKay, Jan Monk, Doracie Nantes, Rhacel Parreñas, Gary Peters, Nicola Piper, Laura Pulido, Curt Roseman, Nanda Shrestha, Rachel Silvey, Nobue Suzuki, Richard Ulack, Richard Wright, and Brenda Yeoh. Over the years, I have benefited also from working with many outstanding graduate students: Steve Butcher, Sutapa Chattopadhyay, Donna Houston, Josh Inwood, Rob Kruse, Olaf Kuhlke, Aron Massey, Gabe Popescue, Steve Oluic, Rob Schwartz, Andrew Shears, and Stacey Wicker.

In the Philippines, I have been greatly assisted by a number of individuals, many of whom devoted considerable time and patience in helping me understand the dynamics and politics of overseas employment. Special thanks are extended to Tess Laurel, Ricardo Casco, Jay Francisco, Max Garming, Nestor Nario, Carmelita Nuqui, and Alfredo Palmiery. At Kent State University, I thank my chair, Jay Lee, for his support of my research; I thank my many colleagues, both within the department and across the university; and lastly, I offer special thanks to Mary Lou Church, for her assistance and patience in the front office.

I thank the many editors and publishers with whom I've worked over the years. The following articles have been revised and updated for inclusion here, and appear with permission. I am sincerely grateful to the editors, publishers, and journals for their permission to expand upon these earlier works. Chapter 2 is a revised version of "Migrant Labour and the Politics of Scale: Gendering the Philippine State," *Asia Pacific Viewpoint* 41, 2: 131–154. Chapter 3 is based on "Global Cities and Circuits of Global Labor: the Case of Manila, Philippines," *The Professional Geographer* 52, 1: 61–74 and on "Laboring in the Periphery," a chapter that previously appeared in *Relocating Global Cities*, edited by M. Amen, K. Archer, and M. Bosman (Boulder, CO: Rowman & Littlefield, 2006), 101–116.

Chapter 4 is based on "Asian Labor Recruitment and the World Wide Web," *The Professional Geographer* 50, 3: 331–344 and "Pan-national Identities: Representations of the Philippine Diaspora on the World Wide Web," co-authored with Olaf Kuhlke and appearing in *Asia Pacific Viewpoint* 41, 3: 231–252. Chapter 5 is a revised and expanded version of "The Globalization of Transnational Labor Migration and the Filipino Family: A Narrative," *Asian and Pacific Migration Journal* 11, 1: 95–116.

My deepest appreciation, however, must go to my family. For all of the long days I've spent at the computer, traveling the Philippines, or attending conferences, my family has been so supportive and understanding. I thank my parents, Dr. Gerald Tyner and Dr. Judith Tyner, for their continued inspiration and advice; I thank also David Tyner, Karen (Tyner) Owens, and Bill Owens. All of these individuals, in their own way, have shaped me into the person I am. As always, I thank my late-night companions: Bond (my puppy) and Jamaica (my cat).

My greatest debt remains with my wife Belinda. She continues to be my greatest supporter and, at times, my harshest critic. For Belinda, migration from the Philippines is truly a global reality; having left the Philippines over twenty years ago, she continues to experience the consequences of "being at home in the world" on a daily basis. And through her, and her family—which has become my family—I appreciate the immediacy of migration within a globalizing world. And lastly, I thank Jessica (aged 5) and Anica Lyn (aged 6), our daughters. Together, we look at maps and we find our various "homes": California and Ohio, the United States and the Philippines. However, we also recognize that "home" is not always a dot on a colored map, or even a house on a street. Home, rather, is mobile. Home is where we are. To Belinda, Jessica, and Anica, *mahal na mahal ko kayo.*

Preface

Nearly five million migrant workers from the Philippines are employed in over 190 countries and territories. They work as doctors and domestic helpers, engineers and entertainers, seamstresses and surveyors. It is through their collective labor that the Philippines has assumed a global presence.

For over five centuries the Philippines has been integrated into the world economy. Only recently, however, has the Philippines been a proactive agent in the production of a global economy. Since the 1970s the Philippine state, in connection with myriad private institutions, has recruited, trained, marketed, and deployed a mobile work force. Annually, approximately one million Philippine migrant workers travel to all corners of the world. *The Philippines: Mobilities, Identities, Globalization* seeks to understand how the Philippines has become the world's largest exporter of government-sponsored temporary contract labor and, in the process, has dramatically reshaped both the processes of globalization and also our understanding of globalization as concept.

To understand the place of the Philippines within a globalizing world requires an in-depth examination of the machinations of particular institutions. Through a focus on the emergence of the Philippines' state migratory apparatus, and its relationship with private agencies, I first question how overseas migration facilitates globalization as a process and an idea. Next, I indicate how this global presence is manifest *within* the Philippines. Specifically, I contend that Manila has emerged as the epicenter of the Philippines' active production of a global diasporic presence. Furthermore, I demonstrate that the Philippines' global presence is found not only in the "real" world, but also in cyberspace. In particular, I illustrate how the Philippine migration industry has utilized the Internet in its promotion of overseas employment, but also how migrant communities have used electronic communications to promote a rearticulated global identity. Lastly, through a detailed discussion of one migrant worker, I explore how "globalization" is experienced at the individual level. For the millions of workers deployed from the Philippines, globalization is not an academic concept; rather, it is very personal, something that is lived day by day. Throughout *The Philippines*, I hope to capture some of this immediacy.

Foreword

In the earlier years of a millennium that can no longer be called new, the peoples of the planet are well aware that something that cannot be measured calendrically is happening. The word that comes to mind is "globalization." But this mushy, indefinite term explains little beyond what some people experience in the daily grind—sleeping in hotbeds warmed by workers from another province trying, like you, to make a new life at such a high cost; children of a greater privilege surfing the air waves for bits torrenting from LA by way of Beijing through copyright-free havens in Central Asia; mothers without diapers to comfort the bleeding bottoms of their starving babies.

Globalization—some of it good for some of the people; some of it bad for many of the people; most of it good *and* bad in irregular measures poured mindlessly into the daily mix. It is far better, for the time being, to use "globalization" as shorthand for what we experience and know, but cannot explain. If we must use an expression to name transformations in how the world's parts and people relate to each other, we might do better to choose one at once more vague and concrete; hence, the title for this series: *Global Realities*. We know that something real is happening and that whatever else it is happening in a strange transfiguration of the relations between the real concretes of local, daily living, and some shape-shifting global process that is headed the gods know where.

Hard workers and refugees on the ground, no less than the high-flying corporate and cultural shakers, must all contend with the global that who (and in a sense what) one becomes is bound up with where one goes. More even, it appears that the going is a must that does not discriminate between the very poor on the margins and the high and mighty. One of the many virtues of *The Philippines: Mobilities, Identities, Globalization* is James A. Tyner's acute sensitivity to the complex but definite changes in the relations between obligatory global mobility and personal and social identity. He is prudently harsh in his criticism of simplistic references to immigration, as if global realties are one-way forces that drive individuals from their home lands. Without denying that global forces work this way, Tyner wants us better to appreciate the equally powerful effect of emigration—of, that is, people in large numbers, whether poor or wealthy, leaving their native lands of their own determinations. "Migrants must be made," he says, in a particularly apt phrase.

There are eight million people from the Philippines living and working abroad and nearly another million abroad in temporary contract labor positions. Manila, says Tyner, may well be considered a global city but, if it is, it is one of several of the kind and, perhaps, one unlike any other. Manila is, at least, a global center of labor recruitment—one of the places in this world where emigrants are made. They are not, however, made in the abstract; hence another alluring feature of this book is its dramatic concluding chapter. In "Performing Globalization" Tyner tells the personal story of a young woman, Lisa, who, after heavy recruitment and much skepticism on her part, makes the decision to *emigrate* to Japan for work in the entertainment sector. She understood very well that sex work was the risk, if not the necessity of her choice. The point Tyner makes is that as scandalous as a great deal of labor recruitment practices are, there are many instances where individuals like Lisa are neither forced to leave their native lands nor caught in a relentless system. Lisa, according to Tyner, had a choice and made it. He does not mean to suggest that there is no evil in the migration of workers. But he wants us to understand that the global realities of human mobility is a complex social thing—one that is indeed bound to strong economic forces, but also one that affects, and is effected by, changes in the way individuals like Lisa see and come to remake themselves.

Charles C. Lemert
Wesleyan University
Series Editor, *Global Realities*

One

Local Contexts, Distant Horizons

> POEA connects to the world, and in partnership with all stakeholders, creates and provides annually a million decent jobs overseas, and helps transform the Filipino worker, as world's Number One.[1]

Unlike the regimented, disciplined streets of Singapore or Kuala Lumpur, travel within Manila is downright chaotic. Indeed, with the possible exception of Bangkok, no other city in Southeast Asia is as famous—or infamous—as Manila for its traffic. Throughout the day, and frequently well into the night, traffic grinds slowly through the maze of highways and fly-overs, the alleys and avenues that constitute Manila's road network. Brightly-painted *jeepneys*, dilapidated and diesel-spewing city buses, and sparkling-clean luxury sports-utility vehicles all jostle for space in bumper-car-like fashion. Turn lanes and even stoplights are largely ignored.

In recent years, the congestion and chaos of Manila have only worsened.[2] Manila, similar to other "mega-cities" of Southeast Asia, is plagued by both extreme social *and* spatial inequalities. It is not happenstance that pedi-cabs and Land Cruisers sit side-by-side, idling in the mid-morning traffic. Nor is it by chance that squatter houses, with corrugated tin roofs and plywood sidings, are constructed just beyond the gated communities of air-conditioned mansions with private golf courses and armed sentries.

And the spatial inequalities of Manila are replicated throughout the country. The Philippines is a country of haves and have-nots. It is a country of the super-rich and the abject poor. It is a land where the richest 10 percent of the population hold over 40 percent of the total income, while the poorest account for less than 2 percent. Overall, nearly half of the population lives on less than US $2 a day. Urban-rural disparities are equally stark. Although poverty is pervasive in Manila and other urban centers, many rural areas exhibit considerably higher rates of poverty. The causes of rural poverty are many, but in general result from a history of land displacement, exploitative land-tenancy and sharecropping systems, and civil strife.

In part, the economic gaps between urban and rural areas have sustained a substantial inflow of migrants to Manila. Increasing rural poverty, combined with the failures of agrarian land reform, has pushed many people to the city seeking a better life. This, in turn, exacerbates the problems of the city. Many in-migrants are unable to find adequate work or shelter; they become part of Manila's ever-growing population of "urban poor." If they are lucky, in-migrants may obtain low-paying jobs in construction, transportation, or other services. Many others though become homeless, living and scavenging in the many squatter settlements that are pervasive throughout the metropolitan area. Government statistics indicate that approximately 14 percent of Manila's population lives as squatters; non-government sources suggest that the number of squatters is probably twice that figure.[3]

Just as poverty may impel rural populations to move, many residents of Manila, whether born in the city, or recently migrated, look for opportunities beyond the shores of the Philippines. For these individuals, overseas employment provides the lure of a better life. To work as a domestic helper in

Singapore, or a pipe-welder in Kuwait: these foreign employment opportunities hold the promise—although not always the reality—of a steady paycheck and the chance to escape poverty. And for many, the path to global futures begins at the Philippine Overseas Employment Administration (POEA).

The POEA building sits at the corner of Epifanio de los Santos Avenue (EDSA) and Ortigas Boulevard. The location itself is symbolic. In 1986 millions of Filipinos lined EDSA, the 12-lane perimeter road that rings Manila. Then, they gathered in protest at the dictatorship of President Ferdinand Marcos. Their peaceful uprising culminated in the "People's Power" revolt that led to the president's downfall. Now, Filipinos gather at the site in search of jobs. Indeed, on average over four thousand Filipinos arrive—every day—seeking foreign work.

The POEA building is an imposing concrete and glass structure, not tall by modern standards, but massive; it is a bulldog of a building. Visually, the POEA building evokes stability and a dogged determination. It is outward-looking, gazing beyond the Philippines to distant horizons. But it is also defensive in appearance, with its surrounding concrete wall topped with a wrought-iron fence. Armed security guards, likewise, provide a constant vigil over those who pass between the metal-detectors and the locked gates. Two contrasting images: forward-looking, seemingly open to the world, and yet protected, insular, guarded against unseen forces.

Literally and symbolically, the POEA building is the face of globalization within—and beyond—the Philippines. For millions of Filipinos, the POEA is the portal to the world's labor markets. For others, however, the POEA constitutes much that is wrong with globalization: the commodification and exploitation of labor, the sacrifice of people for profit. Statistics tell part of the story. Currently, over eight million Filipinos live and work in over 190 countries and territories. Each year, approximately one million Filipinos move to other countries. Some go willingly, while others are coerced, tricked or trafficked. The majority, approximately 85 percent, are temporary contract labor migrants, processed by the POEA. And these migrants have in some respects supported the Philippines' economy. In 2006, for example, migrant Filipino contract workers remitted over US $12 billion into the Philippines economy. This source of foreign exchange alone accounts for approximately 20 percent of total exports in the Philippines. These monies are also significant not only at the national level, but at the household level. Overall, approximately 11 percent of families in Manila receive their main source of income from abroad; in contrast, only about 14 percent of Manila families earn their main source of income through entrepreneurial activities.[4] Surveys of villages throughout the Philippines provide further evidence. Sheila Coronel, for example, found that 3,500 people out of a total population of 49,000 in one town in the province of Pangasinan were working abroad—or 1 person in 14.[5] As Philip Kelly notes, "Add to this the number who have worked abroad in the past, or hope to in the future, and almost every family has some immediate and personal interest in overseas work."[6]

Many overseas workers, however, do not find the proverbial pot of gold. Each year, thousands of Filipino contract workers are exploited or abused, both in the Philippines and beyond. Within the Philippines, migrants are tricked by unscrupulous labor recruiters, deceived by loan-sharks, and become mired in debt-bondage. Overseas, many migrants are physically, mentally, and sexually abused; they are exploited and disciplined through illegal contract substitutions, non-payment of work, or the confiscation of passports. Women migrants are especially vulnerable. Whereas it is true that all overseas workers are susceptible to some form of exploitation and abuse, it is

Table 1.1 Stock estimate of overseas Filipinos, 2006

Region	Permanent[1]	Temporary[2]	Irregular[3]	Total
World total	3,556,035	3,802,345	874,792	8,233,172
Africa	553	71,503	17,742	89,798
Americas	2,887,129	333,763	356,400	3,577,292
Asia	196,968	789,110	237,600	1,223,678
Europe	229,132	534,748	124,380	888,260
Middle East	3,523	1,723,911	112,250	1,839,684
Oceania	238,730	74,813	26,420	339,963
Sea-based workers		274,497		

Source: Philippine Overseas Employment Administration 2007: Table 29.
[1] Permanent migrants are those immigrants or legal permanent residents abroad whose stay does not depend on work contracts.
[2] Temporary migrants are those persons whose stay overseas is employment-related, and who are expected to return at the end of their work contract.
[3] Irregular migrants are those not properly documented or without valid residence or work permits, or who are overstaying in a foreign country.

Table 1.2 Remittances[1] of overseas Filipinos by world region, 2005–2006

Region	2005	2006	% Change
Africa	4,546	10,272	126.0%
Americas	6,605,231	7,198,212	9.0%
Asia	1,172,373	1,496,120	27.6%
Europe	1,433,904	2,061,067	43.7%
Middle East	1,417,491	1,909,208	34.7%
Oceania	54,573	85,610	56.9%
Others	887	819	–7.7%
Sea-based workers	1,669,358	1,949,290	16.8%
Total remittances	10,689,005	12,761,308	19.4%

Source: Philippine Overseas Employment Administration 2007: Table 18.
[1] In thousand US dollars.

equally observable that women are more likely to be affected. Statistics on gender differences of welfare cases reported by Philippine officials indicate that, routinely, female migrants outnumber male migrants as victims in nearly all forms of abuse, and especially those of rape, sexual harassment, and physical abuse.[7] In light of such evidence, criticism has pointed to the sacrifice of (especially) female migrant workers for foreign exchange. Aurora de Dios, for example, writes of the deployment of female Philippine overseas performing artists (OPAs)[8] to Japan:

> The role of the government in facilitating the [deployment] of young Filipino women which constantly puts them at risk of sexual abuse and organized prostitution, to say nothing of the danger of violent death of which we have many examples[,] must now be seriously reexamined and reassessed. By facilitating through official channels, the employment of women in this type of entertainment, the Japanese and Philippine governments have provided a legal cover for the massive trafficking of Asian women in Japan and are, in effect[,] parties to its perpetuation.[9]

In short, there are few issues as important, pervasive, or controversial to a globalizing Philippines as is international migration.

THE PHILIPPINES AS A GLOBALIZING REGION

For the better part of two decades I have considered the "place" of the Philippines within the world economy and the "function" of international labor migration. Through numerous sojourns in the Philippines, I have discussed at length the possibilities and pitfalls of overseas employment, with government officials, private labor recruiters, non-governmental officials, and also migrants. Now, the opportunity to participate in the Routledge series on Global Realities has enabled me to reflect upon this research. The most significant development in the world economy during the past decades has been the increased "globalization" of economic activities.[10] Concurrently, recent changes in the global political economy have had a profound impact on the lives of people. The current phase of economic restructuring, for example, has been characterized by changes in global investment patterns, with new centers of capital accumulation emerging in previously peripheral locations (e.g., Central America, the Caribbean, and Southeast Asia) and a concomitant decline in industrial production in "core" regions. Advances in telecommunications and transportation systems, especially, have "diminished" the global and facilitated the movement of capital and commodities, people and ideas. The transnational operations of multinational firms, to give but one example, have given rise to a new international division of labor, one that has witnessed a shifting of manufacturing sectors from developed to developing economies.[11] Moreover, the worldwide production and market expansion of these firms has led to an explosive growth of producer services.[12] Consequently, the emergence of new international divisions of labor, characterized by an increased differentiation of labor on the basis of ethnicity, gender, and geography, has occurred.

Changes in the global economy have been mirrored by changes in international migration. As Demetrios Papademetriou writes, "At the dawn of the twenty-first century, international migration touches the lives of more people, and looms larger in the politics and economics of more states, than at any other time in the modern era. With more than 160 million people estimated to be living outside their country of birth, almost no country is untouched by international migration or is immune to its effects."[13] Five mutually reinforcing trends are readily available. First, there has been, quite simply, a *globalization* of migration. Not only are more countries involved in systems of migration than in previous eras, there has also been a reorientation of migration flows. While there has been a relative decline of labor migration to the more traditional receiving states of Western Europe, other Southern European states—long associated with emigration—have become important centers of immigration (e.g., Italy and Greece). The oil-rich countries of the Middle East (e.g., Saudi Arabia, Kuwait), as well as the newly industrializing regions of Asia (e.g., South Korea, Singapore, Malaysia) likewise have become important sites of both capital accumulation and labor in-migration. Second, there has been an acceleration of migration, in other words, an increase in the volume (and turnover) of migration for both sending and receiving countries. Third, migration systems have become more diversified. Not only are more countries incorporated within systems of migration, there is a greater diversity of migrant "types," including settler migration systems, student migration systems, and temporary contract labor migration systems. Furthermore, these migratory systems have had a tremendous impact on family formation and continuity. Researchers now speak of "seasonal orphans," "solo parents," "flexible citizens," and "shadow households."[14]

Transnational migration, fourthly, has become increasingly feminized. This is seen not only in the Philippines, but throughout other migratory systems in Asia, Europe, and the Middle East. In part, the feminization of transnational migration reflects the pervasiveness of *globalizing* gendered stereotypes as well as the international division of labor. Female migrant workers, in particular, are often concentrated in certain occupations, such as domestic work and health care services.[15]

Lastly, transnational migration has become increasingly commodified.[16] Government and private institutions assume an important regulatory function in the global mobility of labor and the trend, at least within the Asian region, is toward even greater institutional involvement.[17] While it is true that earlier systems of labor migration, including both the Atlantic slave trade and the movement of indentured servants to British North America, were highly regulated, it is also true that we now see a more globalized, interconnected, and integrated system of institutional control. Private labor recruiters in the Philippines, for example, may facilitate the movement of Indian textile workers to South Korea. Indeed, the institutional mechanisms of transnational labor migration are so interconnected that some researchers now allude to the existence of a labor migration "industry."[18] Participants within this industry, whether they are government officials, private labor recruiters, or foreign employers, interact to promote, manage, and regulate the global circulation of over 160 million workers. In short, globalization per se does not create this global presence of laborers; rather, this circulation is what makes globalization.

Any discussion of the Philippines as a globalizing region, or of international labor migration as a global reality, must fully take into account the government-sponsored export of contract labor migrants. To be sure, the processes of globalization entail much more than the movement of workers. The influx of foreign investment into new territories, the growth of export processing zones, the cultural dimensions of media diffusion: all of these are occurring and are significantly transforming the lives of billions of people. However, less understood within the voluminous writings on globalization, has been any sustained and explicit focus on *the productions of migration* on a global scale.[19] The Philippines provides an ideal setting in which to examine these productions. With an annual deployment of over one million *newly-hired* workers, the Philippines is the world's largest exporter of government-sponsored temporary contract labor.[20] This circulation of labor is a billion-dollar industry, composed of hundreds of thousands of government institutions, private recruitment agencies, foreign employers, non-government organizations (NGOs), migrant welfare centers, as well as the millions of migrant workers themselves.

The Philippines' active promotion of a global presence, however, is of recent vintage. Indeed, although the Philippines is, in the words of Philip Kelly, "no stranger to the global," its introduction to the world economy has been fraught with difficulties. In the remainder of this chapter, therefore, I emphasize the decidedly uneven way in which the Philippines was colonized, occupied, and thrust onto the international stage.

LIMITED HORIZONS

Situated between the South China Sea and the Philippine Sea, the Philippines is an archipelago of 7,107 islands. Only about one thousand of these islands, however, are populated and just 11 islands constitute 94 percent of the Philippines' total landmass. Stretching north to south, the geography of the Philippines is arranged into three major island groupings. To the north lies Luzon, the center of political and economic power in the Philippines. At 105,780 square kilometers (40,842 square miles), Luzon is the largest, most populous island and home to the capital city of Manila. The Visayan Islands, which include Cebu and Leyte, encompass the central Philippines, while the southern Philippines is dominated by the large island of Mindanao and numerous smaller islands, including the Sulu archipelago stretching toward Malaysia.[21]

Prior to the arrival of Spanish colonizers in the sixteenth century, there was no unified "Philippines." Nor was there a unifying pre-colonial empire or any other unifying element or political structure in existence as was present in other parts of Southeast Asia. Rather, there existed many dispersed and largely autonomous settlements throughout the archipelago. Known as *barangay*, after the Tagalog[22] word for "boat," these settlements were composed of 30 to 100 households (or 100 to 500 people). As Kelly explains, the term *barangay* actually provides insight into the initial settlement of the islands. Individual boatloads of extended families and kinship groups, themselves originating from other places of the Malay world, migrated to the islands, forming strong local communities.[23] These *barangays* were highly stratified, reminiscent of European feudalistic society. At the top was the local chief, or *datu*, and the various chiefs formed an aristocratic class, known in Tagalog as *maginoo*. Next in line was a class of "freemen," known as *timawa* or *maharlika*. These individuals had rights to a portion of agricultural lands, and owed the *datu* nothing but occasional labor. At the bottom of society was a class known as *alipin*. Although this term is frequently translated as "slave," it is, in fact, more complex. While it is true that those persons who comprised this class were often held in a form of debt-bondage, it is also true that *alipin*, much like the *timawa*, could claim and inherent land.[24]

Spatially, *barangays* were concentrated along either riverine or coastal locations. Both engaged in subsistence production. Toward the interior, communities practiced shifting cultivation, supplemented with hunting and fishing activities. *Barangays* that were sited along the coast, not surprisingly, exhibited a more outward orientation, participating in various forms of maritime trade. Indeed, trade with China, Siam, and other Southeast Asian kingdoms and empires was common. This general settlement pattern differed mostly in the southern Philippines. Since the thirteenth century, Muslim traders and scholars had made considerable inroads into the indigenous communities and, in time, a number of highly organized sultanates were established.

Overall, therefore, the pre-colonial Philippines was only partially integrated into the Sino-Malay regional economy, and only indirectly tied to the rapidly interconnecting world economy. The arrival of Spanish *conquistadors* and missionaries, however, would irrevocably change the economic orientation of the islands. Initiated by the voyage of the Portuguese navigator Ferdinand Magellan (sailing under the Spanish flag) and sustained by subsequent Spaniards such as Miguel Lopez de Legazpi, the Philippines came into existence as both an object and an opportunity.

Spain's initial interests in the Philippines—the islands were named *Felipinas* by Ruy Lopez de Villalobos in honor of Philip, the Spanish crown prince—were threefold. First, Spain sought entry into the lucrative (and Muslim-dominated) spice trade; second, Spain looked to use the Philippines as a springboard to trade with China; and third, Spain hoped to exploit the natural riches and treasures of the islands. These objectives, while only marginally met, would have a lasting effect on the people of the islands. There was, firstly, no instant wealth to be found in the Philippines, certainly nothing on the order of that "discovered" in Mexico or Central America. There were no vast deposits of gold and silver ready for the taking, and the Philippines had no troves of desirable spices comparable to those found in the Moluccas (present-day eastern Indonesia).

It is important to situate Spain's colonial project in the Philippines within its proper historical and economic context. Beginning around the sixteenth century, Spain (along with most other European states) pursued an economic strategy known as mercantilism, or merchant capitalism. The doctrine of mercantilism is premised on the idea that a nation's wealth is determined by the amount of precious metals (e.g., gold and silver) it had in its possession. Colonialism was fundamental to mercantilism. Colonies (it was hoped) provided instant wealth, access to resources, cheap labor in the form of indentured servitude and slavery, and ready-made markets.[25] Merchant capitalism also was a self-propelling growth system in which the continued expansion of trade was vital: Without such growth, neither merchants nor those dependent on their success (e.g., producers, consumers, financiers) could maintain their economic position, let alone advance it.[26]

In an attempt to capitalize on its colony through the mobilization of labor and the collection of tributes, Spanish colonial authorities needed to socially and spatially reorganize the settlement geography of the Philippines. In a process called *reducción*, Spanish administrators, by force if necessary, regrouped individual *barangays* into towns (termed *cabeceras*). These were organized around a newly-built church and served to facilitate the imposition of colonial rule. *Datus* who brought people into the *cabeceras* were rewarded with elevated positions, as *gobernadorcillo* ("little governor") or *cabeza de barangay* (village head) in the new state. Consequently, through a spatial reorganization of Philippine society, Spanish administrators facilitated the collection of taxes and the establishment of work forces.[27]

These spatial changes contributed to a transformation of the Philippines' social structure. Throughout the period of Spanish rule, social strata emerged and developed, with the *peninsulares* (Iberian-born Spaniards) sharing authority with the Catholic Church and the friar orders. Next in the hierarchy were the *insulares*, the Spanish descendants of the *peninsulares*, followed by the Filipino landed elites: The *gobernadorcillos* and the *cabezas de barangay*. Together, these formed an emergent class known as the *principalia*. Somewhat on a par with these Filipinos were Chinese and Chinese-Filipino merchants, the *mestizo*, who frequently rented lands from the *principalia*. At the bottom were the *tao*, the common people, known to the Spaniards as either *indios* or *naturales*.[28]

Such social and spatial changes dramatically altered the economic structure of the Philippines. Initially, Spain ruled by means of the *encomienda*, a land grant arrangement contrived to attract Spanish migrants to the archipelago. *Encomiendas* were administrative units established for the purpose of exacting tributes and taxes from Filipinos. Spanish landowners, in effect, could tax the areas they settled. Feudalistic in orientation, the system required the assigning of annual quotas to local communities.[29] Because the uprooted and resettled *barangays* had little surplus and no access to currency, tribute was paid "in kind" in the form of unprocessed rice, salt, chickens, eggs, and so on. The *encomenderos*, though, would arbitrarily assign low value to the tribute products and, in turn, sell them at higher market prices in the larger towns. If payment could not be made, labor would be substituted in a form of debt-bondage.[30] Later, a partnership also ensued between the Spanish Crown and the Catholic friars. The friars established *haciendas*, large landed estates that produced crops both for local consumption and for sale in Manila. These estates were worked primarily by sharecropping tenants, known as *kasama*. These church-based enterprises were able to attract sizeable work forces, since they could exempt Filipino peasants from the practice of forced labor required of all households by Spain.

And herein lies the primary change introduced by Spain, one that impacted the trajectory of the Philippines' incorporation into the world economy. In conformance with a doctrine of mercantilism, Spanish colonial authorities imposed severe tax obligations on the indigenous Filipinos. These included, for example, the *tribute*, or head tax; the *donativo de zamboanga*, a periodic special levy to help fight the Muslims; the *vandala*, a forced delivery system by which certain goods had to be delivered to the government at set prices; tithes to the Church; and an assortment of other municipal and tax obligations.[31] As Abinales and Amoroso conclude, "residents of the Philippines paid for their own colonization and religious instruction, as well as subsidizing Spain's wars and its China trade."[32] Most onerous, however, was the imposition of the *repartimiento*, or *polo*, system. According to this forced-labor policy, all Filipino men aged 16 to 60 were required to render service to the state for a period of 40 days every year. Under this system, Filipinos were required to build and repair roads, cut and transport timber for the construction of ships, or work in the shipyards building and repairing ships. This forced labor was crucial for the continuance of the galleon trade (discussed below), Spain's main economic activity in the Philippines.

The *repartimiento* was frequently abused by both Spanish overseers and the Filipino *gobernadorcillo*. As Stanley Karnow describes, Spanish officials "would form brigades of seven or eight thousand men, whom they fed badly, paid poorly and sometimes flogged to death for indiscipline or indolence. Natives often bribed their way out of the conscription, sinking into endless debt by borrowing money at exorbitant rates from local usurers. . . . Village chiefs, pressed to furnish taxes to sustain the projects, squeezed their impoverished communities into ruin."[33] Lorraine Crouchett describes also the hardships imposed by the practice: "Because the construction of ships took priority over everything else and because of the polo system, many Filipinos were drafted into shipbuilding during the planting season or harvest time and lost their crops."[34]

As indicated earlier, prior to the arrival of the Spaniards, many *barangays* participated in limited trade relations throughout the Sino-Malay world. And indeed, by the time of Magellan's arrival in the archipelago, Spaniards were well aware of this extensive trading network, stretching from the Arabian Gulf to China. The galleon trade was thus an attempt on the part of Spain to co-opt and monopolize these trade patterns.[35]

Between 1565 and 1813 Spain's economic interests in the Philippines centered almost exclusively on the Acapulco–Manila trade. Kathirithamby-Wells explains how this system adversely affected the Philippines. Coincident with a growth in external commerce was a concomitant internal economic stagnation in the Philippines. That this occurred is a reflection of the nature of the galleon trade. Manila itself did not emerge as a major manufacturing center. Rather, the city served as an entrepôt, with the exchange in Manila of Mexican silver for Chinese silks and porcelains, and other products, such as spices and ivory, from Vietnam, Siam, India, Japan, and elsewhere. These goods were destined for markets in New Spain and Europe. However, Chinese merchants controlled the Canton–Manila arm of the trade while Spanish officials—the *peninsulares*—controlled the Manila–Acapulco route. The Philippines played no direct role in this system of international commerce.[36]

The galleon trade contributed to a substantial and significant early migration system. As part of the *repartimiento* system, tens of thousands of Filipinos participated in the construction and repair of the large ocean-going galleons. Several thousand, however, also served as crew on the galleons. Later, when the opportunity arose, many Filipinos would desert at the various ports-of-call throughout California and Mexico.[37]

Political and economic changes of the late eighteenth-century Europe, but especially England's industrial revolution, profoundly influenced events in the Philippines. Spain's reaction was to reorient its colonial policies and practices to permit—indeed, to encourage—foreign investment and trade. Whereas previously Spain sought to retain a tight grip on its Philippine colony, toward the nineteenth century colonial administrators worked to expand the production of cash crops, such as tobacco, abaca, and sugar, for the world market. Spain, however, had by this time lost its position as a major world power and, consequently, British and American business interests would dominate the Philippines' colonial market. For the indigenous Filipinos, however, it mattered little. For many Filipinos, the expanded integration of the Philippines into an incipient capitalist-based world economy led to increased impoverishment and landlessness.

Resultant in part from Britain's occupation (1762–1764) of Manila following the Seven Years War, the Philippines was abruptly opened to foreign capital. In 1790 English, American, and other foreign ships began to call at the Philippines and take on cargoes of sugar, indigo, rattan, and other cash crops and in 1809 a British commercial house was opened in Manila. By 1834 the city was opened completely to free trade and throughout the subsequent decades, more than a dozen other foreign commercial houses had opened in Manila. Outside Manila, numerous other provincial ports were likewise opened to direct foreign trade.

The opening of the Philippines to the world economy through the promotion of cash crops was both a cause and an effect of land-use changes. As the colonial state penetrated Philippine society, the *indios* were increasingly, and unfavorably, incorporated into a cash-based economy. Abinales and Amoroso explain that even as late as the nineteenth century, most Filipino families lived in rural areas and tilled their own family plots. Farmers produced mostly for subsistence needs.

In time, however, farmers were impelled to participate in the cash-economy. Birth, marriage, illness, and death required cash and farmers had no other recourse but to turn to the growth of cash crops.[38]

When peasants required hard currency, they often were forced to seek out loans, usually obtained from a member of the *principalia* class. Under the *pacto de retroventa* system, the farmer's land was "sold" to the lender, who agreed to sell it back at the same price within a specified period of time. The borrower, although seriously in debt, continued to have usufruct rights on the land. These loans, though, were exceedingly difficult to repay. If crops failed, for example, the farmer would be forced to take out additional loans. Often, after numerous loans were obtained, the farmer would actually owe more on the land than the land itself was worth. The farmers eventually would forfeit on their loans and lose their land. Many would stay on, however, as sharecroppers or tenants, thus providing surpluses of labor that other landowners might tap into. In short, with the promotion of cash crops, the *indios* soon found themselves landless, in debt, or both.[39]

The *principalia* likewise saw the transition to export production as an opportunity for personal gain. These more wealthy Filipinos, along with the Chinese *mestizos*, increasingly leased lands from friars and apportioned these to sharecroppers. The institutionalization of sharecropping entailed the leasing of land owned by an absentee landlord to an *inquilino* (lessee), who was charged a fixed rent in the form of a share of the harvest. These *inquilinos*, however, did not cultivate the land; rather, they in turn apportioned the land and subsequently received a share of the harvest from a landless farmer. In consequence, landowners recognized that they could increase their profits further not from intensified yields, but simply from the acquisition of more land. Previously, under traditional conditions of subsistence agriculture, labor requirements beyond the means of the immediate household were met by reciprocal labor exchanges—a form of familial and communal cooperation. With commercialized agriculture, however, landlords—who now, more than ever, were absentee—began hiring labor from other regions. This initiated far-reaching changes in the spatial economy of the Philippines. Areas that previously enjoyed labor surpluses became labor-scarce; areas that formerly exported agricultural products now experienced food shortages.[40]

In short, the opening of the Philippine economy throughout the eighteenth and nineteenth centuries set in place a number of structural conditions that contributed to the impoverishment and landlessness of the masses of Filipinos. In particular, the rural restructuring of the Philippines, and the concomitant concentration in landownership, growth in plantations, and the promotion of export crops, severely undermined the development of the Philippines. Kathirithamby-Wells describes the result:

> Capitalist exploitation in the privately managed plantations, with compulsory cultivation for the government, contributed to widespread economic distress among the peasantry. A system of forced cultivation, introduced in the Cagayan Valley, Gapan in the province of Pampanga and the island of Marinduque, supported a Spanish tobacco monopoly, so lucrative that by the mid-nineteenth century it rendered the Philippines financially independent. Under this system each family was required to raise 40,000 plants annually, for sale exclusively to the government. Shortfalls were subject to a fine, while anything in excess of the stipulated quota was systematically destroyed. Government inspections ensured that no part of the crop was held back, even for personal consumption. Pilfering from the

> homes of cultivators while conducting searches for concealed tobacco, and substitution for cash payment of promissory notes which were never honoured, were commonplace. . . . Life was not vastly different even for *indios* outside the forced cultivation system. Under Spanish administration, each family was liable to payment of a tribute or poll-tax, collected in produce, and the system was open to many abuses. . . . Periodic floods and the ravages of locusts which destroyed the paddy were other factors that affected peasant welfare. ("The Age of Transition," 266–267)

In sum, as the Spanish empire waned, the Philippines was unevenly integrated into the world economy. Alfred McCoy suggests that the archipelago "emerged as a series of separate societies that entered the world economic system at different times, under different terms of trade, and with different systems of production."[41] And how did the "global" impinge at the "local"? Elizabeth Eviota concludes that the

> situation in the last hundred years of Spanish rule was one of labour scarcity, land surplus and abundant natural resources, so that the struggle to survive was rarely a matter of life and death. But the local population must never have been far from poverty or hunger. It must have been an endless effort to maintain a certain minimal standard of living—food, clothing, shelter and an occasional celebration. The struggle was exacerbated by the continuing transfer of food and food products to a non-producing population of colonials, clergy, Chinese *mestizos* and Filipino *principalia* who owned or controlled the means of production.[42]

A "NON-GLOBAL" WORLD PRESENCE

In 1898 the United States acquired the Philippines as part of the spoils of the Spanish-American War. It was also the result of a longer, gradual process of territorial acquisition and market penetration, preceded by Commodore Matthew Perry's "opening" of Japan and the possession of dozens of remote islands across the Pacific, including the Hawaiian Islands and parts of Samoa. Many of these territorial acquisitions were the result of an enlarged maritime presence of the US, especially as it related to both the whaling industry and the Navy.[43]

America's decision to acquire the archipelago was both strategic and economic. As the US prepared to enter the twentieth century, American policy-makers were well aware of the broader international environment of imperial capitalist expansion, as the industrialization powers of Europe competed for colonies throughout Africa and Asia. Within the United States, for example, imperialists such as Henry Cabot Lodge and Alfred Thayer Mahan advocated for a strong American presence abroad. Extending the idea of America's "manifest destiny," the imperialists argued that only as a world power could the United States trade, prosper, and protect itself against potential enemies.[44]

The decision to "acquire" the Philippines was not bloodless. The Philippine–American War (1899–1902) saw battle losses of over forty-two hundred Americans killed and over twenty-eight hundred wounded. For the Filipinos, between sixteen thousand and twenty thousand died in combat; an estimated two hundred thousand "innocent" Filipinos died of famine, disease, and other war-related calamities. These deaths do not consider the many thousands of Filipinos who perished during the later "Moro Wars" that ravaged the southern Philippines during the 1910s.[45] Much has been written on the American colonization of the Philippines.[46] Here, I focus specifically on two overlapping themes: (1) the social and spatial changes resultant from America's capitalist penetration of the archipelago and (2) the migration of Filipinos to the United States and its possessions.

Following its violent conquest, America's policy was to remake the Philippines into an opportunity for investment. US advisors recommended a number of programs, including the investment in timber production, road construction, port improvements, and the expansion of railways. The main intent, of course, was to increase agricultural production through the promotion of export crops that were needed in the United States. As Eviota notes, "The Philippines, as an American colony, served the imperatives of capitalist expansion and accumulation well."[47]

American colonialism encouraged the expansion of the capitalist economy, a practice that favored American business and Filipino landowners. Economic policies were enacted that promoted the production of raw materials for US industries, including sugar, coconuts, abaca, timber, rubber, and pineapple. Policies also allowed for the control of the Philippine domestic market for US manufactured goods. Thus, American tariff policies stimulated cash crops for export but, simultaneously, inhibited the development of a diversified Philippine economy.[48] In 1909, for example, the US Congress passed the Payne–Aldrich Tariff Act. This act provided for the free entry of all Philippine products into American markets *excluding* the archipelago's principal crops (i.e., rice, sugar, and tobacco). Rice imports were subjected to regular tariffs, while quotas were established for sugar and tobacco. Later, the Underwood–Simmons Tariff Act of 1913 removed all restrictions on these products.[49] As Kelly concludes, these acts led to virtually free trade with the continental United States as American manufactured goods were imported duty-free and Philippine commodities passed freely into the growing US market.[50] Consequently, the Philippines' integration into the world market became unidirectional, with the Philippine economy increasingly dependent on the American markets and policies.

The colonial state, likewise, facilitated the expansion of US business interests in agriculture. In 1926, for example, the Philippine Packing Corporation, today's Del Monte Philippines, laid the foundation for its huge pineapple plantation in Bukidnon, on the island of Mindanao. Laborers were recruited in Bohol and placed in camps at the plantation site.[51] These economic practices would dramatically alter Philippine society. Indeed, a major consequence of American colonial rule was the transformation of the local elite's relationship to that of the community. Given the capitalist imperatives of colonial rule, American officials entered into close economic relationships with the landed elite. American policy-makers also maintained the existing class structure and kept intact the status quo of landownership. Over time, many Filipino elite, most notably those from the *principalia* class, learned that political power was intimately associated with American support. Consequently, an international patron–client arrangement was established, one that would favor landowning Filipinos and American merchants and investors.[52] For the "modern" landlords, class relationships were business propositions; peasants were simply laborers who would be employed so long as they helped turn land into profits.[53] Given these conditions, landowners were able to demand more and more from their tenants and sharecroppers. High-population densities served as reserve supplies of land. If a tenant complained, other potential laborers were easily found.

Throughout the early twentieth century, therefore, the economy of the Philippines was characterized by overdependence on a few exports, land tenancy, indebtedness, low productivity, corruption and inefficiency, undercapitalization, and miserable working conditions.[54] Consider, for example, land tenancy. Putzel finds that tenancy overall increased from 16 percent in 1903 to 35 percent of the farming population by the eve of World War II. Many regions experienced rates that were considerable higher than the national norm. Throughout Central Luzon, the prime rice-producing area of the Philippines, tenancy rates surpassed 50 percent. In the Central Luzon province of Nueva Ecija, for example, tenancy increased from 38 percent in 1903 to 54 percent in the early 1940s, and to 60 percent by 1948. Other statistics further reflect the deteriorating conditions of the Philippine peasantry. In 1939 only 17,000 farms were run by cash tenants, or 1 percent of the total, while 548,00 were operated by sharecroppers. Usury, with interest rates approaching or surpassing 100 percent, kept sharecroppers in a state of debt-peonage.[55] Most significant, these structural conditions, combined with the institutional linkages developed between the Philippines and the United States, set in motion a large-scale migratory system that continues to the present day.

In her classic study *The Mobility of Labor and Capital*, Saskia Sassen argues that capital mobility creates new conditions for the mobility of labor. Contravening more traditional studies that posited international migration as simply responses to population pressures and poverty, Sassen proposed that the internationalization of production directly influences patterns of international labor migration. Understanding why a migration begins, she writes, entails an examination of conditions promoting out-migration in countries of origin and the formation of objective and subjective linkages with receiving countries that make such migration feasible. Conditions of poverty, unemployment, and overpopulation are not sufficient as explanatory factors. Nor do these factors alone account for the geographic dimensions of international migration. In other words, even if we do surmise that out-migration is a factor of poverty and population growth, these conditions do not in and of themselves explain where the emigrants go. By focusing on specific institutional linkages associated with the circulation of capital, Sassen provides the missing "link."[56]

Beginning in the early twentieth century, opportunities for emigration from the Philippines were influenced primarily by the activities of US institutions in a colonial and, later, post-colonial, context. These opportunities were developed and maintained by US institutions, although the initial patterns were subsequently reinforced and altered through the emergence of social networks and chain migration. Combined, both institutional conditions and social relations contributed to a geographically-circumscribed migratory pattern that significantly tied the Philippines to the United States.[57]

Perhaps the most profound impact of American rule in the Philippines, according to Kelly, was exercised through the education system.[58] On the one hand, the imposition of public education was utilized as a pacification technique. The US government, after taking possession of the Philippines, initiated that country's first public schools—albeit to effectively assimilate the Filipinos to American control. Through novels, songs, and American teachers in public schools, education provided many young Filipinos with an awareness of opportunities outside of the Philippines. On the other hand, the subject matter taught in these schools also served to a cultural orientation toward the West in general, and the United States more specifically.

Educational institutions, however, also established a direct migratory route between the Philippines and the United States. In 1903 the *Pensionado* Act, passed by the US Congress, provided support to send the children of prominent Filipino families—whose loyalty the colonial regime hoped to win

—to the US for education.[59] The *pensionados*, as they became known, earned degrees through the United States, in institutions of higher learning, such as Harvard, Stanford, Cornell, and the University of California at Berkeley. From an initial cohort of approximately 100 *pensionados*, the number increased to over 14,000 by 1938. Many of these individuals founded student organizations in the United States, some of which remain in existence today. Upon completing their education, most *pensionados* returned to the Philippines where they assumed positions as political, social, and economic leaders. Indeed, returning *pensionados* provided models for younger Filipinos. Furthermore, as Barbara Posadas explains, in Philippine classrooms American teachers assured eager pupils that those lacking scholarships or family wealth might work their way through school and, additionally, young Filipinos were taught that even if schooling was not a goal, work in the United States offered an attractive alternative when set against growing tenancy and landlessness in the rural Philippines.[60] In other words, Filipino youth were trained from an early age to contemplate the possibility of laboring in the United States.

A second migratory system was initiated through the militarization of the Philippines. Beginning with the Philippine–American War, the United States established its first military bases in the Philippines.[61] In part, this military presence was an extension of America's broader strategic positioning within the Asia-Pacific region. However, the continued presence of US military bases in the Philippines served as recruiting stations. Significantly, Filipinos were the only foreign nationals who were allowed to enlist in the US armed forces; and the Navy was the only military branch they could join.[62] Those Filipinos who enlisted, however, often faced discrimination and were segregated into the most menial of occupations.

Most were employed as stewards, cooks, waiters, pantrymen, dishwashers, or bedmakers. Nevertheless, a sizeable contingent of Filipinos availed themselves of the opportunity and by 1930 there was an estimated 25,000 Filipinos serving in the US Navy. Because of this military connection, many Filipinos would acquire US citizenship and eventually settle in the United States.[63]

By far, however, the most significant migratory system established between the Philippines and the United States centered on the recruitment of labor. In line with Sassen's contention that international labor migration is strongly associated with the internationalization of capital, this migratory system was the result of a series of economic and political transformations that were occurring throughout Asia, the Pacific, and North America.

American business interests were, throughout the nineteenth century, becoming global. With its own industrial revolution well underway, American capitalists set their sights on markets and materials well beyond the shores of the United States. Asia and the Pacific, in particular, loomed large on their western horizon. In 1835 the US Navy had established its first "East India Station" in the Western Pacific. Subsequent decades saw the acquisition of more stations, as American policymakers and military advisors sought to gain access to the China trade and to "enlarge the opportunities of commercial intercourse" in the region.[64]

Early on, considerable attention was focused on the exploitation of the Hawaiian Islands. Since 1852 American entrepreneurs had been establishing sugar plantations there. Considerable sums of money were to be made, especially through the 1860s as plantation owners were poised to reap the benefits of a potential economic boom bolstered by the blockage of Southern sugar growers during the American

Civil War. However, the successful development of the sugar industry required a large, dependable, and cheap labor force.[65] Native Hawaiians were unable to provide such a ready supply of workers, in part because introduced diseases had decimated the population.[66] Confronted with a potential labor shortage, plantation owners began recruiting workers from elsewhere. Between 1852 and 1909 nearly 220,000 laborers were imported to Hawaii. More than half originated from Japan, with other larger contingents from China, Portugal, and Puerto Rico.[67]

In August 1898 Hawaii was annexed to the United States. Two years later, however, the passage of the Hawaiian Organic Act made the islands subject to US labor laws. Such legal changes posed a serious threat to the continued viability of the sugar plantations in that most sources of contract labor were now barred from entry. The 1882 Chinese Exclusion Act, for example, prevented Chinese laborers from entry into US labor markets and the Gentlemen's Agreement of 1906 likewise prevented the entry of Japanese workers. Faced with the possibility of acute labor shortages, Hawaiian plantation owners turned elsewhere for replacement labor.[68] Filipinos, classified as US nationals, were exempt from federal immigration law, and thus seemingly provided an ideal solution.

In 1906 the Hawaiian Sugar Planters' Association (HSPA) began recruiting in the Philippines. Early attempts proved unsuccessful, however, largely because the recruiters limited their efforts to Manila and Cebu City. Most of these initial recruits were part of the urban unskilled labor poor and thus lacked agricultural experience. Consequently, labor recruiters explicitly targeted agricultural areas, most notably the Ilocos region on the island of Luzon. Here, conditions were ideal for recruitment. In both the provinces of Ilocos Norte and Ilocos Sur, recruiters found an area with limited amounts of land on which farming was difficult and productivity was low. Moreover, the region had a history of out-migration.[69]

Large-scale recruitment was established in 1909 and, over the next two decades, 120,000 Filipinos migrated to work on the plantations. Indicative of recruitment efforts and chain migration processes, most Filipino laborers originated from just a few provinces. The majority were recruited from the northern and central regions of Luzon. Indeed, over 68 percent of these early migrants came from just six provinces: Abra, Ilocos Norte, Illocos Sur, La Union, Pangisinan, and Tarlac. Beyond this region, the central Visayas were most heavily targeted; 27 percent, in fact, originated from the Visayan provinces of Bohol, Cebu, Leyte, and Negros Oriental.[70]

Over time a secondary migration system developed as Hawaiian-employed Filipinos sought better employment opportunities throughout the western continental United States. Still later, as social networks were reinforced and as US labor recruiters became more active, direct immigration from the Philippines to the United States was established. During the 1920s, for example, about 45,000 Filipinos migrated to the United States. Most found employment in the agricultural regions of California and other Pacific coast states. They would travel season to season, from one farming community to another, following the harvest. Filipinos would also find employment in the fish canneries throughout the Pacific Northwest and Alaska. Gradually a permanent Philippine population was established. The 1930 census reported approximately 45,000 Filipinos residing on the mainland, and over 63,000 Filipinos in Hawaii.[71]

The migration of Filipinos to the United States and its possessions, however, was dictated largely by US policies and practices. And just as American officials could initiate migratory systems, so too could they curtail or even halt such systems. Similar to the exclusion of Chinese and Japanese immigrants in the late nineteenth and early twentieth centuries, Filipino migrants likewise were targeted for exclusion.[72]

Philippine immigrants, like other ethnic groups arriving in the United States, encountered racial discrimination and violence. Racism and prejudice were especially pronounced in the western United States during the depression years. Filipinos were perceived as stealing American jobs, but also suspected of stealing American (white) women. And with virtually all immigration from Asia barred (following the 1875, 1882, 1917, and 1924 immigration acts), questions arose as to why Filipinos, legally classified as "Orientals," were still entering the United States. Roy Malcolm, for example, asked in the journal *Current History*: "America has successfully dealt with the threat of Chinese immigration . . . [and] the immigration of Japanese labor. How will it meet this third wave of Oriental immigration that beats so persistently upon its western shores?"[73] Paul Scharrenberg decried, "It is extremely puzzling to the average American worker . . . [who] does not understand why the Filipino had been made a privileged character under the immigration laws."[74]

The exclusion of Philippine immigrants, however, was not a straightforward proposition. As US nationals, Filipinos could travel legally to and from the United States. Until the Philippines was granted independence, the US Congress could not exclude Filipinos. And therein was the problem. If independence was declared, many US corporations in operation in the Philippines were liable to be adversely affected. As Bill Hing writes, an unlikely coalition of exclusionists, anticolonialists, and Filipino nationalists banded together to promote the passage of the Tydings–McDuffie Act in 1934.[75] This act provided for a *10-year* transition period to independence, during which there would be established the Commonwealth

of the Philippines. The commonwealth would draft its own constitution.[76] However, as further specified in the act, Filipinos were no longer classified as US nationals and were thus *immediately* subjected to federal immigration law. The Philippines, although a commonwealth of the United States, was also considered a separate country. As such, the Philippines was allocated an annual quota of just 50 migrants, thereby effectively eliminating migration from the Philippines. Numerically, the effect of Philippine "independence" on immigration was dramatic. Whereas Philippine arrivals in the US totaled 36,525 in 1931, only 72 entered in 1936.[77] American business interests were not so negatively affected. Donald Seekins explains that although the commonwealth was in principle self-governing, all foreign policy decisions would be the responsibility of the United States and laws passed by the Philippine legislature affecting immigration, foreign trade, or the currency system had to be approved by the United States president. Furthermore, the trade provisions of the act allowed for 5 years' free entry of Philippine goods during the transition period and 5 years of gradually rising tariff duties thereafter, reaching 100 percent in 1946, while United States goods during the full 10 years could enter the islands unrestricted and duty-free.[78]

America's own global capitalist expansion brought the Philippines more deeply into the world economy. However, from the standpoint of the Philippines, this incorporation was exceedingly circumscribed. At the time of independence in 1946, the Philippines' economy was firmly dependent on agricultural exports—just four crops accounted for nearly 90 percent of all Philippine exports—and trade was almost exclusively directed to the United States.[79] Emigration from the Philippines, likewise, had reached a size incomparable to any other period in the history of the archipelago. And yet, here again, Philippine international migration was directed near exclusively toward the United States.

As of the mid-twentieth century, therefore, the Philippines was certainly *integrated* into the world economy. Peasant farmers in the Philippines grew pineapples, sugar, tobacco, and other cash crops for sale in the United States; Filipino migrant workers cut asparagus and other vegetables in the fields of California and processed fish in canneries stretching from California to Alaska. Such integration, though, was severely limited. These conditions would continue for decades to come following independence.

THE OUTLINE OF THE BOOK

Our story begins here. In Chapter Two I consider how the Philippine state, since the 1970s, has promoted, through the deployment of overseas migrant workers, a global presence. However, in so doing I question both how this presence contributes to globalization *as a process* and, concurrently, how globalization *as an idea* has been used to promote overseas employment. Globalization, on the one hand, is a material process. It includes the physical movement of goods and people; it includes also the various networked computer systems, telecommunications, information-based technology, and transportation systems that permit the movement of goods and people. But, on the other hand, globalization is also an *idea*, or a discourse. As Kelly argues, globalization is a construction; the *idea* of globalization creates a particular "representation" of space that is deployed to substantiate or legitimate certain strategic practices. This is significant in that "By constructing a particular vision of global space and the 'place' of individuals, national economies and so on within it, it has been argued that the idea of globalization forms part of a rhetoric to legitimize certain political strategies."[80] Indeed, according to Kelly, globalization "serves as a particular discourse of development that is used to justify neoliberal economic policies in which the state is viewed as a hindrance to economic development. Globalization [as discourse] gives authority to neoliberal arguments for market access and free trade . . . [and] creates the context in which openness to the global market is seen as the inevitable and common-sensical route to prosperity and progress."[81]

Manila is the subject of Chapter Three. Drawing on the *global cities* literature, I highlight the consequences of the Philippines' *globalized* overseas employment program on the *local* urbanization processes within Manila. In particular, I reveal how the actualization of overseas employment, predicated on a discourse of globalization, is manifest at the local level, as indicated by the increased concentration of administrative structures and institutional apparatuses. Concurrently, these spatial agglomerations materialize in the production of Manila as a global city.

Chapter Four addresses two concerns. First, I examine the use of the Internet, and specifically the World Wide Web, as a means to facilitate the global recruitment and circulation of migrant labor. Information technologies such as the Internet have evolved in parallel to the evolving spatial network of international flows of labor and capital. How have private recruitment agencies, in particular, incorporated these technological innovations into their day-to-day operations? What are the implications of this confluence of technology and labor recruitment? Second, I consider how Filipino migrants have likewise embraced the Internet. Technological advances and the development of the Internet, in particular, have affected real-world spatial interactions and the (re)formulation of identities. This is seen especially in the creation of virtual- and cyber-communities.[82] Increasingly, members of transnational migrant communities, or diasporas, have employed the Internet to maintain social linkages with their homeland, as well as other migrant communities.[83] Thus, I consider how the global diffusion of Internet technology has facilitated the creation of Filipino "cyber-communities" and how these technologies have contributed to a (re)constitution of what it means to be Filipino "in the world."

In Chapter Five I consider how globalization affects the life of one migrant in particular. I concur with Steven Flusty who argues that "The persistent focus on globalization, extrinsic and overhead, must be redressed by conceptions of global formation that look to specific *in situ* everyday activities. Such activities must be treated not just as informed by the global, but as formative of globalities and, through their interoperation, the global."[84] This chapter, therefore, provides a descriptive and theoretically informed discussion of one woman as she maneuvers within an increasingly interconnected world. Through her experiences I discuss how the current forms of institutional regulations are a consequence of global economic reorganization, and how these materially and discursively impinge on her day-to-day activities. Thus, through her migration "biography," I provide insight into the intricate associations between institutional controls, individual agency, familial contexts, and globalization.

Lastly, in Chapter Six I outline a series of conclusions drawn from this study of the Philippines, international labor migration, and globalization, asking what the Philippines may tell us about the processes, and study, of the movement of workers within a globalizing world.

Manufacturing a Global Presence
Two

> . . . the global presence of Filipino labour is our strategic contribution to . . . global development . . .[1]

> As more and more Filipinos choose to explore work opportunities abroad, globalization has opened up the world's doors to accommodate them more readily.[2]

Filomeno Aguilar, Jr., asks: "Are Filipinos at home in the world?"[3] His question is motivated by the fact that approximately eight million Filipinos currently live and work outside of the Philippines—a figure that does not include the estimated 875,000 Filipinos working abroad as "irregular" or "unauthorized" migrants. Furthermore, the geographic scope of the Filipino diaspora[4] is astounding, with migrant workers residing in 197 countries and territories. Thus, as Philip Kelly writes, "a sense of life lived at a larger scale than the village, town or nation is seldom absent from the everyday experiences of a large proportion of the population."[5]

On the one hand, a global Filipino presence is hardly new. Throughout the Philippines' long colonial past—and even before—Filipinos moved and worked beyond their homeland. On the other hand, the contemporary global dispersal of Filipinos is different. Since the mid-1970s, for example, the Philippine government has actively encouraged and promoted a global presence. The efforts of both state and private institutions are manifest not only in the increased number of workers processed and deployed, but also in the geographic destinations of migrant workers.

To be sure, changing patterns of Philippine overseas employment reflect changes in the world economy. In the 1970s, for example, Overseas Filipino Workers (OFWs) were deployed primarily to the oil-producing states of the Middle East, and in the mid-1980s, this region accounted for over 80 percent of all deployed Filipino workers. During the late 1980s, however, Asian-based destinations began to account for an ever-increasing share of Philippine migrant workers. Indeed, by 1997 Asia as a destination region surpassed the Middle East as the primary recipient of Filipino OCWs.

During the twenty-first century, however, the Middle East has recaptured the lion's share of Filipino OCWs. In 2002, for

Table 2.1 Top ten host countries of Filipino overseas workers, selected years

Rank	1975	1987	1994	2006
1	Japan	Saudi Arabia	Saudi Arabia	Saudi Arabia
2	USA	Japan	Hong Kong	UAE
3	Hong Kong	Hong Kong	Japan	Hong Kong
4	Papua New Guinea	UAE	Taiwan	Kuwait
5	Saudi Arabia	Kuwait	UAE	Qatar
6	Italy	Singapore	Malaysia	Taiwan
7	Saipan	Qatar	Kuwait	Singapore
8	Nigeria	Bahrain	Singapore	Italy
9	Singapore	Oman	Brunei	UK
10	Bahrain	Libya	Qatar	South Korea

Sources: Gonzalez 1998: Table 2.3; Philippine Overseas Employment Administration 2007: Table 4.

Table 2.2 Deployed land-based Filipino overseas workers by region, 1984–1997

	Middle East	Asia	Other	Total
1984	250,210 (83.3%)	38,817 (12.9%)	11,351 (3.8%)	300,378
1985	253,867 (79.2%)	52,838 (16.5%)	13,789 (4.3%)	320,494
1986	236,434 (73.1%)	72,536 (22.4%)	14,547 (4.5%)	323,517
1987	272,038 (71.2%)	90,434 (23.7%)	19,757 (5.2%)	382,229
1988	267,035 (69.3%)	92,648 (24.1%)	25,434 (6.6%)	385,117
1989	241,081 (67.8%)	86,196 (24.3%)	28,069 (7.9%)	355,346
1990	218,110 (65.1%)	90,768 (27.1%)	26,005 (7.8%)	334,883
1991	302,825 (63.5%)	132,592 (27.8%)	41,540 (8.7%)	476,957
1992	340,604 (65.8%)	134,776 (26.0%)	42,252 (8.2%)	517,632
1993	302,975 (59.4%)	168,205 (33.0%)	38,473 (7.5%)	509,653
1994	286,387 (55.3%)	194,120 (37.5%)	37,155 (7.2%)	517,662
1995	234,310 (53.6%)	166,774 (38.2%)	35,800 (8.2%)	436,884
1996	221,224 (52.1%)	174,308 (41.1%)	28,727 (6.8%)	424,259
1997	221,047 (45.4%)	235,129 (48.3%)	30,451 (6.3%)	486,627

Source: Tyner 2004: Table 2.2.

example, the Middle East accounted for 46 percent of all Filipino OCWs. This dominance has continued and, indeed, it has increased to the present. Equally important, however, has been the increased presence of Filipino OCWs in non-Middle Eastern and non-Asian destinations. In recent years, both European and American (i.e., Canada and the United States) have increased in importance as sites of Philippine migrant workers. However, as discussed later, this shift is directly related to specific policies and programs initiated by the Philippine state.

Another recent trend readily evident is the feminization of

Table 2.3 Deployed land-based Filipino overseas workers by destination, 1998–2006

	Middle East	Asia	Europe	Americas	Africa	Other
1998	279,767	307,261	26,422	9,152	5,538	10,201
1999	287,076	299,521	30,707	9,045	4,936	9,046
2000	283,291	292,067	39,296	7,624	4,298	9,807
2001	297,533	285,051	43,019	10,679	4,943	8,884
2002	306,939	292,077	45,363	11,532	6,919	7,992
2003	285,564	255,287	37,981	11,049	8,750	6,721
2004	352,314	266,609	55,116	11,692	8,485	10,200
2005	394,419	259,209	52,146	14,886	9,103	10,462
2006	462,545	222,940	59,313	21,976	9,450	11,582

Source: Philippine Overseas Employment Administration 2007: Table 20.

Philippines' international migration. Out-migration from the Philippines has historically been male-dominated. This is true not only of the migratory systems initiated during the period of Spanish and American colonialism, but also of the substantial migrations to the Middle East in the 1970s. Since the 1990s, however, both settlement migration and temporary overseas employment from the Philippines have been female-dominated. Indeed, as of 2006, Filipino OCWs accounted for 72 percent of all Philippine contract workers.

This feminization is further reflected when figures are disaggregated by sex and occupation. Female workers, for example, are highly concentrated into two sectors: service occupations (e.g., domestic workers) and professional occupations.[6] Male workers, conversely, are largely employed in production-related occupations (e.g., plumbers, pipe-fitters, welders). Occupational segregation, moreover, is manifest spatially. Despite a ubiquitous presence, patterns of Philippine out-migration are highly concentrated. For example, the 39,460 Overseas Performing Artists (OPAs) deployed in 2005 found employment in just 16 countries. However, of these countries, Japan alone accounted for 98 percent of all deployed OPAs. Filipino domestic workers, conversely, were deployed to 54 countries and territories in 2006 while production workers, likewise, were deployed to over 50 countries and territories.

These channels of occupational segregation have been remarkably stable. Since 1992, for example, Japan has remained the primary recipient of Filipino OPAs. More specifically, between 1992 and 2005 Japan accounted for 98.8 percent of all deployed Filipino OPAs; and between 2000 and 2003 this proportion exceeded 99 percent![7] Other occupations reflect similar concentration. Between 1992 and 2006, for example, 84 percent of all Philippine nurses were deployed to just five countries: Saudi Arabia, the United Kingdom, the United States, the United Arab Emirates, and Singapore. Domestic helpers, likewise, are highly concentrated in their deployment destinations. Approximately 75 percent of all Filipino domestic workers are destined to just five countries; Hong Kong alone accounts for nearly one third of all Filipino domestic workers.

Combined, these statistics provide a glimpse of the Philippines' global presence. These spatial and temporal patterns, however, are neither "natural" nor "inevitable." Despite claims to the contrary, these patterns are not the result of globalization per se. They are evidence of globalization, certainly, but only insofar as they reflect materially the activities of an aggressive Philippine "migration industry."

In this chapter I detail the genesis, maturation, and alterations of the Philippines' state migratory apparatus. It is my

Table 2.4 Land-based newly hired Filipino overseas workers by skill and sex, 2005–2006

	2005			2006		
Occupation	**Male**	**Female**	**Total**	**Male**	**Female**	**Total**
Professional	17,212 (41.7%)	24,042 (58.3%)	41,254	11,953 (19.8%)	48,356 (80.2%)	60,309
Managerial	528 (64.6%)	289 (35.4%)	817	381 (77.8%)	109 (22.2%)	490
Clerical	3,271 (41.3%)	4,640 (58.7%)	7,911	1,985 (35.8%)	3,553 (64.2%)	5,538
Sales	2,405 (43.6%)	3,111 (56.4%)	5,516	1,288 (30.2%)	2,972 (69.8%)	4,260
Services	16,135 (11.2%)	128,160 (88.8%)	144,295	10,666 (8.0%)	123,219 (92.0%)	133,885
Agricultural	716 (88.7%)	91 (11.3%)	807	311 (88.9%)	39 (11.1%)	350
Production	80,240 (77.5%)	23,338 (22.5%)	103,578	51,694 (69.1%)	23,096 (30.9%)	74,790
Total	120,507 (39.6%)	183,671 (60.4%)	304,178	78,278 (28.0%)	201,344 (72.0%)	279,622

Source: www.poea.gov.ph (accessed November 12, 2007).

Table 2.5 Deployed newly-hired performing artists by selected destination, 1992–2006

	Japan	South Korea	Hong Kong	Singapore	Bahrain	Other	Total
1992	49,216	107	259	21	53	342	49,998
1993	41,410	174	220	33	28	189	42,054
1994	52,386	194	265	81	29	347	53,302
1995	22,940	28	134	24	20	306	23,452
1996	18,232	4	11	52	24	241	18,564
1997	31,071	50	27	131	32	361	31,672
1998	35,335	46	8	55	58	274	35,776
1999	43,822	47	1	60	65	301	44,296
2000	59,568	3	18	60	36	174	59,859
2001	70,244	94	13	90	43	151	70,635
2002	73,246	256	4	54	9	116	73,685
2003	57,605	237	5	41	0	113	58,001
2004	70,628	615	22	24	12	188	71,489
2005	38,533	687	75	2	9	189	39,495
2006	6,672	487	42	19	24	187	7,431
Total	670,908	3,029	1,104	747	442	3,521	679,709

Source: Philippine Overseas Employment Administration 2007: Table 25.

Table 2.6 Deployed newly-hired nurses by selected destination, 1992–2006

	Saudi Arabia	UK	USA	UAE	Singapore	Other	Total
1992	3,279	0	1,767	271	6	755	6,078
1993	4,202	0	1,987	47	47	1,025	7,308
1994	3,332	0	2,853	270	85	631	7,171
1995	3,246	1	3,690	94	162	761	7,954
1996	3,071	0	270	137	549	1,450	5,477
1997	3,794	0	11	209	586	645	5,245
1998	4,098	63	5	279	371	583	5,399
1999	4,031	934	53	378	214	362	5,972
2000	4,386	2,628	91	305	418	513	8,341
2001	5,275	5,388	304	249	413	2,193	13,822
2002	6,068	3,105	322	424	338	2,078	12,335
2003	5,996	1,544	197	267	326	940	9,270
2004	5,926	800	373	250	166	1,364	8,879
2005	4,886	546	229	703	149	1,255	7,768
2006	2,886	139	133	398	56	4,916	8,528
Total	64,476	15,147	12,285	4,281	3,886	19,471	119,547

Source: Philippine Overseas Employment Administration 2007: Table 22.

Table 2.7 Deployed newly-hired domestic helpers by selected destination, 1992–2006

	Hong Kong	Saudi Arabia	Kuwait	UAE	Qatar	Other	Total
1992	13,584	17,517	666	6,035	4,138	15,963	57,903
1993	17,903	17,800	316	8,882	3,742	22,436	71,079
1994	22,625	16,522	611	6,771	3,618	21,229	71,376
1995	22,134	14,520	376	4,795	2,677	18,961	63,463
1996	17,430	15,135	148	4,233	2,091	22,846	61,883
1997	25,986	2,005	78	3,749	2,291	13,425	47,534
1998	22,439	2,575	4,281	4,410	2,044	11,300	47,049
1999	19,590	9,620	6,309	4,940	1,677	11,255	53,391
2000	27,713	10,660	9,225	5,422	1,329	13,921	68,270
2001	27,513	10,902	10,212	5,228	1,585	15,938	71,378
2002	22,870	11,934	12,835	4,950	1,899	8,946	63,434
2003	13,874	8,652	11,070	4,314	1,736	6,304	45,950
2004	16,501	7,741	17,054	5,826	2,438	13,258	62,818
2005	17,514	9,227	19,707	9,113	4,998	21,908	82,467
2006	19,532	11,898	19,097	11,844	6,524	22,517	91,412
Total	307,208	166,708	111,985	90,512	42,787	240,207	959,407

Source: Philippine Overseas Employment Administration 2007: Table 27.

contention that the origins of this "industry" are found in the radical transformations of the Philippines' political economy that occurred during the martial law years (1972–1986) of President Ferdinand Marcos. To set the stage, however, I pick up where I left off in Chapter One, namely the Philippines' uneven incorporation into the world economy as a result of American colonial and neocolonial practices.

AFTER INDEPENDENCE

World War II inflicted a tremendous toll on the Philippines. Four years of conflict and occupation resulted in a loss of life approaching one million. And in terms of infrastructure, the war left the country devastated. Manila especially suffered. In the immediate post-war period, water, sewage, and electrical services operated intermittently at best; six bridges spanning the Pasig River were in ruins; and most hospitals were destroyed beyond repair. Port facilities and factories, also, were damaged. Many residential areas were uninhabitable.[8]

In light of this devastation, American capital moved in. In 1946, for example, the Rehabilitation Act was passed by the United States Congress. These actions, though, were far from altruistic. In fact, the return of American business and political interests was but a continuation of US involvement in both the Philippines and Southeast Asia as a whole. On the one hand, American activities in the Philippines were strategic. With the dawning of the Cold War, American officials recognized the necessity of maintaining a strong but subservient political ally in Asia.[9] On the other hand, the dispersion of funds was intended to support and benefit American interests in the country, as opposed to affecting genuine change in the former colony.[10]

As part of the rehabilitation of the Philippines, the American Congress provided $620 million to the Philippines. However, only $120 million was allocated for the repair of the country's infrastructure. Of the remaining funds, $100 million was to be supplied in the form of surplus US military property and the rest (US $400 million) allocated to individuals for the restoration of their property. This served to reaffirm the unequal distribution of land and wealth that characterized the pre-war Philippines. Even more so, at least one quarter of the value of war damage claims exceeding US $50,00 were submitted by US citizens. As Stephen Shalom writes, the implications of the Rehabiliation Act meant that rather than using the destruction of the war as an opportunity to reconstruct Philippine society on a more egalitarian basis, those who were economically dominant in the pre-war period were to be maintained in their preeminent position.[11]

The destruction of the Philippines became an opportunity for the expansion of US capital. As argued by Shalom, the lack of sufficient aid to completely cover the war damage was not an oversight; it was a conscious element of American policy to leave as much of the job of rehabilitation as possible to private capital. This practice, in return, necessitated the imposition of one-sided and highly preferential trade relations for Americans and provided incentives to American investment in the islands.[12]

Rehabilitation was also used as a form of political leverage. The dispersal of funds was conditional on Philippine acceptance of unfair and unequal economic and military agreements, most notably the Bell Trade Act. This act specified that US exports were to be admitted into the Philippines free of duty, with no limitation on quantity, for a period of 8 years. Tariffs would then be incrementally increased over the next quarter-century until full duty was paid. This arrangement gave US goods an advantage in the Philippines over goods of other states and, consequently, would reestablish the Philippines as one of the best customers for US goods.[13] Philippine exports to the United States were to follow a similar pattern, but with notable exceptions. Absolute quotas were placed on the entry of Philippine sugar, cordage, cigars, scrap tobacco, coconut oil, and pearl buttons. Not surprisingly, this list included most of the Philippines' major exports. As Jasper Bell, responsible for the legislation, explained, "One of the purposes of this bill . . . is to see that American capital has an opportunity to go down [to the Philippines] and invest on the basis that they will be safe in their investment."[14]

The preferential trade conditions of the Bell Trade Act afforded considerable protection to US domestic producers of these goods and marked especially a victory of the American vegetable oils and fats industry. Other sections of the act permitted the US president to establish quotas on any other Philippine products that were likely to come into substantial competition with American products. This had the effect of further stunting the Philippines' incorporation into the world economy as the Philippines remained tied to a limited and tightly controlled product base.[15] Kelly concludes that the result of these conditions was to establish a post-war economy that retained its dependence on agricultural commodity exports, continued the dominance of Philippine politics by the landed oligarchy, ensured American control over significant areas of the economy, and allowed the US some powerful economic sanctions with which to exercise its influence as political and military "patron."[16]

Throughout the late 1940s and 1950s the Philippine state did begin to exert a degree of independence. During the presidency of Carlos Garcia, for example, the Philippine government advanced a "Filipino First" policy. As part of this effort, the Import Control Act, passed in 1948, became an instrument for an import substitution industrialization (ISI) program. Philippine-owned factories were thus able to take advantage of tax exemptions and liberal credit facilities, thereby setting in motion a transition from an agricultural economy predicated on cash-crops to an economy reoriented toward packaging, assembly, and light manufacturing. Kelly concludes that the implementation of an ISI strategy satisfied both a political and a transnational economic coalition of interests in that an economic program directed toward Filipino-owned businesses partially met the demands of a growing nationalist movement in the country.[17]

By the late 1950s, however, the Philippine economy experienced a slowdown in growth. Many of the older, established manufacturing industries were unable to expand beyond the limited, protective domestic market, and industrial growth could not absorb the expanding labor force—estimated at 700,000 new workers per year.[18] Furthermore, transformation of the world economy, including a decline in the value of Philippine exports and the growth in overseas borrowings, converged to stunt economic growth.[19] Equally important, though, was the revelation that the ISI strategy failed due to the dominant presence of the US in Philippine firms.[20]

Beset with a balance of payment deficit and a mounting external debt, the Philippine government during the 1960s experienced increased intervention by external institutions, such as the International Monetary Fund (IMF) and the World Bank. Citing the "South Korean Miracle" and the "Brazilian Miracle," IMF and World Bank officials concluded that rapid industrial growth could only materialize through a strategy of export-oriented industrialization.[21] Consequently, export-oriented industrialization was heavily promoted under the presidency of Ferdinand Marcos during the late 1960s and early 1970s. The Investment Incentives Act of 1967 (Republic Act [RA] 5186), for example, established the Board of Investments and gave a broad range of tax incentives to export producers, including tax credits on raw materials and imported capital equipment. These benefits were enlarged with the Export Incentives Act of 1970 (RA 6135) which allowed for a 10-year tax holiday on most materials and capital goods used in manufacturing and processing. Also passed in that year was the Foreign Business Relations Act (RA 5455) which removed restrictions on the repatriation of profits.[22]

This period also saw the emergence of a class of professionals known as the "technocrats." These individuals, by and large, were Western-educated economists and managers who were without independent political bases and political ambitions. In time, these technocrats would lead to significant changes in government financial planning, revenue collection, national development programs, and agricultural production.[23]

In short, the Philippine economy during this period was oriented toward the production of not only traditional agricultural products (e.g., sugar and copra), but also non-traditional products, such as electronic chips and garments.[24] The export of labor was not yet a component of the Philippines' shifting economic strategy, but the conditions were forming.

"MARTIAL LAW, PHILIPPINE STYLE"

On September 21, 1972 President Marcos declared martial law. Although the causes (e.g., population growth, economic instability, communist insurgencies, separatist movements) and motivations (personal gain on behalf of Marcos) of this action were (and remain) widely debated, one effect is unarguable: By choosing to declare martial law, Marcos cleared the way for a concerted effort to intensify and expand the promotion of export-led industrialization within the Philippines.[25]

Indeed, Presidential Decree No. 1, Marcos's first act following the declaration of martial law, addressed *not* civil unrest or the potential for revolution, but rather administrative reorganization. Specifically, PD No. 1 abolished the National Economic Council and, consequently, all economic planning and implementation was concentrated in the National Economic Development Authority (NEDA).[26]

Following the success of other Asian states, such as South Korea and Singapore, Marcos promised his version of "Martial Law, Philippine style."[27] Thus, under martial law, Philippine development policy became increasingly oriented toward export production. Economic policies were designed primarily to attract new private investment as this increasing orientation of Philippine development policy took place.[28] Presidential Decree 66, for example, established the Export Processing Zones Authority to oversee an existing zone in Bataan and to develop other zones throughout the country; the Mactan EPZ, near Cebu city, was designed in 1978; Baguio City EPZ followed in 1979 and Cavite EPZ, south of Manila, in 1980. Other decrees included: The reversal of the Supreme Court's decision which declared that the right of US corporations and citizens to own and control resources on an equal basis with Filipinos had expired; the opening of the Philippines to foreign oil corporations for the exploration and exploitation of petroleum products; and the setting up of a free trade zone in Bataan, for the expansion of exports.[29]

President Marcos, legislating through presidential decrees, directives, executive orders, and letters of instruction, facilitated also a major overhaul of labor relations within the country. The net effect of these actions was a weakening of labor's position in the Philippines. In 1973, for example, Marcos created a committee from the Department of Labor whose task was to codify for the first time all existing labor laws in the country. The committee was instructed to gear the Labor Code toward the development thrust of the government, which was for the expansion of exports and the creation of labor-intensive industries for export. Chaired by Undersecretary of Labor Amado Inciong, the committee was subsequently directed to codify the labor laws to conform to the recommendations suggested by the Ranis Mission. This latter mission, a project of the International Labor Organization (ILO) and supported by the World Bank, had released a report in 1973 calling for significant changes in policy. In particular, recommendations included not only the continued expansion of export-oriented industrialization, but also the use of wage restraints as an effective policy to enable employers to expand operations, thus easing unemployment.[30]

Some of the most far-reaching changes resulted from the passage of the Labor Code, signed by President Marcos on May 1, 1974. On signing, Marcos declared that a new "Magna Carta of Labor" had been won by the Filipino working class.[31] Subsequent events suggest otherwise. The 1974 Labor Code, and the attendant presidential decrees combined to favor foreign investors, selected members of the landed oligarchy, and Marcos personally, to the detriment of the Philippine masses. One key to the Philippines' economic strategy was the discursive marketing of an "internationally attractive labor force," i.e., a cheap and docile work force prevented from forming unions or going on strike. Thus, for example, for a 5-year period (1974–1979) the Labor Code made unfair labor practices such as "union busting" administrative offenses rather than criminal offenses; the upshot of this, Villegas argues, was to further weaken workers' stance against management. As a corollary to the declaration of martial law, moreover, Marcos issued General Order No. 5 which imposed a total ban on strikes and other forms of public assembly.[32]

This was later amended to limit the ban on strikes to only "vital" industries which, not surprisingly, included companies engaged in the production or processing of essential commodities or products for export. The Labor Code, likewise, permitted employers to pay new employees only 75 percent of the basic minimum wage during a 6-month "probationary" period.[33] By releasing workers after this period, multinational corporations effectively instituted a high turnover rate. Multinational corporations further benefited from the selective recruitment and hiring of (often young and single) female workers. Hence, this capitalization of patriarchal structures, which encouraged reduced labor costs, led to women's comparative disadvantage in the capitalist wage-labor market and enhanced the comparative advantage of firms that employed women in labor-intensive industries.[34]

According to Kelly, the declaration of martial law, the abolition of Congress, and the suppression of labor organizations and dissident intellectuals, enabled the president to give his technocrats a free hand in reorienting the economy.[35] Martial law resulted in the unprecedented centralization of state power in the executive branch, and specifically in the hands of Marcos and his cronies. The president became responsible for all law-making and all important administrative and judicial decisions.[36] Equally important, however, was that martial law resulted in the increased importance of the technocrats who, arguably, provided for the globalization of the Philippines. As Timberman explains, these economists gave the regime considerable credibility with domestic and international business communities, foreign governments, and international development and commercial banks; they spoke the same language as foreign officials, their plans and presentations were impressive.[37] Combined, these changes brought about by Marcos' political machinations set the context for the emergence of the Philippine state migratory apparatus.

DEVELOPMENT DIPLOMACY AND PERSONAL SACRIFICE

Throughout the 1970s the restructuring of the Philippine economy toward commercial agriculture and export-oriented industrialization radically altered domestic labor market conditions and relations. Denied access to traditional economic forms of subsistence (through the lack of landownership), yet more fully incorporated into the waged labor force, many Filipinos found in-country employment opportunities unavailable or untenable due to low wages. Indeed, Jane Hutchinson notes that approximately 82 percent of the non-agricultural work force was outside the formal sector.[38] As Jamie Peck identifies, in capitalist societies the preparedness of workers to offer their labor in the labor market is largely secured by the systematic erosion of possibilities of subsistence outside the wage system.[39] By extension, the erosion of subsistence-level wages within local labor markets serves to incorporate workers into the global labor market.

As codified in the 1974 Labor Code, all labor policies and programs were to be realigned with overall development goals—including the promotion of overseas employment. Article 3 of the Labor Code specifies that the "state shall afford protection to labor, promote full employment, ensure equal work opportunities regardless of sex, race or creed, and regulate the relations between workers and employers." Additionally, as indicated in Article 12, it is the policy of the state to (1) promote and maintain a state of full employment through manpower training, (2) protect every citizen desiring to work locally or overseas through the securing of the best possible terms and conditions of employment, (3) facilitate a free choice of available employment, and (4) facilitate and regulate the movement of workers in conformity with the national interest. Last, as mandated in Articles 17.1 and 17.2, the Philippine state was to promote the overseas employment of Filipino workers through a comprehensive market promotion and development program and, in the process, secure the best possible terms and conditions of employment of Filipino contract workers on a government-to-government basis.[40] The emergence of the Philippine state migratory apparatus was thus firmly situated within the Marcos regime's policy of *development diplomacy*. This policy perspective was predicated on the observation that "less-developed" countries contained large population bases as well as vital natural resources. In the case of the Philippines, the Marcos regime attempted to utilize the country's "surplus" labor and the high demand for labor in oil-producing countries to demonstrate the feasibility of "interdependent development."[41]

Situated within a discourse of development diplomacy, overseas employment emerged as an attractive opportunity to satisfy a variety of goals. First, as discussed earlier, the strategy was expected to promote Philippine development and to alleviate balance-of-payments problems through mandatory remittances. As indicated in Article 22 of the Labor Code, all Filipino workers were (and still are) required to remit a portion of their foreign exchange earnings to their families, dependants, and/or beneficiaries in the Philippines. The amount which workers are legally required to remit varies by occupation: sea-based workers are mandated to remit 80 percent of their earnings; doctors, engineers, teachers, nurses, and other professional workers whose contracts provide for "free" board and lodging must remit 70 percent; domestic and other service workers are required to remit 50 percent. Second, overseas employment was expected to reduce levels of unemployment and underemployment (especially of the educated, professional surplus population). As discussed, the number of annual entrants to the Philippines' labor force throughout the 1970s exceeded 700,000. Third, it was presumed that overseas employment would improve the stock of human capital, as workers returned to the Philippines (upon completion of their contract) with skills acquired from abroad. Lastly, a promotion of overseas employment offered (potentially) many political benefits. Overseas employment, for example, was perceived by the government (at least initially) as a politically safe and advantageous strategy. It was presented in such a way that the government was portrayed as providing jobs—in a foreign country, yes, but still, a job—to the masses of unemployed and underemployed workers.[42]

In terms of form, the initial Philippine state migratory apparatus was composed of three sub-apparatuses: the newly created Overseas Employment Development Board (OEDB) and the National Seaman Board (NSB), and the existing Bureau of Employment Services (BES), which was housed in the Ministry of Labor and Employment (MOLE; later renamed the Department of Labor and Employment, or DOLE). The OEDB and the NSB were responsible for market development, recruitment, and the securing of the best possible terms of employment for land-based and sea-based workers, respectively. The BES was a government-run temporary employment agency that placed workers in domestic firms. Villegas finds that the majority of Filipino workers drawn by local capital from BES employment offices replenished the production and assembly lines of Philippine industry, dominated by American interests.[43] Hence, the one existing agency prior to the promulgation of overseas employment already had a history of catering to foreign interests.

Consistent with the increasingly centralized regime of Marcos, and similar to development in the export sectors, the form of the Philippines' overseas employment program was envisioned to be a government monopoly benefiting, first and foremost, the Marcos regime. This was to be accomplished by the gradual phase-out of all private recruitment agencies. The public justification for the government monopoly, however, was that "since the Labor Code provided for the network of public employment which is supposed to be the premier vehicle for [the] national employment program, all tactical measures, including the overseas employment program, must serve to strengthen the network."[44]

The state monopoly of overseas employment failed to materialize for four interconnected reasons. First, the OEDB and the NSB were marred by corruption and inefficiency; second, the over-centralized government apparatus began to atrophy; third, the OEDB and the NSB were unable to manage effectively all facets of overseas employment; and fourth, the private sector and coalitions of private recruitment agencies legally challenged the government's proposed monopoly. In short, in its desire to more fully exploit the dynamic global labor market, and to profit from the mandatory remittances of overseas workers, the Philippine government allowed for greater private sector participation. By 1978, following Presidential Decree No. 1412, the government relinquished its proposed monopoly. The impact of this shift is clearly evident in the rise of the private sector. At the outset of the Philippines' overseas employment program, there were 19 licensed agencies involved with recruitment and deployment; by 1979 the number had grown to 75.[45] Consequently, the magnitude of overseas employment increased rapidly. Between 1975 and 1982, for example, the total number of processed workers increased by 772 percent. Moreover, state–private union significantly transformed the day-to-day practices of the Philippine state migratory apparatus. State institutions, specifically, assumed more regulatory functions and worked to strengthen the state–private sector relationship. The bulk of the daily nuts-and-bolts activities of recruitment and deployment, conversely, were carried out by the private sector.

The incipient Philippine state migratory apparatus capitalized on newly-emerging employment opportunities throughout the Middle East and Asia. Prior to the mid-1970s, the Middle East labor market was characterized by a high degree of inter-Arab migration. In general, workers from oil-deficient but labor-surplus states (e.g., Yemen) supplied labor to other, relatively well-off oil-producing states (e.g., Saudi Arabia, Kuwait, the United Arab Emirates, Bahrain). Moreover, the limited scale of industrialization and development was such that regional migration systems could well meet any labor demands. However, the 1973 oil embargo and subsequent spike in oil prices changed the Gulf labor market. Increases in the cost of crude oil, and subsequent government royalties, combined to drive up revenues accruing to the oil-exporting states of the region by over 600 percent in constant dollars between 1972 and 1984. With increased revenues, many Arab states initiated massive infrastructure projects.

With the massive infusion of capital into the region, relative and absolute labor shortages ensued. Regional systems of inter-Arab migration could no longer match the needs of capital. In response, many Gulf States began recruiting foreign workers from East Asia, South Asia, and Southeast Asia. South Korea was an early contributor, followed by other countries, including Pakistan, Sri Lanka, and Thailand. Local governments throughout the Middle East were quick to realize the enormous advantages of hiring temporary, foreign, and non-Arab work forces. Migrant workers could be confined to isolated work camps and then sent home when the projects were completed. This was particularly attractive to the smaller, less-populous states, such as the UAE. Also, there had been a growing uneasiness toward Arab migrants who could potentially decide to resettle after migration. This was not the case with Asian workers who, culturally estranged from the local populations (and physically separated), often had no desire to stay and settle. Government officials in the Philippines were all too eager to take advantage of these changing conditions.

A doctrine of neoclassical liberalism supported Marcos' development diplomacy and the Philippines' overseas employment program. Neoclassical approaches to migration postulate that population movements arise as a "natural" response to regional disparities. Usually approaching from individual-oriented perspectives, they presume that people make cost-benefit decisions based on preexisting regional imbalances in wage and/or employment rates. In the aggregate, neoclassical models predict that, through population movements, economic disparities between sending and receiving areas will lessen and, concurrently, migration will eventually cease. The adoption of a neoclassical understanding of migration leads to two conclusions: First, that migration is beneficial and, second, that governments should intervene to facilitate population movement. Such intervention may appear in the provision of information on employment opportunities and/or a reduction in bureaucratic barriers to mobility (e.g., visas, medical clearances, and other forms of worker documentation). As former Philippine Secretary of Labor Blas Ople explained, "When . . . I started the overseas employment program in 1974, I premised this on the theory that in less than two decades . . . the Philippine economy will have grown so robust the program could then self-destruct."[46]

Ople's neoclassical understanding, though, was not the only discursive formation in operation. It is also evident that the Philippine state migratory apparatus was predicated on a discourse that sacrificed "bodies" for a more global vision of the nation-state. This is seen, for example, in a 1976 speech delivered by Marcos:

> We have provided jobs for our people not only in our new and expanding industries but also in the world labour market. Filipino talents and skills are becoming ubiquitous in many parts of the world. Returning Filipino workers have helped improve our skills and technological standards.[47]

The emergence of overseas employment was thus situated within a nationalized development discourse coupled with a discourse of "personal sacrifice for national good." In short, therefore, the reorganization of the Philippine political economy was predicated on a discursive formation that emphasized individual and national discipline and, concurrently, the sacrifice of personal liberties for economic development.[48] The "New Society" was built on a repressive labor policy which banned strikes, eliminated unions, and entailed a downward revision of existing labor protection standards.[49] Marcos claimed that the loss of civil liberties was regrettable, but was a temporary price that Filipinos would have to pay for political stability, economic growth, and social reform.[50] As quoted in Villegas, Marcos proudly explained that the Philippines "now has one of the lowest average [wage] levels in this part of the world. We intend to see to it that our export program is not placed in jeopardy at an early stage by a rapid rise in the general wage level."[51]

The imbrication of martial law, the 1974 Labor Code, and a strategy of Export Oriented Industrialization (EOI) provides the context for the emergence of overseas employment as a development strategy in the Philippines. Reflecting what David Harvey would term a "spatial fix," the emergent Philippine state migratory apparatus attempted to resolve internal economic problems through a disciplinary technique of labor exportation. To better understand this practice, it is worthwhile to consider Harvey's stretching of Marxism to understand how overseas contract workers *become* sites of capital accumulation.

Unlike slave owners, capitalists do not purchase workers per se, but rather the capacity to work, or "labor power."[52] Following Marx, the term *variable capital* refers to the sale, purchase, and use of labor power as a commodity. Moreover, as Harvey explains, there is a distinct circulation process to variable capital, in that the laborer sells labor power to the capitalist to use in the labor process, in return for a wage which permits the laborer to purchase capitalist-produced commodities in order to live, in order to work, and so on. Within systems of international labor migration, however, the state is, in effect, in the position of selling labor power in return for foreign exchange. The significance of this is further illustrated with reference to Harvey's critique of classical location theory. It is commonly understood that the "spatial range of a good" is defined by the radial distance from a point of production where the market price places the good beyond what consumers are willing or able to pay for that good. Thus, for example, a consumer is more likely to travel a greater distance for a valuable commodity (i.e., an automobile or jewelry) than for a loaf of bread. Harvey explains, however, that goods do not take themselves to market; merchants do. To follow with the example, the automobile, jewelry, or loaf of bread must be transported from the site of production to the site of purchase: The market-place. Spatially, this is what contributes, in part, to the continued expansion of capitalism, as firms continue to search for alternative markets to sell their goods and services.[53]

International labor migration provides an interesting twist

on the mobility of capital. On the one hand, we can speak of the migration of capital to sites of labor.[54] In this case, capitalists may seek out locations where labor costs are lower or, alternatively, where labor is more disciplined (e.g., strikes and unions are banned). And indeed, it was this relationship that spurred the Marcos administration to reduce the power of labor within the Philippines as a means of attracting foreign investment. On the other hand, however, it is possible to speak of the migration of labor to sites of capital accumulation. Here, migrant workers literally embody the circulation of variable capital in that, through their remittances, the sending country is able to tap into locations of surplus capital. Accordingly, through mandatory remittances the Philippine state is able to use migrant workers as a form of mobile capital accumulation. Filipino workers are *placed* in the many localized labor markets around the world and, thus, the Philippine state is able to tap into the shifting sites of capital accumulation, wherever these may appear. In short, the promotion of the international labor market constitutes a highly specialized and flexible system of capital accumulation.

A significant institutional transformation of the Philippine state migratory apparatus occurred in 1982 with the merger of the OEDB, the NSB, and the BES into the Philippine Overseas Employment Administration (POEA). This reorganization, as Maruja Asis writes, signaled an intensified effort on behalf of the Philippine government to capitalize on the globalizing economies of other world regions and to use overseas employment as a national development strategy. As a sub-apparatus of the overall state migratory apparatus, the POEA today remains the most important government institution in the regulation of overseas employment.

Presidential Decree No. 797 assigned the POEA with the formulation, implementation, and monitoring of overseas employment, hence intensifying the state's regulatory functions. Operationally, the POEA concentrated mostly on the regulation of private recruitment agencies and on the global marketing of workers, leaving to the private sector almost the complete operation of the actual recruitment and placement of overseas workers. Statistically, the declining role of the government in the daily processing of workers is readily apparent: In 1975 the OEDB processed 48 percent of all overseas contract workers; following the creation of the POEA, however, the government's share declined to just 2 percent.

As codified in the *Rules and Regulations Governing Overseas Employment*, it is the policy of the POEA:

1. to promote and develop overseas employment opportunities in cooperation with relevant government institutions and the private sector;
2. to establish the environment conducive to the continued operations of legitimate, responsible, and professional private agencies;
3. to afford protection to Filipino workers and their families, promote their interests, and safeguard their welfare; and
4. to develop and implement programs for the effective monitoring of returning contract workers promoting their retraining and reemployment or their smooth reintegration into the mainstream of the national economy.

These policies effectively constructed the framework of overseas employment, from the incorporation and allocation of workers into the global economy to the reintegration of workers to the Philippines. Significantly, though, these policies suggested that overseas employment was not part of the mainstream of the national economy, indicating perhaps a deviation from the early connections between overseas employment and development. Rather than discursively connecting the export of labor with broader national development goals, overseas employment was gradually being portrayed as a means unto itself: The generation of capital for capital's sake.

The increased regulatory function of the POEA, combined with broader structural changes of the world economy, resulted in significant changes in the spatial patterns of deployed contract workers. A primary mission of the newly formed POEA, for instance, was to actively diversify the occupational and geographical makeup of overseas employment. Subsequently, the overall number of destinations of Filipino workers increased from 74 countries and territories in 1975 to 130 in 1987. Moreover, although the majority of destinations remained in the Middle East, throughout the 1980s and 1990s Asian destinations were more common. Indeed, during the 1980s the proportion of Middle East-bound contract workers from the Philippines steadily decreased whereas, concurrently, the share of Asian-bound workers increased. This indicates, on the one hand, the "success" with which the Philippine state migratory apparatus was able to penetrate the dynamic Asian labor markets (Skeldon 1992). Within Asia, for example, economic and demographic trends conjoined to produce a tremendous demand for domestic work. Throughout Singapore, Malaysia, and Hong Kong, in particular, the incorporation of local women into the paid labor force generated a particularly high demand for domestic servants (Skeldon 1992; Huang and Yeoh 1996; Constable 1997). Consequently, governments in both the Philippines and in destination locations produced bilateral agreements and other programs to facilitate the in-migration of maids from the Philippines and elsewhere. In 1978, for example, the Singapore government initiated a Foreign Maids Scheme which was designed to provide low-cost foreign domestic workers for dual-income families. And even today, the labor force participation rate of skilled women in high-growth economies, such as Singapore, is still being sustained in part by the continued immigration of women from low-growth countries (Huang and Yeoh 1996, 488).

Migration as Self-Fulfillment

The political downfall of Marcos and the concomitant ascension of Corazon Aquino as president heralded significant changes for the political economy of the Philippines. In particular, Aquino came to power with promises of democratic rule and the renewed participation of the masses, as her presidential slogan of "People's Power" signified—or at least suggested—a shift away from the authoritarian rule of the previous regime. As Chant and McIlwaine (1995) conclude, however, the overthrow of the Marcos regime was not a "social" revolution which would lead to fundamental changes in the political or economic organization of the government. Hence, despite mounting criticism of overseas employment as a program that "trafficked" Filipinos, the new government effectively maintained and in fact expanded the existing policy of labor export. Indeed, a renewed emphasis on labor in relation to social and economic goals was proclaimed in the first policy speech made by President Aquino (Khan 1988, 9).

The constitutional mandate and labor policy recommendations under the Aquino government were, though, framed as national development goals in the Medium-Term Philippine Development Plan for 1987–1992. Those applicable to overseas employment include:

1. Overseas employment will continue to provide interim employment until such time that the domestic economy can generate enough jobs. Greater protection will be accorded to overseas contract workers against violations of

contracts to ensure that they are employed under reasonable terms and conditions. More systematic processing of employment contracts shall be pursued, while productive investment schemes will be devised to generate additional revenues to finance welfare programs for overseas workers.
2. Labor market facilitation for both local and overseas workers shall be improved to bring people and jobs together. Local employment services, public employment programs and job exchange centers shall be revitalized and upgraded to cope with the demands of an expanding labor force.

Thus, as a means of combating rising unemployment, the Philippine government continued to rely on overseas employment as an outlet. The state migratory apparatus, also, continued to view contract migration as a temporary stop-gap. The thrust of the new administration's stance on overseas employment is summarized in Executive Order (EO) 247, passed in 1987:

> Whereas, it has become necessary to institute changes in the functional structure of the Philippine Overseas Employment Administration in order to enhance its effectiveness in responding to changing market and economic conditions and to the call of the national development plan for the strengthening of the worker protection and regulation components of the overseas employment program.

Moreover, Section 4 of EO 247 states that the POEA will be "established along the areas of firstly market development and then employment, welfare, licensing, regulation and adjudication." Significantly, EO 247 makes reference to the contradictions embedded within the Philippine state migratory apparatus, namely the penetration of foreign labor markets and the provision of migrant welfare and protection. However, the discursive and pragmatic emphasis clearly leans toward the marketing side. This is reflected in materials disseminated by the POEA in its marketing of workers.

In 1987 the Marketing Branch of the Pre-Employment Services Division of the POEA launched its Overseas Employment Info Series (OIS). As part of the "Information Network" of the International Labor Organization (ILO), the OIS regularly published articles on overseas employment, special sections such as "market situationer," and statistical information. In the inaugural issue of the OIS, the POEA indicated that the administration was on the "verge of greater intensive market planning and strategizing" (POEA 1988, 5). Accordingly, the philosophy of the POEA was to adopt a "discriminating marketing approach" in the "development of labor markets for Filipino overseas contract workers" (1988, 5). This was to be accomplished through the penetration of "non-traditional markets" throughout the world, defined as either skills-based or geographic-based, in the search for "high benefit, high-growth areas suited for grooming [the] international image for the Filipino workers" (1988, 5). Moreover, it was the POEA's mission to "equip itself with suitable surplus labor to fill demand trends" and to "ensure that no one market spoils [the Philippines'] overall image and/or blocks . . . entry to newly emerging opportunities" (1988, 5).

Through this philosophy, the Philippine state, under the auspices of the POEA, sought to explicitly globalize its labor force through intensive, deliberate, and concentrated marketing efforts. Subsequent practices, including the streamlining of bureaucratic procedures, bilateral agreements, and memorandums of understanding, were all designed to open new market opportunities for capital accumulation.

Second, and related, an overt concern with the globalized representation, or image, of Philippine contract workers is apparent. Government documents reflect a concern that any one particular occupation might spoil the *international image* of the "ubiquitous" Filipino worker. The POEA was apprehensive that it might be typecast as a provider of only one type of worker, such as domestic workers. Such a singular image, it was felt, would jeopardize the POEA's ability to exploit more fully other labor niches, such as technical and information sectors. Accordingly, the POEA, through its marketing division, developed occupation-specific strategies to diversify more concretely the type of worker exported. The POEA's guiding mission was to avoid *fixing* or *essentializing* the Filipino contract worker.

As corollary, the POEA intensified its promotion of Filipino workers as "heroes and heroines" rather than as "victims." In March of 1987, for example, Aquino signed Proclamation No. 91 which declared the last week of March as "Overseas Filipino Contract Workers' Week." Additionally, in June of 1988, Proclamation No. 276 heralded December as the "Month of Overseas Filipinos." Combined, these two proclamations reaffirmed the government's intention of maintaining overseas employment as a vital development strategy.[55]

A third component of the POEA's revised marketing philosophy was to equip itself with a suitable supply of surplus labor. This statement would suggest, therefore, that the primary concern of the POEA was not *ceteris paribus* to utilize existing unemployed or underemployed labor, but rather to generate further surpluses of labor. This was to be accomplished through the enticement of Philippine citizens to participate more actively in overseas employment, as well as through the continued emphasis of job training programs on "marketable" occupations.

Last, the POEA's attempt to diversify markets was also related to foreign affairs. Especially following the 1991 Gulf War, for example, the economic benefit of narrow geographic distribution of migrant workers was threatened by military conflicts. Thus, as an economic safeguard, efforts were launched to increase the spatial dispersal, the global reach, of migrant workers.

Accordingly, although the rhetoric of self-sacrifice—prevalent during the Marcos administration—was missing, the Aquino government remained unresponsive to demands of critics to eliminate the program of overseas employment. Concurrently, numbers of processed and deployed workers steadily increased. Whereas in 1986 the POEA registered just over 323,000 workers deployed, for example, in 1992 this figure had increased to nearly 550,000.

This favorable and supportive attitude toward overseas employment remained throughout the Aquino administration (1986–1992) and into the presidency of Fidel V. Ramos. Indeed, as Gonzalez (1998, 124) concludes, the Ramos administration's policy on overseas employment remained similar to the past governments' stance—strong in stating that it would maximize the economic benefits but weak in voicing its determination to minimize the social costs. According to President Ramos, "Overseas employment remains a strategic development program of our government" (1992, 6). To Ramos, "the overseas employment program is a major pillar of national development" and aside from easing the employment situation, it "also generates invaluable foreign exchange which is necessary to fund development projects and strategic programs." Moreover, Ramos asserted that "Overseas employment . . . helps rectify world imbalances of income and human resources" and that "countries with large incomes but inadequate skilled manpower are able to help and get help from low-income countries with labor surpluses through international labor migration."

The Ramos administration, similar to past governments, also viewed overseas employment—now in its second decade of existence—as a temporary program. President Ramos was of the opinion that labor export would dwindle away as more industries located in the Philippines, an assumption articulated a decade earlier by Blas Ople. Perhaps indicative of a discursive shift, though, the POEA did claim in 1994 that "Overseas employment remains a viable and legitimate alternative for Filipino workers. However, it should be among many available options—not as a single, almost desparate, path to social mobility and personal growth" (1994: 3). This quote is revealing in that it simultaneously introduces a discourse of legitimacy, but also a discourse of empowerment. Over the next few years the POEA in particular, but the Philippine state more broadly, would continue to reposition overseas employment as a path toward "social mobility" and "personal growth." Hence, overseas employment was, and would continue to be, discursively framed as a means to provide self-fulfillment rather than simply jobs or money for the state. In the post-Marcos political environment, blatant assertions of self-sacrifice would not suffice.

The Embodiment of Globalization

The year 1995 marked a turning point in the development of the Philippine state migratory apparatus. Two highly publicized trials of Philippine Overseas Contract Workers (OCWs) seemingly threatened the very existence of the country's overseas employment program and further challenged the legitimacy of the broader Philippine state. The first case centered on Flor Contemplacion, a female domestic worker employed in Singapore; the second centered on Sarah Balabagan, also a female domestic worker, though employed in the United Arab Emirates (UAE).

In 1991 Contemplacion was charged with the double murder of a Filipina domestic worker—Delia Maga—and a 4-year-old Singaporean boy. Contemplacion had pleaded guilty to both charges, and in 1995 she was sentenced to death. Rumors surfaced that Contemplacion had been framed and forced to confess to both crimes. R.J. May, though, suggests that with the upcoming government elections in the Philippines, politicians seized on the Contemplacion case. Throughout the trial, Contemplacion was repositioned as a martyr. President Ramos requested a stay of execution from the Singaporean government; Catholic Church leader Jamie Sin—who had been instrumental in the People's Power revolution that ousted Marcos—sought Pope John Paul's intervention. All attempts, however, proved futile and on March 17, 1995 Contemplacion was executed.

Public outcry was tremendous in the Philippines. Protests were held; the Singaporean flag was burned. Adding to the furor, on the day of Contemplacion's execution, President Ramos was in West Asia and Europe negotiating for trade and investment in the country, fueling arguments that the government willingly sacrificed Contemplacion for monetary reasons.[56] Criticism of Philippine officials was widespread, including the denouncing of the Philippine ambassador to Singapore and various top-ranking officials of the POEA. Congressional committees initiated inquiries into the Contemplacion case, as well as the broader context of overseas employment.

During the summer of 1995, just months after the execution of Contemplacion, Sarah Balabagan went on trial for murder. Balabagan was a 15-year-old girl who entered the UAE on a forged passport (she claimed to be 28 years old in order to bypass POEA regulations). In July of 1994 Balabagan was allegedly attacked and raped by her 85-year-old employer. In self-defense, Balabagan overpowered her employer and killed him. At the conclusion of the trial, Balabagan was found guilty of manslaughter and sentenced to 7 years' imprisonment. Paradoxically, she was also awarded US $27,000 as compensation for being raped.

The judgment, not surprisingly given the verdict, was challenged by both the prosecution and the defense. Relatives of the slain man insisted that 7 years' imprisonment was insufficient punishment for "murder"; Balabagan's lawyers reaffirmed that the domestic worker had acted in self-defense and thus could not be guilty of manslaughter.

In September of 1995 the 7-year sentence was overturned; however, Balabagan, incredulously, was resentenced to death. Following the political furor of the Contemplacion case, the potential execution of another Filipina domestic worker initiated another round of substantial public protest throughout the Philippines and the global Filipino community. Ultimately, the president of the UAE personally intervened. As a result of his negotiations, relatives of the slain employer dropped their demand for execution in return for a monetary "blood" payment of approximately US $41,000. In October, Balabagan was sentenced yet again, this time to 100 cane lashes and a 12-month imprisonment (of which she served approximately 8 months).

These two cases followed another highly sensationalized case, that of Marcris Sioson.[57] Sioson was an "entertainer" who died in 1991 in Japan under suspicious circumstances. In many ways, the death of Sioson crystallized the plight of female overseas performing artists and ushered in a radical reorganization of the legal deployment of female entertainers. The two cases of Contemplacion and Balabagan, however, resulted in more far-reaching changes. As Gonzalez identifies:

> Contemplacion's death heightened long-standing debates in the Philippines and exposed the lack of adequate government attention to the plight of Filipino overseas contract workers, not just in Singapore, but in all the labour-receiving countries. As a result, opposition parties, church associations, women's groups, labour unions, and other OCW-oriented non-governmental organizations, assisted by one of the freest presses in the world, capitalized on the Ramos administration's political vulnerability during the election campaign period.[58]

The events of 1995 resulted in the most significant reorganization of the Philippine state migratory apparatus since the formation of the POEA in 1982. In April of 1995, following the execution of Contemplacion and during the trial of Balabagan, the Department of Labor and Employment (DOLE) disseminated a "White Paper on Overseas Employment" to provide the Philippine Congress with background information for subsequent deliberations of bills to protect migrant workers. Subsequently, the drafting of House Bill No. 14314 and of Senate Bill No. 2077 was eventually consolidated into RA 8042 and signed into law by President Ramos on June 7, 1995. Hailed as the "Magna Carta of Overseas Employment" (an ironic title, given Marcos' proclamation of the 1974 Labor Code), the Migrant Workers and Overseas Filipino Act of 1995, as RA 8042 was titled, signaled ominous transformations of the Philippine state migratory apparatus. Specifically, RA 8042 was an explicit avowal by the government that it did *not* promote overseas employment as part of the country's development program. However, it was also *not* an act designed to eliminate the export of labor. Rather, it was a clarion call to reposition the government's responsibilities. As articulated in RA 8042:

> While recognizing the significant contribution of Filipino migrant workers to the national economy through their foreign exchange remittances, the State *does not promote overseas employment as a means to sustain economic growth and achieve national development.* The existence of the overseas employment program rests solely on the assurance that *the dignity and fundamental human rights and freedoms of the Filipino citizen shall not, at any time, be compromised or violated.* The State, therefore, shall continuously create local employment opportunities and promote the equitable distribution of wealth and the benefits of development. [Italics added]

As stipulated in this act, Filipino migrant workers embodied a key element in the national economy, but, more importantly, the state ostensibly did not promote or capitalize on the global movement of migrant workers as a mobile source of capital accumulation. Specifically, Section 29 of the act mandated the DOLE to formulate a 5-year comprehensive deregulation plan on recruitment activities, while Section 30 mandated a gradual phase-out of all regulatory functions, to occur within 5 years. This act, as Rochelle Ball and Nicola Piper (2002, 1022) suggest, was based on the strong endorsement of a neoliberal stance of deregulating the responsibility of its institutions—the POEA and the Department of Foreign Affairs (DFA)—for worker welfare. Neoliberalism is an economic philosophy that can be traced to the classical liberal ideas of Adam Smith, David Ricardo, and Herbert Spencer. These philosophers considered that any restraint on free competition would interfere with the natural efficiency of market mechanisms, inevitably leading to social stagnation, political corruption, and the creation of unresponsive state bureaucracies.[59] And the contributions of Spencer, as discussed below, are especially salient in the promotion of neoliberalism by the

Philippine state. Spencer's liberalism was concerned with the "welfare" of society, but from an economically competitive orientation. Modifying the writings of Charles Darwin, Spencer argued that welfare programs were tampering with the "invisible hand" of evolution. In doing so, Spencer argued that free-market economies constituted the most civilized form of human competition in which the "fittest" would "naturally" rise to the top. Consequently, he denounced socialism, trade unions, and social regulation insofar as these, according to him, would inhibit rational progress and individual freedom.[60]

Given this legacy, in sum, the central features of neoliberalism include the primacy of economic growth, the importance of free trade to stimulate growth, the promotion of an unrestricted free market, individual choice, privatization of business, the reduction of governmental regulation, and the advocacy of an evolutionary model of social development anchored in the Western experience and applicable to the entire world.[61] Harvey summarizes that neoliberalism is, first, a theory of political economic practices that proposes that human well-being can best be advanced by liberating individual entrepreneurial freedoms and skills within an institutional framework characterized by strong private property rights, free markets, and free trade. Furthermore, if markets do not exist, then they must be created, by state action if necessary.[62]

Ironically, the death of a migrant worker and the quest for worker welfare provided the impetus, and justification, for the Philippine state to foster an environment that would lead to a greater globalized presence of its labor force.

In October of 1998 the POEA disseminated a "White Paper" on overseas employment. Entitled *Managing International Labor Migration and the Framework for the Deregulation of the POEA*, this paper was written to "allay fears about POEA deregulation and clarify deep seated concerns on [the POEA's] new paradigm of managing migration" (Casco 1997, 2). Within this document, the POEA emphasizes its legal mandate as articulated by the 1974 Labor Code. More fundamental, however, is that the document outlines a specific discourse legitimizing the state's existence as well as "migration." Indeed, this discourse could very well have come straight from Herbert Spencer himself. As indicated in the White Paper, "Managing a global phenomenon starts with understanding the philosophy of humankind, dynamics of migration, history, and natural laws which cannot be repealed." The POEA, and other constituent parts of the Philippine state migratory apparatus, are portrayed as being "controlled" by natural global laws. The document continues:

> The economic law of supply and demand is an irrepressible force in the global labor market, [more so] now with the globalization era. Unfortunately, this reality seems overshadowed by the application of national labor laws and administrative systems that perpetuate a pathological fallacy that labor migration is a program creation or innovation of government to address employment gaps. (Casco 1997, 2–3)

This discursive position of migration as a "natural" feature appeared earlier; in a 1994 policy statement, the POEA indicated that "overseas employment is an inherent structural feature of the international economy." Combined, these discourses of globalization deflect attention away from the actions of government institutions, suggesting that with or without governmental intervention, migration will continue. This essentialist explanation frames migration as a natural feature not only of the global economy, but also of humankind, and that migration operates beyond the reach of institutions.

According to this discursive remaking, the POEA emerges not as a specific program of capital accumulation, but rather as an institution to "manage" a natural process. Indeed, this is evidenced by the POEA's Web site where it boldly asserts that "Labor migration is a global phenomenon that should be managed."[63]

Compare this statement, however, with the earlier pronunciation of a "discriminate marketing approach." During the Aquino and early Ramos administrations, the POEA was clearly concerned with doing more than just managing a natural phenomenon. Rather, the POEA was actively producing a global migration through specific policies designed to exploit new labor markets, and to maintain existing markets or eliminate non-profitable ones. Unlike the emergent globalization discourse, earlier statements indicated that the POEA articulated a proactive policy that attempted to shape itself to the changing contours of the global labor market. Now, however, the Philippine state claimed to simply manage from afar the Philippines' global presence of migrant workers. No efforts were made to curtail the ever-widening scope of Philippine OCWs.

Aside from reference to "natural laws," the White Paper also discursively situates the Philippines within a particular global economy:

> What is the Philippines' standing in the global imbalance of human resources? Media sensationalism tends to overshadow the fact that the global presence of Filipino labor is our strategic contribution to the global development, from which we reap net rewards central to the goals of our social economy. *Managing means being able to objectively recognize and subsequently dominate our niche and comparative advantage* and empowering from our weaknesses.[64]

This statement vividly illustrates two key points. First, not only is international labor migration now represented as an inherent feature of the global economy, the Philippines likewise has been relegated by some natural law to be a labor supply niche. Just as other countries are "blessed" with abundant supplies of natural resources such as coal or petroleum, the Philippines has been blessed—according to the POEA—with abundant supplies of labor. The legacy of colonialism, and structural conditions, such as the promotion of export-oriented industrialization, the expansion of agribusiness, and the failures of land reform, fade dimly into the background. According to this newly-manufactured discourse, the Philippine state migratory apparatus must, for the benefit of the country, capitalize on this market niche; it must take advantage of its natural comparative advantage in the global economy. Of course, this discourse denies any complicity on behalf of the Philippine government, or any other government for that matter, in (re)producing conditions of global inequality.

At another level, this statement is revealing in its allusion to the POEA's ability to "objectively" recognize the economic playing field. The POEA, consequently, draws upon a stock of representations associated with objectivity and the scientific understanding of migration. As Arturo Escobar (1995, 20) explains, science and expert discourses produce powerful truths and ways of creating and intervening in the world. The POEA in effect has repositioned itself not as a tool for capital accumulation, but rather as an omniscient authority that seeks objectively to manage a natural, global, process. This objectivity, accordingly, masks the capitalist rationale underlying the promotion of overseas employment. Globalization is presented not as process, but rather as cause; the Philippine state, subsequently, is presented not as an active agent, but as a neutral mediator.

A corollary discourse accompanies the globalization discourse, this being a shift from broader structural features to that of the "migrant" body. This embodied discourse subsequently hinges on the concept of "empowerment" and contains allusions to the recent political history of the Philippines. As stated in the "Declaration of Policies" of RA 8042: "The right of Filipino migrant workers and all overseas Filipinos to participate in the democratic decision-making processes of the State and to be represented in institutions relevant to overseas employment is recognized and guaranteed" (POEA 1996, 2).

The POEA's reading of RA 8042 is that the act "introduces a new legal paradigm, cognizant of an emerging trend in the global economy whereby individuals are becoming more and more empowered to freely access . . . global information and avail [themselves] of new modes for interactive distance communication."[65] This statement reveals continuities with earlier statements of the POEA, such as a 1995 stance that "the empowerment of the worker populace in making well-informed decisions for which they will be held primarily responsible has been and is a key recognition."[66] In both of these documents, Casco's 1995 and 1997 position papers, a discontinuity exists in that a movement away from migrant workers as being portrayed as "heroes and heroines" sacrificing for the country is evident. Now, symbolically, the POEA's discourse refers back to the revolutionary spirit that captivated the Philippines throughout Aquino's "People Power" movement and the subsequent overthrow of Marcos. In another apparent reference to the dictatorial regime of Marcos, the 1997 White Paper explains:

> As human rights with democratic ideology, our migrant workers assert their constitutional rights and exercise their faculty of

> judgment to satisfy their socioeconomic needs and wants. No amount of legislative or other structural barriers can effectively suppress these natural drives and human rights unless enforcement of such barriers is undertaken strictly under an authoritarian regime.[67]

Thus, in an ironic twist of historic interpretation, to deny Filipinos the right to seek overseas employment is equated with the very same authoritarian regime that contributed to the emergence of large-scale, government-sponsored overseas employment. Migrants are no longer discursively framed simply as heroes, sacrificing their bodies for national development. Rather, "migration" is framed more as an essential feature of one's identity, and to deny individuals from acting upon these "natural drives" would be a violation of their basic, universal human rights.

Through a discourse of the body the Philippine state migratory apparatus claims to facilitate the empowerment of individuals in expressing their constitutional and human rights of movement. Empowerment, furthermore, is to be fulfilled through non-discursive practices that are predicated on a discourse of "full disclosure." As outlined in a 1995 POEA position paper, full disclosure

> calls for the policy norm that: honesty is the best policy. To promote a culture of a well-informed public is to stimulate a universal environment conducive to it. . . . Full disclosure is not a matter of recognizing and accepting one provision of the employment contract and rejecting the others. It is laying the cards on the table and when one makes a decision, he [*sic*] is primarily responsible for that decision.[68]

Through a neoliberal policy of full disclosure, therefore, all government and private institutions are tasked to provide all information—wages, working conditions, and so on—to empower potential workers to make informed decisions regarding overseas employment. The POEA thus seeks to empower individuals to make free and rational employment choices. However, the POEA further notes that migrant empowerment will still require the verification of information. Hence, "only a regulatory intervention which establishes legal liabilities of contracting parties [i.e., employers, employees, labor recruiters] and mandates an accountable institution to conduct verification can address this point of doubt."[69] Accordingly, the POEA maintains a prerogative to impose and sustain standards, but the ultimate decision is that rendered by the employer and the employee, each with "full" understanding of the "rewards and risks."[70]

Following the neoliberal logic of this policy, abused women and men are therefore considered to be "willing" participants in overseas migration through free and rational choice; accountability for cases of exploitation is thus transferred to the migrants themselves. As such, rather than increasing worker welfare, and despite the rhetorical claims to the contrary, the full disclosure policy can be regarded as an undermining of worker welfare through the state's retreat from its responsibilities and culpabilities. The exploitation and oppression underlying many systems of international labor migration within a globalized capitalist system are thus camouflaged. The exchange of labor power for wage remuneration as codified in employment contracts appears benign and natural: A simple agreement among individuals within a free market system.[71]

The emergence of an "empowered migrant worker" occurred simultaneously with other efforts of the Philippine state. As Kelly identifies, the Ramos administration elided the prescriptions of neoliberalism with the cause of personal freedom. Kelly finds, in the Medium-Term Philippine Development Plan of 1995 (MTPDP), that

> The efforts of communicating the MTPDP/Philippines 2000 have been pushed into a more personal but dynamic dimension through the conceptualization of a modern Filipino role model—Juan Kaunlaran [John Progress]. As conceived, Juan Kaunlaran is the modern Filipino, empowered and globally competitive, who has risen above the self-deprecating images of the indolent Juan Tamad [John Lazy] and the submissive Juan de la Cruz.[72]

As portrayed by the POEA, "Juan Kaunlaran" becomes an empowered, globally competitive migrant worker. Publicly, the POEA's website reaffirms this position:

> The Overseas Filipino Worker is the heart of our existence. He [*sic*] is competitive and employed productively. He continues to hone his skills through education and training. He contributes to the country's economic, social and cultural development through technology application in local industries and sharing of international experiences. . . . Recognizing that labor migration is a global phenomenon, we maintain overseas employment as one option for the fulfillment of his aspirations.[73]

A discourse of the body reveals both a continuity of earlier discursive formations, namely viewing migrants as rational decision-makers, but a discontinuity in the specifics of decision-making. Previously, "migrants" may have decided to move as part of a grand altruistic motive, that of a hero or heroine, to help the ailing Philippine economy. Following RA 8042, the decision to move is seen as liberating, empowering, a personal choice made in the context of a full understanding of the risks and rewards to participate in the global labor market. The government, subsequently, promotes itself as an organization committed to the protection not of migrants per se, but of the migrants' *right* to choose overseas employment. Discursively, this counters the criticism that the state promotes or "exports" its workers in a quest for foreign capital. Consequently, the state effectively upholds the "democratic" principles of free choice and the freedom of movement.

A Moral Globalism

On May 3, 2002 the POEA celebrated its 20th birthday. The event was marked by inspirational messages delivered by high-ranking officials of the DOLE, POEA, Overseas Workers Welfare Administration (OWWA), and other state apparatuses. Discursively, the POEA began its third decade of existence under an altered mandate, one that is discordant with its earlier policy of "managed migration" but nevertheless continues to resonate with earlier positions. In effect, the current discursive formation, one that I term a "possessive market society," underlying the Philippine state migratory apparatus reveals both continuities and discontinuities with earlier formations.

This discursive shift is evident in recent government publications, such as the *Medium-Term Philippine Development Plan, 2001–2004*. As articulated in this document, "Good governance operates under an investor-friendly and transparent regulatory framework and a level playing field."[74] Reference to a transparent framework clearly forms a bridge with the POEA's earlier full disclosure policy; reference to "investor-friendly" practices, though, signifies something entirely different. In particular, the MTPDP trumpets a greater incorporation of Philippine labor into the global economy—an incorporation predicated not only on full disclosure and globalization, but also on aggressive marketing. Abandoning somewhat its earlier discourse of "managed migration" and of migration being a natural process, the current state migratory apparatus is committed to an intensified program of worker-deployment. Efficiency, based on a minimization of bureaucratic red tape, becomes a defining feature of contemporary discourse and practice.

President Gloria Macapagal-Arroyo has been instrumental in these shifts. Since her inception as president in 2001, Macapagal-Arroyo has rearticulated the philosophies of the POEA and the overall export of labor. She has retained the neoliberal philosophies of full disclosure, transparency, and migrant empowerment. However, the Macapagal-Arroyo administration is also determined to utilize overseas employment as a means to sustain economic growth and to achieve national development. Abandoning earlier discourses of "managed migration" and of migration being a natural process, the current administration is committed to an intensified global program of worker deployment. Indeed, Macapagal-Arroyo has consistently set as a target the number of one million workers to be deployed in a single year. Likewise, she has promoted a philosophy based on increased efficiency and the removal of bureaucratic red tape. She has been forthright in her assertion that "Filipinos overseas will continue to play a critical role in the country's economic and social stability."[75]

In part, the Philippine president views the global export of transnational labor as a vital part of the country's overall anti-poverty efforts. In her 2001 "State of the Nation" address, for example, she outlined the coordinates of an "anti-poverty" ideology. This consisted of four components: (1) an economic philosophy of free enterprise; (2) a modernized agricultural sector; (3) a social bias toward the disadvantaged; and (4) increased moral standards for government and society. To address the economics, Macapagal-Arroyo intimated that the way to fight poverty was through the creation of jobs, not their destruction. Accordingly, "job creation" was to be accomplished through the attraction of foreign capital. A central point of the Philippines' development strategy, therefore, was to "minimize bottlenecks to productivity" which includes "red tape at the national and local government levels."[76] During a 2001 speech delivered at the Second Annual Philippine Business Outlook Conference, also, she affirmed her commitment to fighting poverty. She explained, "Our objective is to win the battle against poverty . . . and in order to accomplish this, we will pursue a disciplined program for economic growth that will entail encouraging free enterprise through an environment of transparency and a level playing field." This position is consistent with the education of the president. As she explained, "As an economist myself, I understand that without a credible policy framework and stability and without good governance, transparency and a level playing field, there is little that can be done to bring progress to our people." Macapagal-Arroyo identified the preferred course of action: "Our basic strategy is to rely on market forces to push economic growth." Accordingly, Macapagal-Arroyo's administration would intervene as little as possible, preferring instead to "let the private sector be the main driving force of the economy." In this way, the approach adopted by Macapagal-Arroyo conforms readily with the earlier strategies of the POEA to relinquish the bulk of recruitment and deployment activities to the private sector. The Philippine state would provide an operating environment conducive to the requirements of private labor recruiters. Consequently, agencies such as the DFA and the POEA would concentrate on the securing of bilateral agreements and other multinational arrangements that involve foreign labor markets. This state–private relationship is made clear in Macapagal-Arroyo's statement that her administration would "reduce government intervention and competition from the marketplace."[77]

The sentiments of the Philippine president are reflected in the MTPDP. As outlined in that document, the "private sector is the primary engine for employment generation," whereas the government's role is to "develop a competent, professional and productive bureaucracy that effectively enables the private sector to perform its role."[78] Hence, the present discursive formation exhibits continuity with earlier (circa 1980s) modes of incorporation of migrant workers in that the state (as typified by the POEA) fosters greater interaction between government and private agencies. In line with a neoliberal philosophy, overseas employment was, at the day-to-day level, still a privatized operation. However, reflecting a discontinuity from positions forwarded since the mid-1990s, the state does not portray migration as a natural process, but instead as something that is supported and controlled, not simply managed. Indeed, as specified in the MTPDP, one strategy entails the "forging of multilateral and bilateral labor agreements and arrangements for overseas employment." Also, similar to earlier programs during the aggressive marketing of workers in the 1980s, employment enhancement strategies target education and training programs in priority areas, such as export-oriented industries, economic zones, the agricultural sector, and the overseas labor market.[79]

Throughout the Macapagal-Arroyo presidency, the government has aggressively pursued overseas employment as an economic tool, thereby manufacturing an even greater global presence of Filipino labor. The POEA, specifically, has adopted a three-pronged strategy to operationalize its production of overseas employment. One component is to sustain existing markets. Thus, the POEA works to ensure that it continues to deploy contract workers to traditional markets, such as

Singapore and Saudi Arabia. This is to be effected through specific practices, including marketing missions, the establishment of bilateral agreements, direct-mail campaigns, more effective promotional materials, employer recognition programs, and focused training programs. Consider, for example, the practice of marketing missions. These reflect a variety of purposes. Some, for example, may be welfare-related, or in response to a particular legal case. Labor market assessment, however, is often the principal reason. Participants involved on any particular mission depend on the situation and type of mission, although generally will include representatives of the POEA, DOLE, DFA, and OWWA. These market-oriented missions are designed to obtain current information on potential labor markets, or to negotiate a particular labor contract. In recent years the Philippine state has conducted marketing missions in Saudi Arabia, the United Arab Emirates, Kuwait, Lebanon, Taiwan, South Korea, Malaysia, Macau, Guam, Palau, the Commonwealth of the Northern Mariana Islands, the Marshall Islands, Panama, Malta, Cyprus, Germany, Ireland, Norway, the Netherlands, the United Kingdom, and Greece. Apart from marketing missions, the POEA regularly invites delegates from labor-importing countries and territories.

A second strategy is to expand existing markets. Japan provides a good example. Currently, the majority of Philippine contract workers destined to Japan are employed as "performing artists." Under its new mandate, the POEA is attempting to diversify the Japanese market through the deployment of other types of workers, notably nurses and health care workers. Indeed, in recognition of the aging population of Japan, members of the Philippines state migratory apparatus anticipate an increased need for health care workers in Japan in the years ahead. Accordingly, the POEA is attempting to reposition itself to capitalize on this emergent market. Additionally, bilateral agreements have been reached with Denmark and the Netherlands for seafarers, as well as an agreement with Norway for the provision of medical workers. A shortage of 5,000 foreign medical doctors and 3,500 foreign nurses has been identified for the latter country. The POEA has also endeavored to deploy computer engineers and programmers to South Korea, as well as medical and manufacturing workers to Malaysia.

A third strategy promoted by the POEA is to enter nontraditional labor markets, or markets that have been closed in recent years. The countries of Germany, Ireland, and the United Kingdom, for example, have been targeted by the POEA as sites of potential deployment. And the POEA has made appreciable gains in Europe. Whereas in 1998 only 502 Filipinos were deployed to England, for example, over 10,500 workers were deployed in the first eight months of 2002; deployment to Ireland likewise increased from only 18 to 3,260 during this same period. Overall, total deployment to Europe increased from 26,422 in 1998 to more than 43,000 in 2001. The POEA likewise has been following developments in lesser-developed countries in Asia, notably Vietnam, Myanmar, Laos, and Cambodia, as these countries are projected to require foreign technical and managerial expertise in the years ahead. Between January and August in 2002, the Philippines deployed 1,104 workers to these four countries, up from 978 deployed over the first eight months of 2001.

There is a final angle to the Philippines' global search for nontraditional markets, one that I term *anticipatory reactivism*. Policy-making in the Philippines has been largely reactionary when it comes to overseas employment. Maruja Asis attributes this to two factors. First, governmental management is of recent vintage; as such, its initial policies were fashioned without the benefits of historical precedents or a well-developed database. Second, the Philippines' overseas employment program was not envisioned to last so long. As discussed earlier, the original planners of the program believed that overseas labor migration would be a stop-gap measure, one that could take advantage of the emerging opportunities in the Middle East. Consequently, the approach to policy-making was reactive; policies were modified, or new ones formulated, as new challenges surfaced.[80]

Three decades later, the POEA has learned from past experiences. The POEA, in effect, is in a position to anticipate problems before they arise and, consequently, capitalize on events that may otherwise generate crises. In other words, the POEA is able to develop contingency plans to be utilized in case a particular "market" opens up. These openings may be associated with major infrastructure projects initiated by economic restructuring—such as when Taiwan opened its economy to foreign labor—or in the event of military conflict. Indeed, in anticipation of the war in Iraq in 2003, the Philippine state attempted to capitalize on an anticipated 30,000 to 100,000 jobs that would be required for the reconstruction of a post-war Iraq.[81] The POEA, also, has developed contingency plans to protect its migrant workers. The DOLE and POEA, for example, following the September 11, 2001 terrorist attacks on the World Trade Center and the Pentagon in the United States, suspended deployment to critical areas, including Afghanistan, Iran, and Pakistan. The DOLE also began monitoring the whereabouts of approximately 600 Filipino workers who were working in these areas. Additional contingency plans were enacted following the United States' military intervention in Afghanistan. Coupled with the DOLE and the POEA, other government agencies were poised to participate in the evacuation of Filipino workers, including the DFA, OWWA, and local-based Philippine overseas labor officers (POLOs).

Inherent to these three strategies—sustain and diversify

existing markets, and cultivate new markets—promoted by the POEA has been a major restructuring of the technical aspects of worker recruitment and deployment. In short, the POEA has worked to provide a flexible and streamlined process to more effectively take advantage of changing global markets. Practices include the expansion of in-house processing capabilities, a greater use of the Internet to solicit contracts and to process documents, and a deregulation of migrant restrictions in selected geographical areas. One development is the initiation of a system termed *Bilis Dokumento sa POEA* ("Speed Documentation at POEA"). This computerized system was implemented to ensure the processing of documents of migrant workers within 24 hours; likewise, a "Quality Management System" was launched to ensure fewer documentary requirements and shorting processing times for transactions within operating units of the POEA. As an indication of institutional efficiency, the POEA is currently able to process worker contracts and overseas employment certificates for land-based workers hired through private agencies within 2 hours while government-placement branch workers are processed in 4 hours. The accreditation processing time of foreign employers has also been shortened, from 3 days to just 24 hours. The processing time for sea-based principals was reduced from 12 days to only 32 hours.

In short, the recruitment and deployment of Philippine overseas contract workers is the epitome of the time–space compression of globalization. Under the auspices of the POEA, the Philippine state has assumed a pivotal role in the globalization of transnational labor migration, thereby making the out-migration of workers a global reality. In the process, as the world's largest exporter of government-sponsored labor migration, the Philippine state has actively constructed a global presence.

Manila's Place in the World

Three

> We are facing globalization and its effects, both within the country as well as relative to the movement of our people. The way we do things, our procedures, really ought to be reexamined in the light of the changes that [are] happening in the world.[1]

Beginning in the 1980s, the "global city" concept has captured the attention of geographers and other social scientists.[2] Global (or world) cities are conceived as "control centers" or "command points" in the organization of the world economy and thus are viewed as critical to the processes of globalization. Cities such as New York, London, and Tokyo, for example, are viewed as sites of "massive complexes of financial firms, producer services, and corporate headquarters."[3]

Much of this early work was characterized by refined definitions of global cities and of the assigning of cities onto a global hierarchy. More recently, this approach has been widely critiqued. Jennifer Robinson, for example, suggests that researchers need "to break free of the categorizing imperative, and to reconsider approaches which are at best irrelevant and at worst harmful to poor cities around the world."[4] Indeed, she argues that researchers should discard Eurocentric concepts and models "including the nomenclature of 'global cities' and instead embark on a project of understanding 'ordinary' cities."[5]

One promising trend has been to theorize cities in terms of

their specific functions, and of their relations to *processes* within the global economy.[6] This has important implications, in that such a focus raises key questions regarding the place of cities within the context of globalization. What, for example, are the processes and strategies by which newly aspiring global cities are hoping and planning to evolve from regional centers to transnational market spaces? Likewise, following Saskia Sassen,what are cities in the periphery doing to become part of the "growth of the cross-border network of cities that constitutes a transnational space for the management and servicing of the global economy"?[7]

As detailed in Chapter Two, the Philippine state has actively promoted a global presence of its work force through an aggressive policy of overseas employment. However, in the study of global cities, international labor migration—as part of the globalization process—has been relatively neglected. By and large, as a topic, the intersection of transnational migration, globalization, and urbanization has neither been critically conceptualized nor sufficiently analyzed.[8] Kevin Cox, for example, identifies that within studies of globalization in general and global cities specifically, there exists a dominant conception of capital as continually shifting locations from one point of production to another, whereas labor is perceived as generally immobile.[9] The positing of labor as immobile, however, discounts the estimated 160 million workers residing outside their countries of origin. Most immediately, though, such a conception flies in the face of the Philippines' annual deployment of approximately one million *newly-hired* workers. As Rochelle Ball and Nicola Piper assert, the role of international labor migration and the large-scale movement of workers from less-developed countries to rapidly expanding economies are indeed significant components of globalization.[10]

In this chapter I highlight the interconnections of overseas employment policies, urbanization, and processes of globalization. My principal concern lies in the articulation of policies and the manifestation of these policies on the urban landscape. My attention is therefore directed toward the social, political, and economic processes that produce global cities as discourses rather than locating them within a static hierarchical ranking. I begin with the assumption that state-level political and economic decisions are manifest within the urbanization process and that the formulation and implementation of these decisions are influenced by the historical growth and current position of the state within the world economy. As detailed earlier, a program of overseas employment as an economic development strategy has led to the growth of a complex agglomeration of government and private institutions that plays a decisive role in the organization and regulation of international labor migration. Most germane to this chapter is the observation that these institutions are spatially concentrated within Manila, thereby propelling the city not only into a key role within the world economy but also into becoming a key site in the globalization process.

THE FUNCTIONS OF GLOBAL CITIES AND GLOBAL LABOR

When international flows consist of raw materials—such as coal, iron, or corn—the geography of transactions is determined in part by the location of natural resources.[11] More recently, however, a new geography of international transactions has appeared, one that is evident in foreign direct investment, the emergence of offshore banking centers, and the development of export processing zones. Summarizing these trends, Sassen contends that while in the 1950s the major international flow was world trade concentrated in raw materials, other primary products and resource-based manufacturing, by the late 1980s the gap between the growth of exports and that of financial flows widened sharply.[12]

In response to these shifts in international trade, the emergence of global markets for finance and specialized services has contributed to the expansion in, and centralization of, command functions. Sassen further notes that global cities are transnational market-places where firms and governments can buy financial instruments and specialized services.[13] One of these services is labor. Clearly, there exists a substantial global market for labor; concomitantly, there exists a definite expansion and concentration of command functions. In Manila, for example, over four thousand workers are literally bought and sold via contracts on a daily basis.

As mentioned earlier, however, labor does not figure prominently in research on global cities, nor on globalization. Andrew Herod, for example, contends that the geographic literature on the emergence of the global economy is marked by a curious omission, an almost total neglect of the international activities of workers and labor organizations.[14] I suggest that research into global cities and globalization with regard to labor migration has been diverted by three false leads. First, as Cox identifies, the dominant themes in the contemporary politics of globalization rest on certain quite basic assumptions as to the spatiality of globalization. These themes, Cox contends, refer to the mobility of productive capital and the immobility of labor power.[15] Accordingly, researchers have devoted considerable attention to the firms that regulate the mobility of capital while downplaying similar functions vis-à-vis labor. Ironically enough, incipient interest in the formation of global cities and processes of globalization did give prominence, albeit theoretically inadequate, to the circulation of labor. Sassen's work, in particular, stands out for its salience. However, despite this early interest, Samers argues that an initial linkage between capital and labor and the role of global cities was transformed (sidetracked?). He notes, for example, that a now leading group of researchers (i.e., the participants of the Globalization and World Cities Network) has been preoccupied with identifying how putatively global cities are networked in terms of law, accountancy, consultancy, and other financial factors.[16] Consequently, I agree with Cox's pronouncement that the immobility of workers is flawed as a fundamental assumption, and this must be figured into a reconstituted understanding of global cities and of globalization.

Second, while Samers' attempts to reposition migration within the literature on global cities and globalization are laudable, he unwittingly perpetuates a related bias when he speaks principally of *immigrants* and not also of *emigrants*. This is more than semantics, even given that, literally, the words "emigrant" and "immigrant" refer to the same migrant. I contend that the continued emphasis in the literature on "immigrants" implies a destination focus and, hence, excludes a priori many cities—most of which are located in the periphery—from discussion. Thus, Samers (and Sassen, to an extent) consider only sites of destination for immigrants and neglect sites of origin. In an attempt to revise the global cities literature, for example, Samers suggests that one must be attentive to the relationship between changes in *immigration policy* and the growth of global cities (my emphasis).[17] But migration is not unidirectional; indeed, there is a substantial circulation of temporary labor (including both *skilled* and *unskilled* migrants). Moreover, this circulation of labor is remarkably well organized and regulated (whether these regulations are always legally followed is a separate question), and cities on the periphery typically assume a large share of this organization. Therefore, we must acknowledge not only *immigration* policies, but also *emigration* policies to gain a more complete portrayal of labor migration, global cities, and globalization.

A third misperception is that labor, when it is considered mobile, simply moves in response to "globalization," that migrants simply respond to wage or employment differentials and, accordingly, gravitate toward sites of capital accumulation. However, as detailed in earlier chapters, and following Sassen, "migrations do not just happen; they are produced. And migrations do not involve just any possible combination of countries; they are patterned."[18] As I explained earlier, state apparatuses and private agencies combine to produce global patterns of contract labor migration. Migrants must be made; they must be incorporated within global circuits of labor. Moreover, this making of migration is part and parcel of the discursive production of globalization. Clearly, globalization is not a natural process; rather, it is a practice derived from economic decisions and political contestations. The fact that these decisions, policies, and regulations must *take place* is what generates our concept of global cities.

Having identified three false leads and, consequently, three reasons for the inclusion of the circulation of labor, let us now revisit the standard criteria used in assessing global cities. Sassen, for example, defines global cities as key sites for the organization and management of a global production system and a global market-place.[19] Friedmann likewise suggests that these cities "serve as centers through which flow money, workers, information, commodities, and other economically relevant variables."[20] There is thus a commonality among definitions of global cities, all of which recognize the concentration of activities required for the control, management, and regulation of the world economy. Among the most important criteria identified I include (1) a spatial concentration of financial and service complexes serving a global clientele; and (2) a hub of international networks of capital and information and communication flows. Based on these criteria, cities such as New York, London, and Tokyo are commonly identified as "control centers" of the global economy; strong "support" also exists to classify Los Angeles and Chicago as global cities.[21] Other cities, such as Cleveland and Philadelphia, are conceived as regional control centers.[22] In the remainder of this chapter I argue that these same criteria of concentration, control, regulation, and management of capital flows are found within systems of global circuits of labor, and that these control nodes are found predominantly in a few key "Third World" cities (i.e., Manila, Colombo, Dhaka, and Hyderabad). Consequently, places like Manila emerge as vital *globalizing* agents in the world economy.

PLACING MANILA

Since its incorporation into the Spanish Empire, Manila's place in the world has been tied to the capitalist world economy. Following the death of Ferdinand Magellan on April 21, 1521 off the island of Mactan, the Spanish Crown continued to seek a foothold in the archipelago. Spanish officials based in Spain's profitable colony in Mexico looked east, and specifically to the Philippine Islands, as a means of increasing trade and profits. A series of expeditions were launched, all of which proved unsuccessful until Miguel Lopez de Legazpi, in 1565, founded the first permanent Spanish settlement, named Santisimo Nombre de Jesus, on the island of Cebu.

The Spanish settlement, however, was far from secure. Food was scarce and the site was vulnerable to attack from both the Portuguese and the indigenous *tao*. Legazpi, subsequently, temporarily relocated to the island of Panay, all the while searching for a more promising site. Small expeditionary forces sailed throughout the islands and in 1570 two frigates entered a sweeping bay. There, they found a small *barangay*, named Maynilad, that was already participating in regional commerce.[23]

At the dawn of the sixteenth century an indigenous urban tradition was largely lacking in the Philippine archipelago. As indicated in Chapter One, settlements throughout the islands consisted of scattered *barangays*. These revolved around the family, and were often extended through marriage and alliances. In the southern Philippines, however, notably on the island of Mindanao and the adjacent Sulu archipelago, the diffusion of Islam contributed to the beginnings of urbanism. Here, Muslim settlers introduced a political concept of territorial states ruled by *rajas* or *sultans*, who exercised suzerainty over the *datu*.[24] Over time, a loose confederation of *barangays* was developed. Maynilad, prior to Spain's arrival, was an emerging center within the political sphere of Brunei, a sultanate on the north coast of Borneo. Maynilad's rulers were Brunei aristocrats who had intermarried with Tagalog elites.[25]

Spanish authorities, through military and missionary action, reorganized the settlements of Maynilad and, over the years, transformed the *barangay* into a key node in the galleon trade. Manila, as the city became known, was transformed into a colony's colony, dominated by the Royal Company of the Philippines. Manila grew rapidly, accruing in size as a result of the money that flowed into and out of the city.[26] From a population of approximately 2,000 in 1570, by 1620 Manila's population exceeded 40,000.

Throughout the long centuries of Spanish colonialism, Manila emerged as a montage of different settlements. At the core was the *Intramuros*, the Walled City that functioned as the economic and political heart of Spain's eastern outpost. Here, populated by the *peninsulares*, the streets were spacious and clean. Large, stately houses were built of hewn stone with iron balconies. With continued growth of the Spanish population, however, wealthier residents began to settle in the nearby suburbs. By the 1620s this process of intra-urban mobility fashioned a distinctive landscape of small country estates along the Pasig River and its estuaries. These palatial houses, complete with private vegetable gardens, fruit orchards, and ornamental plants, symbolized the wealth and status of the Spanish elite.[27]

Beyond the walls of the *Intramuros* lived the Chinese merchants and the masses of indigenous *tao*. Through fear, ignorance, and prejudice, Manila developed into a segregated city, representing a dichotomy between the wealth and power of the elites and the poverty and dependence of the poor and landless. Spanish authorities issued a series of decrees, limiting who might live in the city. It was mandated, for example, that with few exceptions, all Chinese, Filipino, and other non-Spanish persons were required to leave the *Intramuros* before nightfall. Other ordinances contributed to both an ethnic and an occupational segregation of the city. In 1581 Chinese residents were assigned to a single quarter, known as the Parian, located within the *Intramuros*. Within two years, however, this quarter was razed and the Chinese were relocated outside the *Intramuros*, to an estuarial swamp south of the Pasig River. Later, the Chinese were again relocated, this time to an area north of the Pasig River, known as Binondo.[28] Many other sections of Manila originated as indigenous hamlets and villages. Ermita, for example, began as a small fishing village south of Manila and adjacent to Manila Bay. Tondo, north of Manila, was a collection of small Muslim villages. Other communities, such as Parañaque and San Pedro Makati, slowly developed as distant market towns which supplied produce and handicrafts to Manila proper.

Manila's primacy continued throughout the American period. The opening of the United States' markets to Philippine exports and the development of an improved internal transportation infrastructure within the archipelago greatly facilitated the growth of Manila.[29] American investment facilitated the development of a new commercial district with deep-water piers south of the Pasig River; the port of Manila was refurbished; and roads were constructed between Manila and outlying provinces.[30] These physical changes were matched by an increased population; between 1898 and 1946 the population of Manila grew from approximately 200,000 to over 700,000.[31]

Following the devastating occupation of Manila by Japanese forces during World War II, Manila continued to reflect its political and economic primacy. Throughout the 1950s continued in-migration to the city of displaced peasants contributed to the burgeoning population. Ermita, Malate, Paco, Santa Ana, Sampaloc, and Tondo became more densely populated, and squatter settlements were established through the old *Intramuros*. Furthermore, many residents of Manila proper began moving to the surrounding provinces, as the capital region began its inexorable sprawl into its hinterlands. Manuel Caoili explains that these patterns of rural–urban and urban–suburban migration greatly altered Metro Manila's urban landscape. The suburban towns of Spanish colonial Manila—Binondo, Tondo, Santa Cruz, Quiapo, Sampaloc, Ermita, Malate and so on—have become the sites of poor and lower-middle-class residences, while the adjacent cities and municipalities—Quezon City, San Juan, Mandaluyong, and Makati—have become the locus of middle- and upper-class housing. And beyond the capital region, the provinces of Bulacan, Cavite, and Laguna exhibit the modern problems of urban sprawl: congestion, pollution, and poverty.[32]

By the early 1970s, when the Philippine government launched its overseas employment program, the primacy of Manila was firmly entrenched. Now, Metro Manila, or the National Capital Region (NCR), is composed of 17 local government units: 12 cities and 5 municipalities. Initially, the Greater Manila Area comprised four cities: Manila, Pasay, Quezon, and Kalookan. In the mid- to late 1990s, eight of the former municipalities assumed city status.

While occupying an area of only 636 square kilometers (245.5 square miles), or approximately 0.21 percent of the country's aggregate land area, the economic, political, and social dominance of Metro Manila is not in question. With a population of around 10 million inhabitants, Metro Manila accounts for about 13 percent of the country's total population. This translates to a population density of over 15,617 people per square kilometer (0.3 square mile)—three times the density of Singapore! Densities are even more pronounced for specific cities and municipalities within the NCR. The city of Manila, for example, registers a population density of over 41,000 people per square kilometer (0.3 square mile), whereas the municipality of Navotas has a density of 88,617 people.

Large size may qualify a city as a "megacity" but not as a "global city." As such, the primacy of Manila must not be measured only by population or population density. Economically, the NCR accounts for approximately 30 percent of the country's gross domestic product. Moreover, of the top 50 corporations in the country, based on 1998 gross revenues, 41 were located within Metro Manila. Makati accounted for the largest share. The relative strength of Metro Manila is further revealed by the fact that following the 1997 Asian financial crisis, the NCR maintained a growth rate of 0.1 percent compared to an overall decline of 0.5 percent for the country. The NCR accounts for approximately 90 percent of all private businesses, as well as a majority of cultural, educational, and medical establishments. In 2000, for instance, within the NCR were 179 of the country's 1,712 hospitals. Likewise, in the late 1990s the Metro Manila region accounted for just under 17 percent of the total number of institutions of higher education; for the 2000–2001 school year, 256 out of 1,603 higher educational facilities were in the NCR.

The Metro Manila region is also a focal point of transportation and communication technologies, a fact that contributes to the concentration of business activities. Two rail systems service the NCR: The Light Rail Transit and the Metro Rail Transit. With respect to communications, an estimated 70 percent of all households in the NCR have access to newspapers, compared to a national average of just 29.8 percent. Also, in 2000 the National Telecommunications Commission reported a total of just over 6.9 million telephone lines in the country; of these, 43.8 percent were in the NCR. Moreover, the telephone density (the number of lines for every 100 of the population) of the NCR stood at 29.07 compared to a national average of just 9.05.

The over-urbanization of the NCR has, however, contributed to a notable decline in the quality of life for many of its residents. This is seen in rising levels of pollution, traffic congestion, morbidity rates, and more proximate indicators, such as lack of access to sanitary facilities, clean water, and housing. In the NCR during the 1990s and well into the twenty-first century, for example, nearly 5 percent of all households relied on itinerant water peddlers as their main source of drinking water; by comparison, the national average was only 1.8 percent. In addition, over 9 percent of all households relied on pits, pails, or some other primitive system for their toilet facilities (the national average, however, is a staggering 42 percent). Lastly, an estimated 11,000 households were illegally occupying dwellings put up without the consent of the landowner.

In response to the acknowledged over-concentration of activities within the NCR, as well as regional disparities between Metro Manila and the rest of the country, the Philippine government has proposed a number of strategies. Specifically, the past three decades have witnessed numerous attempts to deconcentrate both political power and economic activities; all attempts, however, either have failed or have met with only limited success. These include the development of urban centers outside of Metro Manila, in particular the Cavite–Laguna–Batangas–Rizal–Quezon (or Calabarzon) Corridor of southern Luzon and the Cagayan de Oro–Iligan Corridor (CIC) of Mindanao, and the development of transportation networks linking major industrial centers such as the Subic-Clark Toll Road and the Southern Tagalog Arterial Road.[33] Kelly notes also that certain legislative acts, such as the Local Government Code of 1991, were intended to encourage industrial zones and to attract foreign investment within their jurisdictions. However, given the requirement of adequate infrastructure and accessibility to transportation and communication facilities (which, as indicated, are overwhelmingly concentrated in the NCR), those municipalities closest to Manila have been most successful.[34]

More significant, however, *national* policies formed in the context of globalization continue to augment the (over-) urbanization of Metro Manila. As Sassen writes, a key dynamic explaining the place of major cities in the world economy is that they concentrate the infrastructure and servicing that produces a capability for global control.[35] As discussed in earlier chapters, the martial law period (1972–1981) of the Philippines witnessed significant economic transformations in that country as it was more fully incorporated into the global economy. The declaration of martial law, moreover, produced a sharp increase in the concentration of political power within the government as President Ferdinand Marcos centralized his control through a series of administrative changes. New economic policies were designed primarily to attract foreign direct investment as the Philippines' development policy became increasingly oriented toward export production.[36] Hence, this political period set the stage for what Sassen identifies as a defining feature of the contemporary era of globalization, namely a global *dispersal* of economic activities combined with a *concentration* of regulatory control over these activities. Specific national economic policies, therefore, continue to congregate business activities within a few key locations, most especially in Manila. To this day, investment and production activities continue to be concentrated in the Manila region.[37]

THE SOCIAL ORGANIZATION OF OVERSEAS EMPLOYMENT

Saskia Sassen identifies a trend toward the spatial dispersal of economic activities at the metropolitan, national, and world levels that we associated with globalization as contributing to a demand for new forms of territorial centralization of top-level management and control functions.[38] Given the centralization of bureaucratic functions within the NCR of the Philippines, Manila emerges as a key node in the larger circulation of contract labor. Given the nearly one million workers deployed annually to over 190 countries and territories, it is clear that the Philippines' overseas employment program constitutes a spatially diverse economic program. As this section details, those institutions overseeing this geographically expansive program are highly concentrated within just one location: Manila.

In Chapter Two I discussed the administrative role of the

Philippine Overseas Employment Administration (POEA). Located in Manila, the POEA functions as the "command center" for the export of labor. This position is facilitated through the establishment of both formal and informal guidelines and channels of communication that create a web of information flows. Owing to the dominance of the POEA, therefore, Manila by default occupies the focal point of this web.

The POEA, however, is not alone in its activities. According to the *Rules and Regulations Governing Overseas Employment*, the POEA is tasked with the "establishment and maintenance of effective linkages with other government agencies including Philippine Missions abroad or corps of labor attachés, foreign governments directly or through their Embassies, foreign employers, the local private recruitment sector, and other organizations."[39] In effect, the POEA operates as a conduit; without the cooperation and organization of a multitude of other individuals and institutions, the POEA would be ineffective in the global labor market. Of paramount importance is the symbiotic relationship between the POEA and private recruitment agencies.

The private sector is composed of hundreds of labor-recruitment agencies. These are distinguished primarily by the type of worker recruited and deployed. The most fundamental distinction is between land-based and sea-based workers. *Private recruitment agencies* are those licensed to recruit and deploy land-based overseas contract workers. These agencies are further classified into two categories: *private employment agencies* (PEAs) and *service/construction contractors* (SCCs). PEAs provide Philippine labor to foreign clients with the foreign client as the principal employer. Conversely, SCCs provide labor through the deployment of Philippine companies, with the Philippine company receiving the foreign labor contract. *Manning agencies* are those that are licensed to recruit and deploy seafarers, or

Figure 3.1
Workers gather outside a private recruitment agency in Manila, with hopes of obtaining overseas employment
Kind permission of the author.

sea-based workers, for vessels plying international waters or other related maritime activities.

Further segmentation of recruitment agencies is evident. Because of complex licensing procedures and a desire to capitalize on specific foreign labor markets, private labor recruitment agencies exhibit *labor-niche specialization*. Aside from the aforementioned division between land-based and sea-based workers, recruitment agencies may specialize in the deployment of particular occupations (e.g., nurses, domestic workers, construction workers) and/or in particular destinations (e.g., Japan, Kuwait).

The role of government officials abroad is also especially important to the effective deployment of labor. These officials may not be directly associated with the POEA. Ambassadors and consulate officials, for example, have many responsibilities that are far removed from the movement of labor. Other officials, of course, are more directly involved. Labor attachés are a case in point. The Philippines, for example, maintains a network of approximately two dozen labor attachés around the world, located in many of the principal labor-importing countries and territories, such as Saudi Arabia, Kuwait, Hong Kong, and Singapore. According to administrators of the POEA, government officials stationed abroad act as the "eyes and ears" of the Philippines' overseas employment program. Ambassadors, consular officials, and labor attachés are attuned for any labor-market developments, such as talk of hotels or airports in the planning stages. Much of this information is passed through casual conversation at State dinners, parties, or hallway gossip. Upon hearing of new prospects, government officials may report either to the POEA directly, or to the Department of Foreign Affairs (DFA). If this latter route is taken, the DFA will forward the relevant information to the POEA.

To Sassen, the "maintenance of centralized control and management over a geographically dispersed array of plants, offices and service outlets cannot be taken for granted or seen as an inevitable outcome of a 'world system.' "[40] Rather than an "inevitable" and "natural" manifestation of "globalization," the production of international labor migration must be seen as a direct outgrowth of the interactions of government officials, labor recruitment agents, foreign employers, and potential migrants. The marketing branch of the Pre-Employment Services Office of the POEA, for example, helps promote and develop overseas employment opportunities for various "skills" categories. These tasks are accomplished through marketing missions, governmental promotional campaigns, the pursuance of bilateral agreements, and media advertising.

Marketing missions illustrate well the social organization (and global production) of international labor migration. These missions constitute specific State-sanctioned visits of Philippine officials. The type of participants involved depends both on the situation and type of mission; however, participants usually include officials of the POEA, the DFA, the Department of Labor and Employment (DOLE), and the Overseas Workers Welfare Administration (OWWA).

Although reflecting a variety of purposes, including policy discussions on the welfare and safety of migrant workers, marketing missions are most often designed to obtain current information on potential labor markets. In 1989, for example, as the Hong Kong labor market was opening up, the POEA dispatched two missions to the territory. These missions were the direct result of perceived labor shortages in the (then) British colony. The POEA received word that Hong Kong authorities were liberalizing the importation of temporary contract workers; at the time, there were an estimated 115,000 advertised vacancies, of which 14,700 were approved for foreign workers. There was no quota on the nationalities to be hired, but language ability was considered important. The POEA determined that Philippine workers, because of their English language skills, would be preferred in the service sectors, such as hotels, travel agencies, airlines, and clerical work. Following the completion of the marketing mission, the POEA designed and implemented a four-stage strategy to penetrate the Hong Kong market. First, an active information campaign was launched to transmit the most current information on the new Hong Kong labor-importation guidelines to the many private recruitment agencies in the Philippines. Second, this dissemination of information was accompanied by a direct mailer campaign by the POEA, wherein lists of directories of Hong Kong employers were provided to the private sector.

Third, the Philippine labor attaché in Hong Kong was tasked to monitor developments and to maintain contact with the POEA. Last, the POEA liberalized the processing procedures for Philippine migrant workers bound to Hong Kong. This liberalization of requirements was intended to make the Philippines more "attractive" to potential Hong Kong employers. Efficiency of processing, and the lack of bureaucratic "red tape," are key factors in the hiring of foreign workers.

The critical role of the POEA as "command center" in facilitating international clientele is further illustrated by the functioning of the Client Referral Assistance (CRA) program. The CRA began in 1985 under the auspices of the Market Development Division of the POEA and functions as a state-organized conduit between private foreign employers and the Philippine-based private recruitment agencies. CRA clients are usually "first-timers" in that they have not previously recruited contract workers from the Philippines and thus have not established any contact with specific Philippine private recruitment agencies. Under the CRA program, foreign employers contact the POEA with specific requests for Philippine workers. For example, a hotelier in Amsterdam may be in need of hiring two dozen female chambermaids. Foreign employers may have learned of the POEA through media sources (e.g., the Internet), through promotional campaigns initiated by the POEA, or (commonly) through individual social networks of employers. After a screening of the job request, the POEA provides a list of (usually) three recruitment agencies to the potential employer. The determination of the three agencies is, in part, based on a match between agency specialization and job request. Employers requesting sea-based workers, for example, would be directed toward relevant manning agencies.

Once three agencies have been selected, information pertaining to the prospective labor contract is forwarded by the

POEA to the selected private recruitment agencies. These agencies then make bids to the potential foreign employer. The employer, after a review of the proposals, may either accept one of the agencies' proposals—a successful "tie-up," using the nomenclature of the POEA—to procure a contract, or, alternatively, decline all proposals. In the event that the potential foreign employer does not have a successful tie-up with the referred agencies, the POEA may supply a complete listing of all licensed recruitment agencies in operation.[41]

In sum, the POEA, coupled with the private sector, assumes a central position in the organization, management, and regulation of Philippine international labor migration. This control thus influences the economic development of nearly 200 countries and territories. Spatially, however, this globally-extensive control is overwhelmingly concentrated within Metro Manila. It is to this concentration I now turn.

THE CENTRALITY OF METRO MANILA AS GLOBAL CITY

The social organization of Philippine recruitment and deployment is manifest in the spatial centrality of Manila. As discussed above, the Manila-based POEA is the principal government agency involved in overseas employment. Composed of four sectors (Pre-Employment Services; Licensing and Regulation; Adjudication; and Welfare and Employment), the reach of the POEA extends into all facets of the Philippines' overseas employment program. Consequently, the POEA works closely with other Manila-based governmental institutions as well as the myriad private recruitment agencies.

The spatial distribution of labor recruitment agencies reveals also a spatial concentration within Metro Manila. To demonstrate this geographic patterning, in the late 1990s I examined the location of over 600 private recruitment agencies.[42] Results indicated that the Metro Manila region in

Figure 3.2
Private recruitment agency located in Makati, Metro Manila
Kind permission of the author.

general, and the city of Manila specifically, were home to the lion's share of private recruitment agencies. Of the 633 agencies for which I could identify a location, 627 (99 percent) were located in Metro Manila. However, 46 percent were located in the city of Manila proper. Another 11 and 13 percent respectively were located in Quezon City and the municipality of Makati.

A strong spatial patterning based on recruitment agency classification is also evident. Over 99 percent of all PEAs for which a site could be identified were located in Metro Manila; just under half of these (49.7 percent) were in the city of Manila. One of the two agencies not sited in Metro Manila was located in the second largest city of the Philippines, Cebu City, and the other in the city of Iloilo, on the island of Panay in the Visayas. A finer resolution indicates that of those PEAs located in the city of Manila, the majority (56 percent) were in the Ermita district, with another 29 percent in the district of Malate. Outside Manila proper, an additional 30 percent of

PEAs were located in the municipality of Makati. This spatial distribution is not surprising, given that Makati is the nation's financial center and headquarters of most domestic and foreign corporations. Ermita, conversely, was long considered the "entertainment" district and, indeed, many agencies specializing in the deployment of performing artists were located in this area.[43]

The distribution of manning agencies reveals a similar pattern, with 55 percent of identified agencies located in the city of Manila and another 28 percent in Makati. The most obvious difference is that an additional seven agencies were located in the port areas around Manila, with an outlier in Batangas

Figure 3.3
Recruitment poster for "entertainers." The global reality of overseas employment is indicated by the requirement to speak Japanese or Chinese
Kind permission of the author.

(itself an important port facility south of Metro Manila). Both service and construction contractors were more likely to be found in the municipality of Makati than in the city of Manila. Makati is the home of the Philippine Overseas Construction Board, the principal government agency responsible for the deployment of Philippine construction companies.

By locating in the NCR, private recruitment agencies are able to capitalize on both localization and urbanization economies in the conduct of business.[44] Localization economies are derived in three key areas. First, the localized scale of the Philippine migration industry within Manila permits the subdivision of operations. Certain occupations, for example, require training and testing procedures to be completed prior to departure. Consider the deployment of overseas performing artists (OPAs). As part of a complex pre-departure recruitment system, OPAs are required (legally) to undergo academic and skills training conducted by an accredited training center or talent agency. Ostensibly, these procedures protect OPAs against abuses encountered overseas. An analysis of 315 training/talent agencies revealed a spatial concentration within Manila (18 percent) and the three proximate cities of Quezon (27 percent), Pasay (6 percent), and Kalookan (5 percent). An additional 31 percent of training/talent agencies were located within the 13 municipalities, with the majority (15 percent) in Makati. Of greater significance, however, was that approximately 10 percent of all training/talent centers were located beyond the boundaries of the NCR. Indeed, unlike the spatial distribution of PEAs, numerous training/talent agencies are located throughout the Visayas and Mindanao. This distribution indicates the importance of training/talent agencies, particularly in the deployment of OPAs, as intermediaries between Manila-based PEAs and potential migrant workers. Private employment agencies engaged in the recruitment and deployment of OPAs are legally confined to specific territories; through the subdivision of operations, however, and the use of training/talent centers, these recruiters are able to skirt licensing procedures and canvass a wider geographical coverage in their recruitment.

Second, the creation of a pool of skilled and unskilled labor strengthens localization economies. As primate city, Manila is the destination of thousands of displaced peasants from the rural hinterland. These internal migrants either may arrive in Manila specifically for overseas employment, or perhaps will later take advantage of this opportunity once in the city. Either way, Manila-based labor recruiters benefit from a continual supply of reserve labor. Concurrently, the sheer number of schools and universities within the NCR provides a ready supply of skilled labor which private recruitment agencies can tap. Third, private recruitment agencies in general, but especially those located in Manila, may benefit from a reputation acquired by its workers and it is this "image" that the POEA is careful to cultivate and protect through its marketing efforts (see Chapter Two).

Urbanization economies derive from the close association of many different kinds of industry in large cities. For the labor migration industry, these include the spatial proximity of embassies, consulates, hospitals, and police stations. As evident by now, the export of labor is highly regulated in the Philippines. The bureaucratic efficiency of recruitment agencies, however, is greatly enhanced through the spatial concentration of these regulated activities. Documentary requirements include passports, passport photographs, visas, airplane tickets, and medical and police clearances. Although some recruitment agencies handle most of these requirements, at other times the costs and responsibilities are transferred to the worker-applicants. In either case, recruitment agents and/or potential migrants must be physically present at the relevant facilities (e.g., embassies, consulates, medical facilities). Furthermore, some governments, such as those of Saudi Arabia, Hong Kong, Malaysia, and Italy, require that workers are examined by competent medical clinics that are accredited by their respective embassies; these medical clearances must also be authenticated by the Manila-based Department of Foreign Affairs.

Private recruitment agencies are also able to benefit from the close proximity of services drawn from non-labor-related activities. These include advertising agencies, transportation facilities, and an existing infrastructure (e.g., electrical services for personal computer use). Within Manila, additionally, the proximity of labor recruitment agencies to Ninoy Aquino International Airport, the main transportation node linking the Philippines to the rest of the world, is a significant factor.

Figure 3.4
Manila-based training center for sea-based workers. The Philippines ranks as one of the world's major exporters of seafarers
Kind permission of the author.

In discussing the centrality of Manila to the global presence of Filipino contract workers, it is instructive to consider the nexus between the services offered by Manila with the needs and concerns of foreign employers, as outlined by William McCuskey, Senior Vice President for Marine Services of C.F. Sharp & Co. In addressing the global market for seafarers, McCuskey outlined several major items which foreign employers look for in selecting a "labor supply" country. These include the ability to send and receive communications promptly by telex, telephone, and facsimile transmission; the availability of an international airport; a choice of honest and reputable manning agencies; an efficient seafarer-processing and documentation system; a national licensing and examination procedure; training centers; and a steady supply of qualified and properly motivated seafarers.[45] Manila, not only as the primate city of the Philippines, but more importantly as the primate city of the labor-export industry, is best able to accommodate, regulate, and manage these diverse needs. As the Philippines routinely ranks as the world's preeminent provider of seafarers—supplying nearly 20 percent of the world's million-plus seafarers—it is clear that the Manila-based POEA (combined with the hundreds of manning agencies) assumes a key position in the world economy.

MANILA AS WHOSE GLOBAL CITY?

The Philippines' policy of overseas employment is not a deliberate strategy on behalf of government officials to promote Manila as a global city. Indeed, there is apparently no explicit recognition on the part of relevant state apparatuses (e.g., those tasked with the regulation of overseas employment and those tasked with the management of the NCR) that overseas employment may affect the urbanization of Manila, either positively or negatively. This, in and of itself, is a fundamental

Figure 3.5
Private recruitment agencies often post listings of unfilled jobs outside their offices
Kind permission of the author.

omission in the regulation of both labor market functions and urban planning. Nevertheless, the perpetuation of overseas employment as a global development strategy intensifies the urbanization of Manila through the spatial agglomeration of institutional apparatuses and the in-migration of people in search of overseas employment.

Manila, consequently, provides key lessons in our theoretical understanding of global city formation and the processes of globalization. Jennifer Robinson caustically writes that "the discursive effectiveness of the global city hypothesis depends on the pithy identification of the 'global city'—a category of cities which are claimed to be powerful in terms of the global economy." She further asserts, "If the 'global city' were labeled as just another example of an 'industrial' district . . . it might not have attracted the attention it did."[46] Her comments speak more broadly to the ontological and epistemological basis of global city and globalization research. What exactly is the object of study? And how are we to acquire (produce) our knowledge of this object? In short, what is the referent that the label "global city" denotes? Friedmann, for example, enunciates five traits that define a world (or global) city: (1) world cities serve as organizing nodes of a global economic system, (2) a space of global capital accumulation exists, but not all places are connected, (3) world cities are large urbanized spaces, (4) these cities may be arranged hierarchically in accord with the economic power they command, and (5) the culture of these cities is cosmopolitan, and their ideology is consumerist. Friedmann concludes by suggesting that if no a priori agreement is reached on these five points, then we must part company.[47]

My examination of Manila as a global city, as a key facilitator of globalization, takes seriously these concerns. If, as Robinson suggests, we are trying to fit "structurally irrelevant" cities of the periphery into a Eurocentric-based paradigm (à la Friedmann's five points), then the less developed regions of the world will remain marginal both literally and metaphorically—a similar argument holds for our conceptions of globalization.[48] Consider, for example, Friedmann's position on the categorization of global cities. He notes, "A city's ability to *attract* global investment ultimately determines its rank in the order of world cities" (my emphasis).[49] World cities thus become "end points" (or receptors that *receive* both capital and immigrants), more reminiscent of a production line, rather than nodes in a circular system. Given the malleability of supposedly rigid definitions, therefore, perhaps we are asking the wrong questions. What if, conversely, we forward the argument that global cities (and globalization) is whatever we as researchers define global cities (or globalization) to be. There is thus no natural or essential global city, just as there is no singular, and inevitable, globalization. To do so suggests that we focus, therefore, on the *process of becoming a global city*, just as we focus on the *process of globalization*. This is most decidedly not a clarion call to jettison all research on globalization and global cities. Instead, we should examine the manifestation of social, political, and economic processes at particular (and interconnected) sites. In some circumstances, these sites may reflect an agglomeration of functions, such as those concentrated in Manila that are related to the global circulation of labor. Rather than assigning a ranking (and by implication, a sense of superiority?), we should consider both the material and the discursive consequences of this agglomeration.

The experience of Manila suggests that something is "happening" that has been called "globalization." However, the presence of government and private institutions within Manila also confirms Christof Parnreiter's argument that globalization does not simply "happen" but rather results from the deliberate reshaping of relations of capital, state, labor, and space.[50] As such, a glimpse of Manila within the world economy highlights that the agglomeration of firms is not always a deliberate attempt to "produce" a global city. Instead, it is a post facto rationalization of this agglomeration that researchers, such as Friedmann, have identified as a process of global city formation. To be sure, certain urban planners and managers, as well as marketing agencies, have since jumped on the global city bandwagon and attempted to produce (or, more simply, to promote) cities as global. Nevertheless, we should hold in abeyance any notion of a "natural" process of globalization and global city formation; rather, we should direct attention to specific policies and programs and their respective consequences, irrespective of intent. In the Philippines, the decades-long promotion of overseas employment as a *national* development strategy has, unintentionally, contributed to the *localized* spatial concentration of both government institutions and private businesses associated with the *global* circulation of labor. Such is the process of global city formation and of globalization.

Global-Philippines.Com
Four

During the nineteenth century, international migration was greatly facilitated through advents in steamship technology and postal deliveries. Combined, the quality and quantity of information dissemination was accelerated and widened in geographic scope; potential migrants learned about conditions of distant lands and many of the "mysteries" of migration were dispelled. Likewise, employers of migrant work forces were able to cast their nets far and wide, to take advantage of the millions of people in search of better opportunities.

Following World War II, a similar revolution in technology transformed international migration. Air travel, in particular, expanded and intensified population movements at a global scale. And more recently, transformations in the dissemination of information have revolutionized the migratory process. Nowhere are these changes seen more completely than in the emergence of the Internet and its graphic interface, the World Wide Web. As Manfred Steger explains, the Internet has assumed a pivotal function in facilitating globalization through the creation of the World Wide Web that connects billions of individuals, private associations, and governments.[1]

Now in the twenty-first century, the basic coordinates of the Internet are well understood.[2] Described as a "network of networks," and likened to a spider's web, the Internet is a system for transferring files, in binary form, between computers.[3] The World Wide Web, as a graphical interface to the

Internet, has led to the increased popularity of this communication medium.[4] Conceptually, information is transmitted over the Web between "clients" and "servers." Information is accessed by clients (and provided by servers) in the form of "Home Pages" or "Web Sites." These sites are identified by addresses called Uniform Resource Locators (URLs) and over the past two decades geographers and other scientists have been monitoring the temporal and spatial trends of Web site occurrence, as well as the accessibility of information acquired from Web sites.

Within the global labor market, potential employers of migrant work forces are clients, initially requesting information on potential workers (though ultimately contracting with the actual workers); labor recruiters, on the other hand, are servers, providing information (and again, ultimately, workers). In this chapter I consider the recruitment of contract labor (broadly) through the use of the World Wide Web.[5] There are over 2,000 licensed recruitment agencies in the Philippines. To these are added many thousands of other employment agencies in operation throughout Asia and the rest of the world. To be sure, not all of these agencies are connected to the Internet. However, many agencies are interconnected and their global presence in the cyberworld economy is rapidly transforming the recruitment and deployment of international contract labor migration. This is the subject of the first part of this chapter.

The cyber-realm of international migration is not restricted to the activities of private recruitment agents. Indeed, the migrants themselves have been utilizing the "cyberworld" as a means to facilitate "real-world" interactions. Accordingly, in the second half of this chapter I address how, and for what purposes, the Philippine diaspora community has utilized the Internet as a tool for interaction, what forms of spatial linkages are reflected by representations on the Internet, and how a globalized Philippine identity is represented on the Web. This chapter, therefore, highlights two crucial components of globalization and the Philippines: The use of Internet technology in the production of mobilities—the circulation of overseas contract workers—but also the use of the Internet to facilitate the production of identities.

THE CYBER-RECRUITMENT OF LABOR

The global market-place for contract labor is highly competitive. Thousands of private employment agencies compete with each other. To distinguish themselves, agencies engage in a process known as labor niche specialization. Some agencies, for example, specialize in the deployment of only certain occupations (e.g., nurses, domestic workers) or only deploy workers to a few, select locations (e.g., to Japan or Singapore). Briefly, labor niche specialization results from a combination of factors. Governments, for example, often have complex licensing procedures pertaining to the recruitment and deployment of workers. These assume the form of visa requirements, which differ from country to country and among occupations. Because of these regulations, it may either be too costly to apply for numerous licenses (and thus be legally allowed to process many different occupation types) or too difficult to maneuver through the complexities of different occupational and geographical procedures. Also, labor recruiters may specialize in order to capitalize on rapidly growing markets (defined either occupationally, as with domestic workers, or geographically, as in Taiwan). The early 1970s in the United States, for example, saw the emergence of many agencies attempting to import foreign nurses. Lastly, labor recruiters may specialize in certain occupations or destinations because of previous personal experience. Thus, for example, one labor recruiter with whom I spoke indicated that he was a retired air force officer and was able to use his knowledge and personal connections to facilitate the deployment of aircraft mechanics.

The existence of labor niche specialization assumes an important role in the gendered, racialized, and occupational segregation of migratory systems, one that is manifest in promotional advertisements circulated on the World Wide Web. Agencies such as *Allied Manpower, Apex, Lending Hands*, and *Phil-Thai* deploy only domestic workers. Conversely, *Yeo Koh* and *Achieve* specialize only in the deployment of management-related personnel. *Wang & Li Asia Resources*, likewise, state that their purpose is to place "bilingual & bicultural professionals with multinational companies in Greater China and Southeast Asia." *NYK-Fil*, alternatively, deploys only seafarers and other laborers engaged in maritime activities.

In such a competitive market-place, it is imperative for labor recruiters to be able to offer the "best product," in this case, migrant workers. Many recruitment-related Web sites, therefore, exhibit a process of *agency aggrandizement* and highlight why their agency is superior to all. Text, images, sounds, and animation, can all be incorporated into Web sites. And labor recruitment agencies often take full advantage of these capabilities. Graphically illustrated with colorful pictures and photographs, the Web sites of employment agencies proudly proclaim their qualities in bold fashion.

When selecting private recruitment agencies, employers are often influenced by considerations of cost, efficiency, and length of services. This latter quality suggests a proven track record of providing quality workers. The use of text and images on the Web enables labor recruitment agencies to emphasize these qualities in their marketing efforts. *Lending Hands Employment Services*, for example, states in bold letters:

"With our years of experience since 1989, we solved domestic problems our way—the Lending Hands way!" *KTK Manpower Services*, likewise, "provides you with solution for manpower. We have assisted many companies in their manpower planning needs for many years and WE UNDERSTAND our customers' need[s] very well." *MultiJobs International*, a Singapore-based agency, claims to "have over 30 years of experience . . . supplying foreign workers and professionals to the MNCs and SMEs in Singapore and the region."

To be competitive in the global market-place for migrant workers, recruitment agencies—as "sales" industries—must be able to cultivate the buyers' (i.e., employers) criteria for the product (workers) available. Employers of foreign domestic workers, for example, often "purchase" more than labor-power. Indeed, many employers of foreign domestic workers and nannies seek to obtain a specially cultivated and constructed "image" to match their perceived affluence.[6] Similar to owning the right car, or living in the right community, it has become essential, for some households, to employ the "proper" maid. As Chin finds in Malaysia, "the ability to employ a foreign female domestic worker has come to symbolize the achievement of 'middle-classhood' and status."[7] Female foreign domestic workers become positional goods. And recruitment agencies are quick to fill these demands—often in the form of "guaranteed" package deals. *Noble Maids*, for example, is a Singapore-based recruitment firm specializing in the deployment of domestic workers. They offer a package deal which covers agency and placement fees, insurance coverage, accident insurance, as well as the personal "collection" and "delivery" of the domestic worker. In bold type, *Noble Maids* proclaims that "complete packages start from only $388."

Employers of foreign work forces seek certain characteristics in their labor force.[8] These requests often include technical considerations (e.g., the ability to perform the prospective job), current employment experience, educational attainment, and language ability. *East-West Services*, for example, is a Manila-based agency specializing in the provision of professional workers. Their Web site provides regularly updated information on its supply of worker applicants. The following two narratives of Filipino contract workers are illustrative:

> [Worker ID Number] Top secretarial skills: experience as secretary of over four years in a leading Australian-owned company. Proficient in word-processing, spreadsheet software and other windows applicants such as MS Word (text and tables), MS Excel and MS Powerpoint (slide presentation and organizational charts).
>
> [Worker ID Number] Certified Public Accountant: adept in all aspects of accounting cycle and functions, i.e., preparation of financial statement/credit & collection; experience of over four years as General Accountant, proficient in Lotus, Microsoft, Excel and Macola. Available now.

Agencies deploying domestic workers tend to emphasize personal traits rather than occupational qualifications. *Arcadia Services and Agencies*, for example, provides information on age, language, and "remarks" for its domestic worker applicants. Many prospective domestic workers, for example, are described as "willing to do all" and "pleasant." Nevertheless, those employment agencies specializing in domestic workers do also emphasize the qualifications and training of their worker applicants. The Singapore-based *Filmo* provides vignettes for all of its domestic worker applicants, and includes specific details such as "Experienced in caring of infants and young children"; "2 years domestic helper experience in Singapore"; and "worked 14 years in Philippines as factory worker and supervisor, no overseas experience." *Lending Hands Employment Services* asserts that its worker applicants "undergo strict training and orientation." *Phil-Thai Employment Services*, likewise, provides "reliable assessments" of domestic workers through the use of "psychological tests." Not to be outdone, *Apex Manpower* categorizes domestic workers according to a "personality" profile. Categories include "D" personalities (i.e., dominant/driver), "I" personalities (i.e., influential/expressive), "S" personalities (i.e., steady/amicable), and "C" personalities (i.e., compliant/competent). *Apex Manpower* informs its potential clients that good housemaids are those with strong "S" or "C" personalities, since these workers are "easier to teach and control. They tend to be quieter and good-natured, not busybody or trouble-maker." As such, *Apex Manpower* assures potential employers that its domestic workers are "specially selected and groomed on the general skills pertaining to domestic needs" and that "they are carefully screened before being recruited."

Other intangible qualities are also stressed on the Web sites of private recruitment agencies. Pierrette Hondagneu-Sotelo refers to these intangible qualities as "the right stuff." Not uncommonly, these qualities often assume the form of ethnic (e.g., Filipinas are harder workers) or gendered stereotypes (e.g., women are ideally suited for domestic work). Michael Humphrey, for example, finds that employers in Jordan commonly prefer to hire maids from the Philippines because they have "fairer complexions" than do the "darker skinned" maids from Sri Lanka.[9] Peter Woodward likewise finds that in the Saudi Arabian labor market, statistical prejudgments based on nationality abound. Filipinos are considered to be more productive, compliant, and easier to supervise—traits that the Philippine government has been actively promoting! Thai workers, by way of comparison, are "well-liked" and "able to work with minimal supervision."[10]

Recruitment-related Web sites reveal a similar use of statistical prejudgments. The use of gender-based and ethnic-based statistical prejudgments is most pronounced in the deployment of domestic workers. In general, those agencies deploying domestic workers specify quite clearly the nationalities and religious affiliations of their worker applicants. Agencies deploying only professionals (e.g., managers), on the other hand, rarely describe worker applicant pools in terms of nationality, religion, or sex.

Agencies deploying domestic workers also tend to emphasize more personal characteristics—the "right stuff." *Newway Employment Agency*, for instance, claims that its domestic workers are "selected from good provinces" and the workers are "simple, hardworking, & obedient." Specifically, the docility and reliability of worker applicants are stressed. *Golden Employment Agency*, a Singaporean-based recruiting firm, provides "well-trained, reliable and hardworking domestic helpers"; *Reuben Viton Career Services*, also based in Singapore, supplies "diligent and English-speaking housemaids carefully selected from the Philippines & Indonesia."

Some Web sites attempt to justify their use of statistical prejudgments. The Malaysian-based *Apex Manpower*, for example, explains the supposed advantages and disadvantages of "Indonesian housemaids" as compared to housemaids from the Philippines. According to this recruitment agency, the advantages of Indonesian housemaids include "lower costs in terms of agency fees and salary compared to engaging Filipino domestic help"; "no day-off, hence no disruption to daily work routine"; and "generally more teachable and obedient." Potential disadvantages of Indonesian maids include "language barriers"; "slower in execution of tasks"; and "does not eat pork (Muslims)." *Apex Manpower* quickly notes, however, that "through experience and time" the first two disadvantages can be overcome.

Information is often provided on recruitment-related Web sites about specific workers in the form of "bio-data." Bio-data Web sites are catalogues of specific products—workers—and are designed to provide relevant information for prospective employers to make "informed" decisions. Recruitment-related Web sites, for example, may provide photographs of worker applicants. *Phil-Thai Employment Services* provides eight pages of "constantly monitored and updated" photographs and bio-data of domestic workers. *FOK Employment* provides "100s of Quality New Bio-Data Weekly." This provision appears to be most common in the deployment of domestic workers. Among those sites that provide photographs of potential domestic workers, the photographs are usually in color and show either a "head-shot" or, less commonly, a full "body-shot" of the *female* domestic worker.[11] It is also common for the domestic workers to be shown wearing uniforms. This homogenization of women is cultivated by recruitment agencies; as Nicole Constable finds, applicants are advised to "look the part" and in so doing, conform to the agencies' body disciplinary practice.[12]

Appearances, especially vis-à-vis the recruitment of domestic workers, are very important selling points.[13] Not infrequently, these play upon racial, gendered, and even sexual stereotypes—many of which have themselves become "globalized" in recent decades. Some Web sites, for example, classify domestic workers based on skin complexion, or "race". The Singapore-based *Inroads Employment Agency* employs a tripartite classification: *fair*, *tanned*, or *dark*. These statistical prejudgments may influence the "cost" of migrant workers. Many recruitment agencies, for example, emphasize that Indonesian maids are less expensive than those from the Philippines.

Cost-differentials, it is explained, result from the better English-language proficiency of Filipina domestic workers. However, other explanations are also forwarded. *Inter-Mares*, a Singapore-based recruitment agency, explains that "Most Indonesians are willing to work for two years without a day off." Interestingly, *Inter-Mares* also provides supplemental information about the Philippines as a country. As specified on their Web site, "It would be an advantage to the employer to know a little about [Filipinos] and hopefully this page will in some small way help the prospective employer to understand them better."

Here we see quite clearly how recruitment firms participate not only in the global distribution of material "products" (i.e., migrant workers) but also in the production and circulation of particular "images" or "representations." On the *Inter-Mares* Web site, the Philippines is graphically represented by two pictures: One of Baguio City and the other of the rice terraces of Banaue. Both of these locations are popular tourist sites and, in the travel literature, have become symbolic of the Philippines. Text provided on the Web site, however, draws a particular connection between these two locations and the employment of Filipina domestic workers. According to *Inter-Mares*, "our [Filipino] girls come from a rather rural background" (as evidenced by the "rural" photographs of the rice terraces and, to a lesser extent, of Baguio City which appears relatively undeveloped). The text continues: "It is because [the Filipinas] are unsophisticated that they are so highly regarded by Singapore employers who, on the balance, prefer more conservative nannies." In reference specifically to the rice terraces, *Inter-Mares* explains that "the ancient architects and engineers did not have the benefit of tractors, excavators or any other mechanical aides. . . . [T]hey had no elephants to help them." And the implications of this narrative? *Inter-Mares* explains that "the tradition of hardwork [*sic*] for little reward in a mountain terrain, with its attendant scarcity in arable land, makes for a hardy race."

Web sites may also provide additional corporeal information, including data on age, height, and weight. Again, these are more pronounced and commonplace for those agencies specializing in the deployment of domestic workers. Some agencies also include information on marital status and family size. This serves multiple purposes for private employment agencies. Such "traits" may indicate a level of "personal debt" assumed by the worker applicant. The assumption is that workers who are more impoverished, or have significant familial responsibilities, are more *willing* (or forced) to work longer hours without complaint. Also, female workers with children may be considered more "qualified" to work as domestic helpers or nannies. Last, a family life in the "home" country might also indicate that the worker will be less likely to seek a social life in the "host" country, thereby suggesting greater docility.

To increase efficiency and to provide greater selectivity, many Web sites are interactive. These sites are also facilitated by the use of statistical prejudgments, thereby reifying the production of gendered and racialized migration systems. *Lending Hands Employment Services*, for example, offers potential employers the opportunity to request the preferred nationality when hiring a maid. Choices include "Filipina," "Indonesian," "Sri Lankan," and "Other." Their interactive Web site also allows potential employers to select maids based on age, income, and priority of duties.

Private employment agencies may also claim to provide intensive screening of worker-applicants. *Newway Employment Agency* contends "we know the Girls personnaly [*sic*]!" Similarly, both FOK and *Kingston Employment Services* assert that their "maids are personally interviewed." *Phil-Thai Employment Services* states that their domestic helpers are "personally interviewed overseas and screened from provinces frequently."

Other services that agencies emphasize in their Web-based marketing include counseling sessions, orientation seminars, and training for their worker-applicants. *NYK-Fil Ship Management*, for example, specializes in the "recruiting, training and deploying" of "qualified Filipino seafarers." Technical expertise among its workers is critical; as such, *NYK-Fil* maintains "state-of-the-art equipment and training facilities," including tanker training rooms and equipment simulators. *Shalom Manpower Management*, an India-based recruitment agency, deploys workers in a variety of occupations, including information technology, telecommunications, and engineering. According to their Web site, *Shalom* "selects the cream of candidates from the Indian sub-continent."

One proffered service, again most commonplace among those agencies specializing in the provision of domestic workers, is that of "worker-replacement" guarantees. Thus, if the "performance" of the work in question is perceived to be unsatisfactory, some recruitment agencies offer guarantees and replacement deals. *CT & J*, for example, provides not only a standard "maid" package, but also a 3-month guarantee with "one replacement worker." *Maid-Power* likewise provides a "free 40 days trial" and *Noble Maids* offers "*Free replacement* of your maid if she is medically unfit and if you find her unsuitable anytime during the year."

Not all recruitment agencies are willing, or able, to provide such assurances. *Maids-Plus*, a Web-based "consortium" of private recruitment agencies in Singapore, prominently displays that their affiliated agencies "do not give anything for free. They do not offer free trial, free six-monthly medical check-up, free watch, free ticket to London, Manila or wherever.

After all, employment agencies, like other businesses, are not in the charity business." *Maids-Plus* does explain, however, that "they do conduct their business in a conscientious professional manner and earn the fee they charge."

In short, the Web-related recruitment of contract workers is both cause and consequence of the processes of globalization. As a medium of communication and representation, the Internet has facilitated the global presence of Filipino (and other) workers, both in the "cyberworld" and the "real world." In the coming years, the "virtual" presence of employment agencies has the potential for revolutionizing patterns and processes of transnational migration. Web sites are essentially "place-less" and yet they physically connect the world by facilitating material linkages in the form of commodities, information, and even people. However, the Internet has also affected how individuals perceive themselves and others. Consequently, these technological advances have transformed the processes of identity formation. As Elkins writes, as "virtual communities take form and become more visible to their members or observers, they offer opportunities for existing ethnic communities to consolidate their diaspora and to facilitate the identities and behavior so difficult to sustain over the generations when small enclaves have been isolated to one degree or another within other societies."[14] It is to this process I now turn.

COMMUNITY FORMATION IN AN ERA OF GLOBALIZATION

The processes of globalization have challenged traditional notions of nationalism and self-identity. National identity and nationalism are powerful social constructs that help create a common will. These identities are also concretely represented by and acted out in certain spaces. However, as millions of people circulate around the world, (re)presentations of national identity have been challenged, contested, and reformulated. Like other media, such as radio, television, and film, the World Wide Web transcends these spaces and thus helps foster the growth of national identity.

Approximately eight million Filipinos live and work in 197 countries and territories. Reflective of the many paths of mobility, "settlement" patterns impart vastly different diasporic experiences, including the live-in maids of Singapore, the construction workers housed in isolated work-camps in Saudi Arabia, and the nurses working in Los Angeles. While some Filipinos enjoy relatively stable lives, other Filipinos reside in ephemeral communities, wherein workers are vulnerable to immediate deportation by the host-government at any time.

Regardless of the "permanence" of the community, within host-societies Filipinos often encounter various forms of discrimination and prejudice. Even as they are heavily recruited to fulfill labor needs around the world, many of these Filipinos are simultaneously accused of stealing jobs from native workers, of bringing in diseases, and of otherwise taking advantage of the "system." It is, in part, this discrimination that spurs the establishment of transnational communities. As Glick Schiller et al. suggest, immigrant transnationalism is best understood as a response to the fact that in a global economy contemporary migrants have found full incorporation in the countries within which they resettle either not possible or not desirable.[15] Yen Espiritu, in the context of Philippine–US migration, argues that "the position of the Philippines within the global racial order and the social location of Filipinos in the United States means that Filipino immigrants—regardless of their class status and familiarity with US culture—are defined as 'non-white' and face the consequences of being so labeled." She continues: "to resist racial categorization, Filipino immigrants in the United States . . . have refused to sever their ties to the Philippines. They have assumed instead the role of *transmigrants*, generating and sustaining multistranded relations between the Philippines and the United States. . . . In so doing, they have created and maintained fluid and multiple identities that link them simultaneously to both countries."[16]

Espiritu's statements are equally applicable to the myriad other destinations of Philippine migrants. Whether living and working in Singapore, Canada, or Italy, Filipinos are often viewed as outsiders. Thus, the linkages between and among these transnational communities, and the connections between overseas communities and the Philippines, are important to consider. All of these sites of the Philippine diaspora entail their own historical and geographical contexts and continuities; each of them is racialized and gendered in its own unique ways, and they impart varying day-to-day experiences, and yet still remain part of the globalized Philippine presence.

Yet another *process of globalization* is at work. As I have routinely emphasized, the Philippine state has actively promoted this global presence of Filipinos. And indeed, since the early 1970s the Philippine government has fostered the extension of overseas Filipino communities. In 1973, for example, as during the martial law years of President Ferdinand Marcos, the Philippine government in cooperation with the travel and tourist industry initiated the politically- and economically-motivated *Balik-Bayan* (homecoming) program. Antonio Pido identifies three reasons for the implementation of this governmental sponsorship: First, the program served as a form of propaganda, to show Philippine expatriates that martial law was beneficial to the Philippines; second, these government policies served to stop the "brain drain" from the Philippines and promoted the use and directionality of the skills and talents of overseas Filipinos to help economic growth; and third, the program helped to increase tourism, playing on the sentiments of overseas Filipinos. Specific practices used to initiate the movement of overseas Filipino expatriates to travel to the Philippines included discounts on hotels, restaurants, shops, and travel, as well as special immigration visa requirements.[17]

There exists, therefore, a dual process of (1) discrimination in host-societies—and often the prohibition of "assimilation"—thereby necessitating strong communal linkages, and (2) the extension of the Philippine nation-state, and the government's active solicitation of contributions by overseas Filipinos. Combined, these two processes have contributed significantly to the construction of transnational communities within the Philippine diaspora. Historically, however, interaction among these disparate communities was rather limited. Although newspapers and other textual media permitted the interchange of ideas, many of these communities remained as isolated islands—a diasporic archipelago—within the Philippine diaspora. The World Wide Web, however, has emerged as a means to more effectively bridge these disparate communities and to foster a new sense of what it means to be a Filipino in the world.

Serving the Filipino Community

Peter Kollock and Marc Smith ask: "Can the social relations created or supported in cyberspace alter the fabric of our physical communities?"[18] In answering this question, I am in agreement with Elkins who maintains that "the technologies which make feasible . . . virtual communities will allow existing dispersed ethnic communities to find new means of support, persistence, and governance."[19] In this way, the Internet provides for the maintenance of distinct communities that transcend the impediments of physical space. To this end, Web sites provide a variety of services for the endurance and interaction among individuals within diaspora communities at a variety of "scales." Although not mutually exclusive, four principal scalar functions can be identified: Intra-diasporic, inter-diasporic, diaspora–host, and diaspora–homeland.

Intra-diasporic Web sites cater predominantly to the needs of locally concentrated expatriate communities. Services provided on these sites typically include information about community meetings, church services, the presence of Philippine doctors and lawyers in the area, the announcements of births, weddings, deaths, and of cultural events, art exhibitions, traditional dances, and so on. These Internet sites, quite clearly, may serve as "survival" guides, or handbooks, for localized expatriate communities.

Web sites that operate mainly on the intra-diasporic scale often reflect the specific needs of localized communities. The Philippine community in Germany, for example, has a migratory history tracing to the shortage of German nurses in the 1960s.[20] Later migrations were dominated by an influx of Filipinas married to German men. As a result, Philippine-German communities are often female-dominated. This characteristic, not surprisingly, influences the functions of local organizations. Consider, for example, the Web site maintained by *Asiana*. This is a German-based site that specifically offers services for Filipinas living in Germany. As the Web site for *Asiana* explains, the services this organization offers are directed primarily toward women, but also toward families. Established in 1991 by a Filipina nurse living in Cologne, the organization quickly expanded its services to the local diaspora community. Originally intended as a support network, the organization now operates a cultural center that offers multicultural education, counseling for women and families, slide shows, group sessions for Filipina single mothers, and support for Filipinas married to German men.

Philippine migration to Australia, likewise, has been dominated by Filipinas married to Australian men: Part of the so-called "bride trade" or "marriage migration."[21] It is not uncommon for these "mail-order brides" to encounter emotional and physical hardships and, consequently, numerous organizations have been established to provide relief and assistance. These organizations are notably present on the Internet. The *Filipinos in Victoria* Web site, for example, provides a hyper-text link to *Buklod-Pinay*, or the "Collective of Filipinas for Empowerment and Development" (CFED). According to its Web site, *Buklod-Pinay*

> was founded in 1990 as a response to three violent deaths of Filipino women in Victoria. . . . Disturbed by the deaths, the scandalous stories about domestic violence where Filipino women become victims and survivors, and the lack of employment opportunities for them, a group of Filipino women decided to form themselves into a support and advocacy group for Filipino women's issues. . . . CFED's work has been on empowerment of Filipino women, lobbying and advocacy. It also serves the welfare needs of the community through direct services, organizing of support groups and providing referrals, information and training workshops.

Intra-diasporic Web sites have also been formed in response to specific occupations or interests. *Nurselink*, for example, is the "official web site of the Philippine Nurses Association of Metropolitan Houston." According to their site, the organization and corresponding Web site constitutes a "full-service professional organization representing Filipino nurses working in and around the Texas Medical Center." The Web site provides information on membership meetings, community outreach programs, and publications. Conversely, an interest-related site is that of the *Philippine Basketball Association of Montreal*. The stated objectives of this site include the promotion of physical fitness, sportsmanship, and fellowship; friendly and closer relations among the Filipino youth in the greater Montreal area; and to teach the merits of competition while stressing the value of sportsmanship.

Other intra-diasporic Web sites are based on school affiliations. The Web sites of the *Association of Filipino Students* (University of South Florida), the *MIT Filipino Student Association*, and the *Marquette University Bayanihan Student Organization*, for example, fulfill a role in providing information not only for local members, but also for the surrounding community. Indeed, as stated on the Web page of the *Association of Filipino Students*, "The purpose of our organization is to promote and conserve the Filipino culture on the campus of USF." The *Filipino Student Association at Georgia Tech* likewise maintains a Web site providing information on local meetings, membership, Philippine culture, and links to other Philippine organizational Web sites.

Several local Filipino church communities are also present on the Internet. These organizations commonly use the Web to announce fund-raising campaigns and religious events in the community. The *Mount Zion Filipino Seventh-Day Adventist Church* (based in Canada) and the *Philippine German Community Oberberg* are good examples of this type. However, beyond the reach of the local community, these sites also provide links to other church communities that share their particular denomination; in addition, they invite members of the host-society to interact. As stated on the *Philippine German Community Oberberg* site, "The PGCO was founded to give all Filipinos and Germans from the Oberbergischer Kreis and neighboring regions, who are interested in Philippine culture, the opportunity to meet and exchange with each other and to celebrate."

Beyond fostering localized intra-disapora interaction, Web sites commonly provide linkages and facilitate spatial interaction at the *inter-diaspora* scale. Through inter-diasporic networking, diaspora communities exist in cyberspace not as isolated "islands" but rather as beacons of guidance and support that shine far and wide. Indeed, this imagery is vividly captured on the Web page of the *Filipino-American Association of the Tri-Cities* (FIL-AM). This Richland, Virginia-based Web site proclaims: "Like a lighthouse standing tall amidst the ocean shore, Fil-Am serves like that guiding light to help you and your family to have fun and a memorable stay in the area be it for a day or for a life time!" Inter-diasporic Web sites thus serve to bring "closer" the many disparate communities around the world. Specific functions, therefore, extend beyond the immediate and particular needs of a localized community, to other expatriate communities. The *Filipino Association of South Australia* typifies this function. Along with a history of the organization, this Web site provides linkages to 22 other Philippine-related Web sites in the region, ranging from women's community health centers to migrant resource centers and the Philippine consulate. Links to local organizations, Philippine radio stations in Australia, schools, religious institutions, and sports organizations are also provided. Indeed, the organization, and, subsequently, its Web site, was established with the purposive goal of inter-diasporic networking: "Over the years, the Filipino community grew in numbers, other organizations emerged to cater for special needs such as sport or geographic convenience. Nevertheless the FIL-ASA maintained its role as the flagship to promote Filipino art and culture. Thus its folk dance, youth choral and senior groups, liaison to government departments and other ethnic groups were established, maintained, and expanded." This site also notes the importance of networking on a national scale, to preserve Philippine traditions and national heritage for future generations of Filipino-Australians:

> In 1975, there were only a few Filipinos in Adelaide but the founders of the FIL-ASA realized that more is required than just social functions. All ethnic groups want to preserve and to pass on their culture to the younger generation. If they live outside their homeland, it is with pride that they want to show to other groups their heritage aiming to enhance their standing in the host country and to create goodwill for their homeland. Filipinos, who have a proud and unique history, are also subject to this desire to ensure the continuity of their heritage.

The *Kumusta Communications* home-page provides information relating to "Asian information" but "mainly on [the] Philippines and Japan." Having long provided "hard-copy" publications, *Kumusta Communications* has established a presence in cyberspace, providing links to the personal home-pages of individual Filipinos living in Japan, listings of "favorite Filipino recipes," and links to Japan-based Philippine clubs and organizations. *Kumusta Communications* also publishes a monthly "on-line" journal, entitled simply *Kumusta Online*, available in either Filipino or Japanese versions. In Canada, both the *Philippine Multicultural Society of Canada* and the *Filipino-Canadians in Manitoba* fulfill inter-diasporic functions. This latter Web site, for instance, serves as an umbrella organization for 19 other Philippine intra-diasporic organizations located in Manitoba, such as the *Bicol Association of Manitoba*. As a last example of inter-diasporic Web sites, *Filipinos in Luxembourg* identifies that "Although Luxembourg is a small country . . . there is, amazingly enough, a sizeable Filipino community. At the moment there is to our knowledge no sign of them in Cyberspace, but we'll provide links if and when this changes." Contained within the Web site are physical (non-Internet) addresses for the Philippine Consulate of Luxembourg, the Philippine Embassy in Belgium, and the Philippines-Luxembourg Society.

Despite the immense importance of inter-diasporic networking, the fostering of interaction between diasporic communities and host-countries (*diaspora–host* linkages) appears to be even more important. By and large, such sites express a goal to promote cultural exchange among Filipino residents and host-country citizens. The *German-Philippine Association in Mainz* (GPA), for example, seeks to "lay the foundations for cultural exchange and enhance the same among the Filipino residents and the German citizens in the Federal Republic of Germany. The GPA has been inviting known Filipino cultural groups and artists and also has been exhibiting Philippine paintings, graphics and ethnic exhibits being presented to the different cities in Germany."

Diaspora–host Web sites also provide information about linkages between the diaspora and the host-country's government institutions. The GPA, as such, serves also as

> liaison between the Filipino community and governmental institutions in the Federal Republic of Germany. The GPA represents the Filipino community as a group of nationals playing guests to a host country. Be it a tourist, a student, or a long time resident or Filipino-turned German, the GPA stands almost between the Filipino and the authorities in cases of resident permits, labor permits, stranded people, mixed marriages, divorce and deportation proceedings and many more. Conscious of these problems confronting the Filipino in Germany, the GPA provides secretarial and translation services and legal assistance.

A final cyberspatial linkage exists between the diaspora community and the homeland. *Diaspora–homeland* Web sites not uncommonly reflect highly focused linkages between localized communities in both the host-country and the

Philippines. The *Gapan Club of San Diego*, for example, is an association of Filipinos and their families living in San Diego County, California, all of whom originated from the same location in the Philippines: Gapan, Nueva Ecija. Activities of this diasporic community thus focus spatially on the nexus of both the destination area and the origin. It is this type of organizational-based Web site that most closely aligns with traditional perspectives of diaspora communities.

The Internet has emerged as a highly effective tool to compress both time and space between diasporic communities and their homelands. With Internet access, for example, it is possible to listen to Philippine radio programs, or to read Philippine newspapers and magazines from any location in the world. The *Filipino Executive Council of Greater Philadelphia*, for example, provides linkages to Philippine newspapers and also information on Philippine basketball leagues. More extensive is the Portland, Oregon-based Web site entitled *Philippines World Wide Web Links Collection*. This site provides hyper-text linkages to hundreds of separate Web sites, classified into 18 categories, such as "Government" home pages, "Philippine" pages, "Travel Links," "Sports," "Philippine Artists Online," "Philippine Newsgroups," and "Filipino Expatriate Pages." Under the heading of "Government," for example, links are provided to the Malacañang Home page (the site of the president of the Philippines), to Philippine diplomatic posts in the United States, and to the Philippine Embassies in London and Japan, as well as to the Philippine Senate. This site also includes links to 14 Philippine radio stations, 14 Philippine colleges and universities, and 27 "on-line" media sites, such as Philippine newspapers and television stations.

In short, the globalized Philippine community has developed its own spider-web of interconnectivity. Hundreds of cyber-places have emerged, providing a range of functions at a variety of "scales." Intra-diasporic Web sites function principally to serve the needs of an immediate local community; inter-diasporic sites, conversely, operate as regional and global "umbrellas," drawing together geographically-separated diaspora communities. Lastly, diaspora–host and diaspora–homeland Web sites function to solidify social interaction along traditional origin–destination axes. Beyond the concrete functions of these sites, however, community formation and practice in cyberspace also have fostered a renegotiation of national identity.

Tahanang Pilipino: A Global Home

The Internet provides a foundation for the use of "home" as metaphor. Indeed, it is remarkable that Internet Web sites are, both literally and figuratively, *home pages*. These cyberspaces thus constitute (and represent) a sense of home, of belonging, a virtual situatedness. This is significant for diaspora communities, as these communities are separated in "real space" from their homelands but, through computer technology, are able to (re)create a notion of home on the World Wide Web. The Internet, therefore, symbolically provides for a spatially enlarged concept of home.

Home as metaphor, however, connotes a deeper meaning for the Philippine diaspora. By way of explanation, consider the German-based Philippine Web site, *Asiana*. This site is actually subtitled *Tahanang Pilipino*, or "Pilipino Home." Although itself evocative of a physical structure, or presence, the phrase refers to the totality of Philippine culture, nationalism, and identity. The name is thus symbolic of the Philippine diaspora, and of the understanding that simply because individual "family" members may reside in different countries and territories, they still remain "under one roof." As explained on *Asiana*'s Web site, "We would like to think that Asiana is here to use the cliché 'to build bridges' that is the reason that within its premises any individual group, club/organization will always find a 'home', a cozy nook at ASIANA." The importance is not simply national identity tied to the Philippines as also a sense of identity based on a local community, but specifically as part of a wider, global diaspora. Thus, the significance of a "home" metaphor constitutes not a dichotomous hybrid identity, but rather a *pan identity*—a deliberate attempt to maintain a more global presence rather than a dualistic identity between a specific diaspora local community and homeland. The Web site of *LakBayan: The Filipino Diaspora*, consequently, is "dedicated to the more than 4.5 M Filipinos living overseas."

Evidence is found elsewhere. According to the home-page of the *Pilipino Organizations Regional Online Network Guide*, the PORONG is "a page for all who trace their roots to the Philippines. It is about the organizations they form wherever they may be." This site also provides a graphic of the Philippine flag, a map of the Philippines, and information about political participation. The goals of *Filipinos in Kansas City* likewise allude to the broader *global* Philippine community: "to promote understanding between the Filipino-American community and the native, majority, and other ethnic cultures in greater Kansas City, to aid in perpetuating the Filipino culture for future generations of Filipino-Americans, and to promote *Filipino community spirit regardless of geographic boundaries*" (italics added). Although this Web site does make frequent mention of a hybrid "Filipino-American," it also emphasizes the notion of a pan-national Philippine identity.

The common usage of *mabuhay* on diasporic Web sites also testifies to the construction of a pan-national Philippine identity. This word is often translated as "May you have life," and is assumed to be equivalent to the English word "greetings." However, within Philippine culture, *mabuhay* evokes more than a simple greeting, for it captures the concept of being alive, and of a collective enjoyment. *Mabuhay* thus speaks to a communal spirit, even among communities physically separated. Therefore, when the Web site *Filipinos in Kansas City* opens with the phrase "Mabuhay and welcome to the Filipino American community in Kansas City," the phrase is not redundant (i.e., "welcome and welcome"), but instead serves to invite one into the larger Philippine community, the *tahanang Pilipino*. Relatedly, the Austrian-based *Mabuhay ang Pilipinas* Web site states as its objective: "we aim to imbibe national unity and motivate Filipinos worldwide to be proud of who they are and to participate in the accomplishment of their nationhood. Mabuhay ang mga Filipinos!"

As the processes of globalization intensify, and ever larger numbers of people gain access to electronic forms of communication, questions of identity will be renegotiated. The Philippine diaspora indicates one possible reworking, namely the promotion of a pan-national identity, one where members of disparate communities around the world can interact near instantaneously. A growing number of Philippine diaspora Web sites foster a specific *geographical imagination* of a pan-national identity. This runs counter to the forwarding of a *trans*-national identity that is currently in vogue among many academics. "Trans" refers to a "crossing," as in crossing nations. The prefix "pan," conversely, is more appropriate. As suggested in the concept of *tahanang Pilipino*, a pan-national identity recognizes that there is a shared history and geography of all Philippine migrants, although their day-to-day experiences may differ substantially. Individual members may travel different paths, and find themselves anywhere from Australia to Zimbabwe, but they remain "under one roof."

National identity, as represented on Philippine diaspora Web sites, is not a simple dualism, reflective of a homeland/

destination dichotomy. Rather, a globalized nationalism is more fluid, more malleable, and made possible, in part, through Internet technology. Consequently, Filipinos living in Vancouver, for example, may retain a sense of community, of home, with Filipinos living in Frankfurt, Singapore, or any of the other locations around the world. Emergent Philippine diasporic identities are thus not limited to a single origin-destination linkage, and the subsequent construction of "hybrid" identities, but rather are oriented to the development of a pan-Philippine national identity, of members all residing under one roof, living within the *tahanang Pilipino*.

Performing Globalization

Five

Recent changes in the global economy have had a profound impact on the lives of people. Current processes of globalization, coupled with the emergence of "migration industries," have significantly impacted the everyday life of individuals and their families. As migrant workers respond to changing conditions of the international division of labor, and of changes in the global labor market, different family formations emerge. Researchers now speak of seasonal orphans, solo parents, flexible citizens, and shadow households.[1] Rachel Silvey notes that migrants' particular experiences, on the one hand, are shaped in part by the different positions of their respective sending and receiving countries in the global economy.[2] The Philippines, for example, attempts to export "surplus" labor and earn foreign exchange, while receiving countries, such as Japan, Canada, or Singapore, attempt to import cheap labor as a strategy of flexible accumulation. On the other hand, migrants' experiences are also a reflection of individual and familial contexts, and how these are likewise affected by the processes of globalization. Consequently, how migrants experience globalization is unique. For the eight million Filipinos who live and work beyond the shores of the Philippines, there are eight million stories.[3] The experience of being a Filipina nurse in the United States is different from being a Filipina nurse in Singapore; the experience of being a Filipina performing artist in Singapore, likewise, is different from being a Filipina performing artist in Japan. And each of these experiences provides insight into the different, but similar, ways in which globalization is acted out in real ways by real people.

Through their spatial mobility, as well as governmental and academic discourses, people *become* migrants. But their lives are filled with the everyday trials and tribulations of simply *being people*: the day-to-day activities of shopping, cooking, and going to work, along with more episodic events such as marriage, divorce, childbirth, and even migration. In this chapter I provide an in-depth narrative of Lisa, a Filipina who worked as a performing artist in Okinawa. Following the influential work of Maruja Asis, Pauline Barber, Geraldine Pratt, Rhacel Parreñas, Deirdre McKay, and Nobue Suzuki, in particular, I believe that life-stories provide an invaluable means of giving voice to participants in viewing and describing their migratory experiences.[4] Indeed, I am in agreement with Deirdre McKay and Carol Brady who argue that "macroprocesses such as globalization only take shape through the particular activities of people in place" but that such "agency is expressed within the limitations defined by particular economic situations."[5] Consequently, through the experiences of Lisa, I hope to articulate how the globalization processes advanced by the Philippine state, and those of Japan and the United States, impinge on the life of a real person.

THE EMBODIMENT OF A MIGRANT ENTERTAINER

Lisa grew up in a small village near a major US military installation in the northern Philippines. Her father, Reynaldo, was a carpenter; her mother, Evelyn, sold vegetables at the local market. Lisa is the third child of six. Her eldest brother, Gerardo, died when Lisa was very young. The other siblings are Lisa's older sister (Maria), two younger brothers (Eduardo and Ben), and a younger sister (Tess).

Life was difficult for Lisa and her family. Lisa describes her family as being relatively poor; she recalls that there were many occasions when they worried whether they would have enough food for the next day. According to Lisa, her parents supported Maria most, to the neglect of the other children. Previous research indicates that parents in the Philippines often rely on daughters to supplement their income because, traditionally, daughters maintain close ties with their birth-family, even after marriage. Lisa explains, however, that her parents looked to Maria for support not only because of gendered expectations, but also because of generational considerations. In other words, if Gerardo had not died, he would have been expected to provide for the family. Lisa's parents used any surplus income that they acquired to provide for a decent education for Maria. In this way, despite their poverty, Maria was able to attend private school. However, Maria later ran off with a boyfriend and did not finish her education.

To help her family, Lisa dropped out of middle school to begin work in a Taiwanese-owned candy factory. In this way, Lisa became part of the Philippines' provision of low-waged workers within the international division of labor. Her decision to work on the assembly line was motivated by a desire, initially, to help her parents. It was also during this time that Tess, then 13 years old (but looking, according to Lisa, much older), was approached by a distant cousin. This cousin talked excitedly about opportunities to work and earn substantial sums of money in Japan. Tess, whom Lisa describes as very impetuous, was eager to look into this possibility.

The migration of Filipina overseas performing artists to Japan is big business.[6] Annually, approximately 30,000 women (and some men) from the Philippines obtain temporary work in Japan, remitting millions of dollars back into the Philippines' economy. According to the Philippine Overseas

Employment Administration, these migrants are employed as dancers, composers, singers, and musicians. In actuality, many of these individuals are engaged in "sex work," working in brothels, nightclubs, and massage parlors.

The large-scale presence of Filipinas in Japan is itself the result of former President Ferdinand Marcos' attempt to globalize the Philippines. As indicated in Chapter Two, the Philippine state, under the authoritarian control of Marcos, sought to increase foreign revenue into the Philippines through the provision of lax labor laws, generous tax incentives, and so forth. Such practices resulted, for example, in the establishment of foreign-owned firms, such as the candy factory where Lisa worked. However, another component of the Philippine state's drive for foreign revenue was through the promotion of international tourism. Tourism was not actively encouraged by the Philippine state until the early 1970s. During the Marcos regime, though, tourism was recognized as a means to boost foreign investment, provide employment opportunities, and increase foreign currency through money spent by tourists. Consequently, the Philippine state, with incentives such as tax breaks under the direction of the Department of Tourism, was instrumental in encouraging partnerships with major corporations in an attempt to finance hotel and resort developments. Tourism, furthermore, was vigorously pursued during the 1970s based on a selected—and sexualized—image. Indeed, as Nobue Suzuki identifies, "Under the ailing economy since the Marcos regime in the 1970s, [the] Filipino ruling elite has exploited . . . women's sexuality for political leverage and economic gain."[7]

Travel brochures, guidebooks, and tourist magazines regularly portrayed the Philippines as a sexual paradise—and Filipino women as openly welcoming. These promotion campaigns translated into massive tourist flows. The number of visitor arrivals in the Philippines increased from 166,431 in 1972 to 1,008,159 in 1980.[8] Tourism was also highly profitable. By 1974 tourism became one of the Philippines' chief earners of foreign exchange. Japanese tourists, for example, spent an average of US $800 on a week's trip to the Philippines.[9]

Perhaps not surprisingly, this massive tourist inflow was later exposed by many non-governmental organizations and activist groups as nothing more than "sex tours."[10] In 1981, for example, protests by the Christian Temperance Union (based in Japan) and the Third World Movement Against the Exploitation of Women (based in the Philippines) led to declines in sex-tours from Japan. In 1983, also, 17 civic, religious, and university organizations formed STOP (Stop Trafficking of Pilipinas), an NGO aimed primarily against "pimps, agents, protectors, recruiters, managers, and brothel owners."[11]

International campaigns against sex tourism did not eliminate the "demand" for sexual excursions, but merely forced a shift in venue. This was made possible through the efforts of the Philippine state migratory apparatus. The POEA, in cooperation with the private sector (including recruitment agencies, "talent" managers and promoters, travel agencies), institutionalized a process to effectively recruit sex workers and deploy the sexuality of the Philippines to global destinations. Patterns of tourist data and migration data provide testimony to this shift. Whereas visitor arrivals from Japan declined from 193,146 to only 126,825 during the period 1981–1987, the number of Filipino contract workers to Japan increased from 11,656 to 33,791. Of those 33,791 workers, 31,292 (93 percent) were female entertainers.[12] Rather than traveling to the Philippines, women were "imported" to satisfy demand in the growing Japanese "sex industry." As Duenas explains, "sex tours from Japan to the Philippines . . . stopped precisely because Filipino women are now imported to Japan like commodities for sale in a modern slave market."[13] Indeed, throughout the 1980s and into the 1990s it was not uncommon to see "Filipina women" advertised on billboards and in films and magazines.

Such was the historical setting that contextualized Lisa's exposure to employment in Japan. Lisa and Tess, accompanied by their father, arranged to have dinner at a nearby restaurant with their cousin. Also present were two Japanese men. Over the course of the meal, the two men from Japan attempted to "impress" Lisa and her father. Enough food was ordered, for example, to ensure that Lisa and her family could take home leftovers for the other family members.

Conversation focused on the "unlimited" possibilities of employment in Japan. Reynaldo, however, grew increasingly suspicious. The two men, Reynaldo ascertained, did not operate through a recruitment agency. They also gave no indication of a manager or other authority figure. Although not having personally worked abroad, Reynaldo knew of many other men from his village who had worked as contract workers. Mostly, though, Reynaldo was concerned that his daughters were too young. The Japanese recruiters, however, attempted to assure Reynaldo that they would take care of all the arrangements, including visas, passports, and work contracts. After the meeting, however, the incident dropped from conversation. Lisa explains that it was simply no longer a topic of discussion. The seed, though, had been planted. For both Lisa and Tess, the prospect of working—and earning lots of money—remained intriguing.

The possibility of working in Japan, for Lisa, was ever present. Through family members, friends, and even strangers, it seemed as if everyone was aware of work in Japan. Television advertisements depicted beautiful women, laden with bulging suitcases, shopping at duty-free stores in airports around the world. And so it was that a few months later Lisa found herself sitting with Tess and another cousin at a neighborhood store. Ironically, this cousin was herself waiting to meet a recruiter to talk about the opportunities of working in Japan. On this occasion, Lisa remembers, the labor recruiter—a Filipino—appeared to visually "inspect" her and her sister. He said that he wanted to recruit both Lisa and Tess to work in Japan. After the earlier incident, however, Lisa was more skeptical. That evening she spoke about the matter with her parents. This recruiter, Lisa explained, appeared to have legitimate credentials.

Unlike in the first instance, Lisa made the decision to pursue a contract in Japan. In some respects, Lisa may be considered an "incidental" migrant, in that her initiation into overseas employment was not planned.[14] Rather, the opportunity arose and Lisa chose to act upon the offer. How, though, are we to interpret Lisa's decision to seek employment in Japan as a performing artist? Certainly her story illustrates a life of poverty and a lack of opportunities. And indeed, discussions of Filipina migrant entertainers commonly emphasize poverty as the primary, if not sole, determinant of their movement.[15] Randolf David, for example, argues that the migration of entertainers reflects the "desperation that extreme economic poverty induces in migrants from an impoverished country."[16] However, these dominant representations risk obfuscating more than they reveal. The movement of Filipinas, specifically, into Japan has been so commonly portrayed as a desperate flight of poverty-stricken women using sex as a means to a better life, that these images have been used to discriminate against *all* Filipinas.[17]

It would be easy to presume, therefore, that structural

conditions impelled her to become a migrant, and that patriarchal norms limited her opportunities to that of sex work. There is more to the story, however, and we may draw parallels with similar studies. Lisa Law, for example, cautions that

> By emphasizing the structural determinants of why women enter the sex industry . . . Filipina dancers are cast as "victims" who have no choice. While it could be argued that this representation victimizes women, denies agency and distorts the complexity of experience . . . it is important to note that the naturalness of the choice issue can be appropriated by women themselves, where having "no choice" simultaneously becomes a source of agency, a resistance to moral judgements and justification for their employment.[18]

Studies on Philippine migration likewise acknowledge the vital role performed by families in the migratory process, and how globalization has affected this traditional role. Within the Philippines, for example, it is commonly asserted that the concepts of obligation and reciprocity are especially salient. Familial assistance patterns within the Philippines are characteristically described as reciprocal and thus carry a sense of obligation, or *utang na loob* (translated as "a debt of prime obligation"). In addition, the social organization of personal obligations is amplified because kinship ties are composed of extended family members, including godparents who become "part of the family" through their participation not only in baptism but also in other rituals such as weddings. Within Philippine society, brothers and sisters often have different godparents or sponsors (*ninongs* or *ninangs*) to look to as their benefactors, and thus an individual's source of assistance, as well as the sense of debt, may not be found within the immediate nuclear family, but rather within a wider kinship network. Furthermore, Philippine society reveals also distinct gender roles whereby daughters, especially, are expected to care for the family.[19]

Although the cultural attributes, the gendered roles, and the affects of the state-sponsored globalization of labor certainly influenced Lisa's decision, it was not deterministic. Lisa did have opportunities to work in the Philippines; she could easily have continued to work in the candy factory, for example. Her decision was thus prompted more by a condition of perceived under-employment rather than by unemployment. At the time, Lisa felt that Japan offered more opportunities than those afforded in the Philippines. Moreover, Lisa explains, she saw in Japan an opportunity to assert her independence, to be on her own. She was tired of asking for new shoes, for example, and being told that there was no money. But in Japan, Lisa hoped, she would have the ability to buy whatever she desired. Yes, she explains, she wanted to help her family. But she looked for her own independence, both financially and personally.

Lisa, moreover, was not swayed by visions of helping her country, of being a modern-day heroine—as the Philippine state often touts its migrant work force. Lisa's action, instead, conforms with other studies of migrant attitudes. Victoria Cruz and Anthony Paganoni, for example, find in their study of 466 migrant and non-migrant women that "the respondents [do not situate] themselves in relation to the nation as a whole. Their decision is certainly not dictated by the government program to reconstruct the national economy. Neither is it understood as contributing to the economic well-being of the host country. The national and international dimensions are simply overlooked by respondents who are . . . acting out their own desire for something different and more liberating."[20] In Lisa's situation, those larger (global) structural conditions did not figure prominently in her decision to obtain overseas employment, though these certainly did provide the (unacknowledged) context. Indeed, at this point Lisa did not view herself as a "migrant"; rather, she was a "middle daughter" who wanted to buy new shoes.

Lisa's decision to obtain overseas employment also challenges another embedded presumption of global migration studies, namely that the *opportunity* to migrate is often taken as given; individuals are presumed a priori to be able to pick and choose among a myriad of destinations. However, overseas employment is highly regulated. Bureaucratic procedures of recruitment and deployment set in place tangible parameters within which individuals must negotiate. As such, the mobility of individuals is neither a simple nor an inevitable process. Lisa became aware of a particular opportunity, that of working in Japan as a dancer. She did not hear of, nor did she seek out, other potential overseas opportunities.

Was Lisa concerned about the stigma of working in Japan? Of being labeled a *japayuki*? Coined by the Japanese filmmaker Yamatani Tetsuo, the word *japayuki* is a combination of *Japa-* (Japan) and *-yuki* (to go). As Nobue Suzuki explains, *japayuki* is also a pun on the word "*Karayuki*" (China-bound), used for Japanese prostitutes who were deployed throughout Asia prior to World War II. *Japayuki* has entered into both the Japanese and Filipino vocabularies as a derogatory term for Filipina prostitutes. Suzuki explains that in Japan, the "continuing domination of such a pervasive 'prostitute' image of Filipinas symbolically places *all* Filipinas in the time-space confinement of the 'sex industry.' " Consequently, when Filipinas are redefined as prostitutes, they are commodified. They are perceived not as being people, but instead as sex objects.[21]

Law finds in her study of Southeast Asian sex workers that the women she interviewed perceived a negotiated tension between their free will to enter sex work and the constraints that make this particular type of employment an opportunity for them. With hindsight, Lisa concedes that yes, at first, some relatives and friends disapproved. However, when she returned from Japan for the first time, laden with material goods, everyone became her friend. With a laugh, Lisa thinks of these people as "plastic." As to her own perceptions of overseas employment as a dancer, Lisa is more circumspect.

TRAINING TO MIGRATE

The Philippine state migratory apparatus produces specific "bodies" for overseas employment.[22] Performing artists, especially, are produced (legally) through a regulated series of training and testing.[23] This is accomplished through the organization and regulation of time, space, and daily activities through which bodies are trained, shaped, and impressed with particular normative ideas of femininity and sexuality.

In the context of producing appropriate "bodies," Michel Foucault discusses the emergence of "observatories," or locations where the techniques of disciplinary power are applied. Such observatories include military camps, schools, hospitals, and factory floors.[24] The exercise of discipline thus presupposes a mechanism that coerces by means of observation. The training centers and testing facilities established and sanctioned by the POEA serve as observatories in the production of Filipina performing artists. The entire system is designed to monitor, track, and chart the development of the entertainer. A visual reading of the "making" of entertainers is therefore possible. It is not, though, simply the physical infrastructure (e.g., buildings and dance stages) that becomes visible, but the entire process. The POEA and the Department of Labor and Employment (DOLE) has designed a system that is apparent and open for all to see. This is concurrently a system that caters to the international demand for "entertainers" and to the production of "legitimate" and "reputable" migrant performing artists. These women (and some men) are made to conform to the economic imperatives of overseas employment.

Once in Manila—the "command center" of the Philippines' global circulation of labor—Lisa and Tess moved into a large dormitory-like building: The talent studio. The building itself was subdivided into living quarters, dance floors, meeting rooms, and various other offices. The owner/manager of the studio was a Filipina; her husband was a Japanese-Filipino. Lisa did not know the history of the owner, or whether she herself was a former performing artist in Japan—something that is, in fact, quite common. What Lisa did know was that the manager owned two homes, one in the Philippines and the other in Japan. Approximately 30 to 40 other women, and a handful of men, lived in the studio. Some of the women were trainees (called "newbies") while others were returning workers (called "timers") who elected to live at the studio during their brief stays in the Philippines. The studio manager tried, though largely unsuccessfully, to keep the "newbies" separate from the "timers."

Life in the studio was regimented. Mornings were occupied with aerobics and other exercises, while afternoons were reserved for dance training. Combined, the activities of the trainees were to produce a specific bodily form. Sandra Bartky writes about the "proper" shape of the feminine body.[25] The training center encouraged aerobics and certain exercises. The particular body that was desired—from the trainer's point of view, as well as that of the potential club manager—was slender and feminine. Overly muscular bodies were to be avoided, as these were perceived as too masculine. Lisa explains that cosmetic surgery was not encouraged in her studio, although she did hear stories that clubs catering for Japanese men preferred women with large breasts; accordingly, Lisa believes that many Filipinas employed in those clubs may have been more likely to have breast enlargements. She also perceives that Japanese men preferred more "Westernized" women. Consequently, some Filipinas had eye and nose surgery to conform to a particular type of body that was thought to be in demand on the international market.

Over the course of her training, Lisa was taught three dance routines. In retrospect, she feels that this training was pointless, in that she was never once asked to perform these routines in Japan. She says, "I asked that to myself—why did we learn those dances? Yeah, it was stupid if you think about it." Rather, in Japan, Lisa and the other dancers were expected to perform "sexy" dances, those typical of strip clubs. For this type of training, which is not specified in official guidelines, the studio manager would take the trainees to nightclubs in Manila so that they could watch other dancers perform. Significantly, recruiters with whom I've spoken indicated that they preferred to recruit women from the provinces and not the clubs of Manila. They explained that the women who were employed in the bars and clubs of Manila were too "professional," meaning that they were already experienced in entertainment work. As such, they were deemed "too hard to control" and if deployed to Japan, they would be "too demanding." Consequently, throughout the training period, the new recruiters were escorted throughout Manila, so that they might learn dancing styles and yet presumably remain naïve about actual employment conditions of nightclubs.

Dancing and exercise were also two components of a wider regime of corporeal discipline. The dance trainees were instructed on particular bodily gestures and movements. Lisa explains that they were taught how to be "lady-like," to be feminine. The women were instructed on the proper (feminine) way to cross their legs, hold drinking glasses, and walk. Facial expressions were also coached. Bartky explains that "feminine faces, as well as bodies, are trained to the expression of deference."[26] The female gaze is trained to look away coyly, to smile demurely when looked upon. These facial expressions, in which Lisa was trained, conform to Westernized representations of Filipinas (and "Asian" women in general) as delicate, docile, and subservient. The training they undergo serves to produce a particular feminine body—one that visibly and visually signifies their submissiveness, passivity, and *willingness* to serve the (usually) man's needs and desires.

Aside from physical changes to the body, other practices that produce a properly ornamented body are also utilized. Bartky, for example, writes of the mastery of certain techniques, and the acquisition of a specialized knowledge, in the construction of the feminine body-subject. She explains that women must learn about regimes of hair-care, skin-care, manicures and pedicures; women must also learn the proper manipulation of devices such as blow-dryers, styling brushes, curling irons, eyeliners, lipliners, mascara brushes, and so forth. For Lisa, her training included just such lessons.[27]

Lisa explains that pimples were certainly to be avoided. In retrospect, she does not remember any women with severe cases of acne. The interpretations of this are many and open. Were women with acne deliberately *not* recruited? Were these women simply not offered overseas contracts? Lisa is unable to answer these questions, but she does explain that heavy applications of makeup were often used to cover temporary or permanent facial "blemishes." Lastly, Lisa mentions that the women received dental care. Clean teeth, as well as the avoidance of bad breath, were a must. Quite literally, these training studios attempt to put "the best face forward" in their promotion of a global work force.

Women at Lisa's training studio were also instructed on the proper etiquette for both "Japanese" clubs and "American" clubs.[28] Once deployed to Japan, the women would be employed either in a club that serviced primarily Japanese clientele or, particularly if deployed to Okinawa, in a club that catered to US military personnel. Lisa explains that, based on her training, work in Japanese clubs was stricter; the Japanese men had very different, and more rigid, expectations than the US servicemen. For example, she was taught that it was very disrespectful for a woman to light the cigarette of a Japanese man.

Lisa and the other trainees would also watch videos on how to work as "hostesses." This type of training included lessons on how to talk to customers; lessons included introductory Japanese language training. I asked Lisa if she ever wondered about this component of training—on the techniques of entertaining customers—when she was to be employed as a "dancer." Lisa, though, knew what her "real" occupation was: That of hostess. Indeed, Lisa explains that the most valuable lessons learned came from speaking with the "timers." Even prior to her arrival at the studio, Lisa had heard stories about work in Japan, and so she had some understanding. Speaking with the veterans of work in Japan, however, helped Lisa tremendously in her preparation.

Did Lisa, therefore, worry about potential abuse and exploitation? Certainly she was aware that many women, and not just entertainers, encountered problems while working abroad. However, she adopted an attitude that conforms with Filomeno Aguilar's discussion of "cross-border gamblings." Aguilar explains that labor migration may be considered a "gamble against life itself and the personal destiny one wants to alter by token of the very act of leaving and seeking a new life." He continues that at a basic level, the expectations may be minimal, such as having the good fortune, or *suwerte*, of working for a good employer. Conversely, the migrant may hope to become a *panalo*, or winner, of making lots of money.[29] As to the risks, Lisa left that to fate.

Lisa's training period lasted for approximately one year. During this time Lisa was able to remain in contact with her family by phone; additionally, her parents were able to make periodic visits. Although Lisa never attended college, she compares her training to the stories and television shows she has seen about moving away from home and living on campus.

The day of Lisa's booking stands out in her memory. Having completed her training, Lisa was asked to perform at a "booking" at the studio. She, along with dozens of other women and men, were required to perform their three dance routines behind a mirrored room divider. On the other side of the screen were various club managers from other countries, though mostly from Japan.

The booking procedure resonates with Foucault's discussion of the examination as a technique of discipline. This procedure is highly ritualized and combines the techniques of observation with those of normalization. The examination, consequently, is the technique by which power manifests its potency, essentially by arranging objects: it is the ceremony of objectification.[30] In the Philippines, overseas performing artists are required to undergo a series of examinations and, ultimately, to perform their routines at auditions. In this "making" of migrant entertainers, it is the successful completion of the Academic and Skills Test, and the subsequent awarding of the Artist Record Book, that makes a migrant performing artist into an object. It is through the training and, subsequently, the examination of bodies that judgment is written—inscribed—onto the bodies of the trainees. As Foucault writes, "all behavior falls in the field between good and bad marks, good and bad points."[31]

PERFORMING MIGRATION

Following her audition, Lisa was offered, and she accepted, a 6-month contract to work in a nightclub in Okinawa. The everyday presence of the US military in Okinawa is pervasive. As of 2000, Okinawa hosted 50,000 US military personnel and their dependants, all on an island that has just 1.3 million inhabitants and is just 1 percent of the land area of Japan.[32] Sexual services have historically been available for US military personnel in Okinawa. Saundra Sturdevant explains that during the American occupation following World War II, Okinawan women "provided" sexual labor; women involved were mainly widows and daughters of families left with few resources. She further explains that, by the 1970s, the total amount of foreign exchange generated by sexual labor was the largest of any industry in Okinawa.[33] Lisa thus came to Okinawa as part of the United States' own globalizing military presence.

Lisa landed in Okinawa during a severe tropical storm. She remembers, vividly, the lightning illuminating the night sky, and the deep rumbling of thunder that seemed to shake the entire island. She was met at the airport and driven directly to the club. Arriving at the club around 8 pm, Lisa assumed that she would not start working until the following day. Instead, she was told to change and to begin work. She says, "I thought they were going to give me a break, like I'm going to start tomorrow, [but] no, right away. They said, 'Give me all your suitcases' and 'Put on your makeup.' I said, 'What?' "

Her first night was filled with a mixture of emotions: fear, nervousness, anticipation, anxiety, exhaustion. She was not required to dance that first night, but rather was told to walk around, talk to customers, to get a feel for the club. At first, she was shy about talking to strangers, even in English. The club, she learned, catered mostly to a foreign (non-Japanese) clientele. Customers were mostly US Marines from a nearby base.

Disciplinary power is exercised through the spatial distribution of individuals. Through enclosure and confinement—whether walled cities, prisons, or nightclubs—the physical confinement of bodies in space serves to restrict social and spatial mobility. Disciplined spaces also provide greater efficiency. These geographies of discipline resonate with the experiences of Lisa. Her worksite/home was a two-story building. Upstairs was the nightclub; living quarters were on the lower level. The living arrangements were dorm-like. Approximately six women lived in each room, with bunk-beds provided. Although some clubs have both male and female performers, including transvestites, this club was staffed only by female performers.

Disciplinary power is also exercised through the control of activities. Within the club, working hours were set by the club owners and were correlated with the activities of the military personnel. Normally, the club opened for business around 6:30 or 7:00 pm; on paydays—meaning the days when the Marines were paid—the club would open earlier, usually around 5 pm. The club would stay open until 2 am but, again, on paydays the club would stay open all night, not closing until 8 am. Even if no customers were in the club at any given time, Lisa and the other dancers were not allowed to sleep or rest during their shifts.

Daily life was routinized. In the morning the women were required to do their chores: Cooking, cleaning, laundry. They had free time between 1:00 and 4:00 in the afternoon. During this time the women could come and go as they pleased.

Other researchers have identified that club owners often require dancers to call up customers during the day. Aurora de Dios, Rosario Ballescas, and Maruja Asis, for example, document instances wherein club owners would pressure the women to go out with clients, a practice known as *dohan*, and for which club owners would exact a fee.[34] Lisa explains that she was not explicitly told to engage in these activities. At the same time, however, she also quickly learned that if you knew a "good-spender," you would call him or visit him during the day, to encourage him to show up that evening.

The club maintained a dress code. While performing, women were required to wear short skirts, high heels, and heavy makeup. Beyond that, the club managers were less strict. Weight, according to Lisa, was generally not an issue, although the women were encouraged to maintain a "feminine" look at all times. Again, this meant that the women were not to be too muscular (hence masculine) nor too "heavy." Bartky writes that, often, the disciplinary power that inscribes femininity in the female body is everywhere and nowhere; the disciplinarian is everyone and yet no one in particular.[35] Lisa explains that within the club the women learned from each other as to how to adorn their faces with makeup, to select the "right" customers, and to wear their hair in the current fashions. For Lisa, it was important for the women to be "hip" and "up-to-date" in their looks. All the women attempted to be popular with the clientele.

The performers were, however, visually inspected before they began work, though apparently not for reasons related to beauty. This was done, Lisa says, to check if the women were pregnant. It was explained to Lisa that a pregnant woman would bring bad luck to the club. Regardless of the specified reason, the women knew that pregnancy meant deportation.[36]

Work in the club revolved around a drinks-quota system. It

was this system, for Lisa, that structured her experiences and became the principal disciplinary technique that permeated the lives of the women. Performers at the club were required to fill a monthly quota of 800 tickets. Lisa explains that each drink was worth a specified number of tickets. A US $10 drink, for example, equated to one ticket. Clearly, this system encouraged the women to entice the male patrons to purchase numerous drinks, and ideally the most expensive ones. The dancers were not required to drink alcoholic beverages, and so usually drank 7-Up or Coca-Cola. It was extremely difficult to fill a quota of 800 tickets; normally the women's monthly tally would be around 500. An incentive was put in place that if the 800-ticket quota was reached, the performer would receive a US $200 bonus. On the other hand, women risked the canceling of their contract and thus deportation if they failed to bring in an adequate number of tickets.

The activities of the women were under constant supervision. The "mama-sans" would patrol the club floor with flashlights. They maintained a 5-minute limit, wherein customers were expected to buy drinks every 5 minutes. Accordingly, the control of activities further permeated the working experiences of Lisa and the other dancers. The time limit, Lisa explains, was the biggest complaint the women had.

Dancing, of course, was required at the club. The women were expected to perform a series of dance numbers on the stage—usually lasting for two or three songs. Nudity was not permitted in Lisa's club, but the women did wear revealing clothes. From the club owners' perspective, dancing was merely the draw, for profits hinged on the purchase of drinks. Whoever sold the fewest drinks would be expected to dance more frequently. In Lisa's view, however, this was not entirely viewed as punishment. In general, she did not object to the dancing, but did complain of having to change costumes so often.

Lisa and the other women attempted to resist within the boundaries established by the club owners, namely as a means of securing more profit for themselves. However, the quota system was extremely regulated; cans of ticket stubs were kept behind the bar and a written record was maintained. One tactic the women employed, though, was to encourage their customers to pay them cash directly, and not to purchase drinks. This was most feasible toward the end of the month, after the entertainers had already reached, or were approaching, their quota. They would hide money in their shoes or some other item of clothing, which, given their attire, was a difficult proposition. This practice, not surprisingly, was discouraged by the club owners since they would not profit from these transactions.

The quota system also engendered competition among the performers. Lisa recalls that downstairs, in the living quarters, women could be the best of friends. Upstairs, however, on the club floor, they viewed each other as competitors. When first starting employment, for example, the "newbies" were not assisted by the "timers." The recent initiates were viewed as competition. Customers, Lisa explains, often preferred, or at least exhibited more interest in, new dancers at the club. Lisa also identifies techniques that women might use to increase their own "productivity." When a woman would leave temporarily, to go to the rest room for example, another woman might approach the customer and whisper in his ear something like "Why are you buying her drinks? Don't you know she's married back in the Philippines and has four kids?" This would discursively reposition the other woman as unavailable, shatter the myth of sexual innocence or, at the very least, availability. Also, in an attempt to reach their quotas, the performers would often attempt to steal customers, especially if the men were perceived to be "good-spenders." A performer might also accuse another woman of being pregnant; hence, their competition for customers was facilitated through the disciplinary rules imposed by the club managers.[37]

Given that contracts for performing artists are 6 months in duration, Lisa made repeated sojourns to Okinawa. On one occasion, while working in Okinawa, Lisa began dating Steve, a US Marine. In hindsight, Lisa explains that she never intended to find a husband in Japan, although this is not an uncommon occurrence.[38] Lisa, furthermore, is adamant that she did not date Steve simply as a stepping-stone to the United States. Nevertheless, Lisa's relationship with Steve resulted in her becoming pregnant and, as a result, she was forced to stop working at the club.

Back in her hometown, Lisa gave birth to a girl. Steve had promised that he would follow her to the Philippines to marry her. Lisa remembers thinking that she would probably never see him again but, to her relief, Steve did come. Lisa's pregnancy, wedding, and subsequent move to the United States, however, brought significant changes to her life.

THE EMBODIED IDENTITIES OF LISA

Lisa's identities were transformed through her experiences in Okinawa and, later, in the United States. Within the literature on Philippine migration, women are traditionally presumed to take the lead in ensuring the family's survival. Daughters, wives, and mothers, for example, are expected to fulfill family obligations. De Dios writes that "Filipinas are primed by orientation and socialization to take on the role of a 'sacrificial lamb.' " Medina contends that women "continue to shoulder the greatest responsibility: it is the wife, mother, sister, or daughter who is the primary care-giver."[39] In Lisa's narrative, we see that her eldest sister Maria was primed to become, in essence, the "sacrificial lamb" for the family. As events unfolded, however, this did not materialize and, in fact, Lisa assumed much of the responsibility. Although spatially separated, Lisa was able to remit money to her family and help support her young siblings' education.

Lisa also utilized this opportunity to assert her own independence. Certainly, economically, Lisa—through her experiences in Okinawa—may be considered a *panalo*. As Ballescas identifies, *panalos* are the entertainers who are most conspicuous upon their return home. They arrive laden with money and material possessions such as stereos and television sets. However, Lisa speaks of acquiring more than simply material possessions. Lisa's own sense of identity was transformed. She saw herself in Okinawa as an independent *woman*; she was not an appendage of her family, but an autonomous woman who could provide for herself and her family in times of need.

In the United States, Lisa's sense of self was transformed yet again. She explains that, following the birth of her daughter, her concept of family shifted from her earlier childhood family, with her parents, brothers and sisters, to her incipient family. Rather than a focus on herself, and her parents and siblings, Lisa transferred her attention toward the health and well-being of her child.

Ironically, as Lisa moved around the world, so too did her perception of her ability to provide for her natal family. Lisa perceives her move to the US as one of downward mobility. Indeed, Lisa reminisces that her life was "best" not in the Philippines, nor in the US, but rather in Japan. In Japan, Lisa was able to move about; in the US, without the ability to drive, Lisa feels constrained spatially and therefore, also, socially. Economically, in the US, Lisa now feels more impoverished than when she lived in the Philippines. More important, however, is that she also feels personally impotent.

Lacking in skills and education, she believes that she has few prospects. Her spatial and financial dependence on her husband does not sit well. After her independence in Japan, and having assumed a familial position as primary wage-earner, Lisa now feels frustrated that she is repositioned in a subservient role. Lisa intimates that this has placed a strain on her marriage.

Lisa's experiences, and identity, must also be contextualized within the realm of her occupation, namely that of being a performing artist. For many, being an entertainer carries a stigma. As Ryan and Hall write, sex workers are often marginalized, as they are seen to be a threat to the fabric of society.[40] And yet, working as an entertainer, for Lisa, constituted an act of partial liberation. Work in the entertainment sector in Okinawa, for Lisa, was assuredly a performance. Admittedly, also, her experiences in Okinawa were largely positive. She was not physically beaten, raped, or abused as has happened to many other entertainers.[41] Nevertheless, Lisa describes a sense of newly acquired confidence. Certainly, sexual work is experienced as an integral part of many women's and men's lives around the world, but it is not necessarily the sole defining activity around which their sense of self is shaped.[42] Lisa has carried this over into her family life, as she is able to maintain a separation between her (previous) employment and her (current) role as daughter, sister, mother, and wife.

In the case of sex workers, as Law writes, sexual and cultural taboos help discursively to produce subjectivities in ways that mark women's bodies with sexuality, class, race, and gender.[43] What empowered Lisa to resist the negative discourses surrounding employment as a performing artist? Consistent with work conducted by and about sex workers, Lisa readily acknowledges her previous employment, but she views erotic dancing simply as a job. It was not, and is not, her defining feature. Dancing, and more broadly sex work, to Lisa constituted an income-generating activity or form of labor, and not an identity. Lisa thus views her former occupation as do many other sex workers: Sex work becomes work, like any other, and this attitude removes stigmas associated with victimization.[44] As Law finds in her study of sex workers in Southeast Asia, the women "do not author themselves as homogenous victims of colonialism, sex tourism or political economy. Prostitution is only one facet of their lives; it is a job they are employed in—often for short periods of time—and cannot be equated with the essence of their personhood."[45] In this way, the experiences of Lisa resonate with the writings of Law. For Lisa, her experiences as an entertainer constitute one chapter of her life—one that only minimally carries over in her current life. She freely acknowledges her former occupation, and exhibits neither shame nor pride.

That said, as Sallie Yea asks, is such a view—for academics—adequate in "understanding the concrete challenges these women face in re-sculpting their identities beyond prostitution-entertainment"?[46] Yea, for example, identifies the ongoing "anxieties" of former Korean-based Filipina entertainers. She finds among the women she interviewed that

> there was no discrete post-entertainer identity that was not affected by their previous status as entertainers (their past work) and the reasons they originally migrated to Korea (their transnationally situated futures). Insecurity expressed around fidelity, conflicts over money, frustrations over financial and personal independence as well as practical questions concerning legal status, visas and financial security all pervade these women's lives beyond the club in Korea.[47]

Significantly, Yea's concerns speak to broader issues of

globalization. Sex work is global and is facilitated through tourism, trafficking, and even the legal "migration" of overseas performing artists. But as with other global circulations, the perceptions of sex work are context-specific and contingent upon individual agents. How being a performing artist is viewed differs between and within countries. How Lisa dealt with her "life" as a performing artist therefore shifted as did her location. In the Philippines, she could be considered a *panalo*, although even there, she would downplay certain facets of her job. Indeed, Ballescas makes a distinction between "winners" and "losers" among entertainers. Winners, the *panalos*, are those women (and men) who were able to remit large sums of money to the Philippines; they may have been able to buy or remodel homes, to send children to school, or to start up businesses. And yet, even among the "winners," there is a tendency to not speak of the specificities of *being* an entertainer. Of these "well-kept" secrets, Ballescas writes that at home in the Philippines:

> No one among them is telling her loved ones . . . that as an entertainer in Japan, she was subjected to unsolicited touches and kisses. No one is, of course, admitting that there were offers for entertainers like her to do sex; while many say they refused, there were many of them also who agreed. However, no one is saying anything too negative about her stay in Japan; no one has completely related the reality of her world and life as entertainer in Japan.[48]

Recall that for Lisa, many of those people who knew of her job as a performing artists were "plastic," or hypocritical. They may turn up their noses in disdain for such employment, but nevertheless eagerly accepted the material goods that Lisa brought home.

And in the United States? There, Lisa's experiences have been shaped certainly by stigmas associated with sex work, but also by the legacy of racial discrimination. Lisa now lives in a small city in the Midwest. She has since given birth to two more children, and now spends most of her time caring for her family. Steve works in a factory, and bills remain an ongoing worry for Lisa. Living on just his salary, and supporting three children, Lisa and Steve are only able to afford a small rental house in a "lower-class" neighborhood.

Filipinos living in the United States must negotiate daily specific instances of discrimination and prejudice in their interactions in the host society.[49] Filipinas, on a day-to-day basis, confront dominant stereotypes of the Philippines, other Asian groups, and even some non-Asian groups. It is not uncommon, for example, for people living in rural, non-ethnically-diverse locations (such as the Midwestern United States) to have never encountered a person from the Philippines; their only source of information is obtained via television, print media, or academia. In January of 1997, for example, the news-program *60 Minutes* aired a report on mail-order brides. During the broadcast the anchor, Lesley Stahl, reported that

> The reason [for mail order marriage] is not only the irresistible charm of American men, it's that marriage is an escape route from poverty. Mired in the Third World, the Philippines relies heavily on exports to the First World, and one of its most valuable exports is its women. Each year close to half a million Filipinas go to foreign countries, many as nurses and maids, some as prostitutes and others as brides. And they send millions of dollars back home. There's an unwritten law that daughters sacrifice for the rest of the family.

Television shows reaffirm these negative representations of Filipinas. In a 1994 episode of the situation comedy *Frasier*, the father of the title character remarked, "For an extra five grand, you could have bought a whole new wife from the Philippines."[50] These representations impart an added dimension to the construction and negotiation of transnational identities—a partial explanation for the emergence of cyber-communities and "real-world" community organizations as detailed in Chapter Four.

Living in the United States, Lisa must constantly negotiate these pervasive stereotypes of Filipinas, of being asked if she is a "mail-order bride" or a prostitute. Filipina migrants are continuously asked questions, such as "How did you get here?", "Did you marry an American?", "Are you a pen-pal?", and "Are you poor?" And even more problematic is that she must confront these representations within the diasporic Philippine community. Lisa speaks of her difficulties in relating with, of feeling shunned by, Filipinas who entered the United States through other avenues (e.g., being petitioned through family reunification procedures). Lisa explains that other Filipinas place considerable stock in the paths of migration. She feels that as a former dancer in Okinawa, she is at times diminished in the eyes of other Filipinas. In this setting, Lisa's identity as a former dancer does transcend her other identities, and even that of being a Filipina. She is, in this respect, marginalized within the immediate Philippine community as well as in the dominant host society. Both Filipinas and non-Filipinas, Lisa believes, do not want to regularly associate with her, and she thinks that they assume that she is less worthy of their respect because of her former occupation. Lisa is thus burdened with the long-standing denigration of sex workers in general. She does not deny her previous occupation; nor does she dwell excessively on that part of her life. Rather, she views her experiences in Okinawa as a temporary moment, a time where she earned money and helped support her parents and siblings. Now, as she negotiates her daily life in the Midwestern United States, she draws strength from these experiences. Having been socially and financially independent while in Okinawa, Lisa is able to transcend the negative and racially- and sexually-defined stereotypes she encounters in her new home.

LEARNING FROM LISA

Pauline Barber suggests that in Philippine communities, global processes are "localized" through the anticipation of departures and the enthusiasm created by returning migrants. However, at such moments, Barber continues, it is possible to overlook that the Philippine state orchestrates and depends upon labor migration and the funds it generates.[51]

What are we able to take away from the experiences of Lisa? How can her life contribute to our understanding of international labor migration and the processes of globalization? Certainly the life of an individual does not permit one to make sweeping generalizations or concrete conclusions. But then again, globalization is an inherently localized—indeed, individualized—process. There are over eight million Filipinos living outside their country of birth; annually, more than one million Filipino laborers embark on temporary sojourns abroad. Their lives are unique, and each would tell its own compelling story. That said, the life of Lisa is also played out many times over across the changing world map of the Philippine diaspora. The experiences of these migrants are shaped by a multitude of factors and are contingent upon local contexts, personal circumstances, particular histories and geographies.

In Lisa's narrative, though, we find verisimilitude with

other studies. Her life touches on the different modes of migration, including both legal and illegal channels. Her migration experiences also inform us as to the actual daily practices that structure migration within an institutionalized context. The Philippine state migratory apparatus aggressively markets its workers to foreign labor markets. The global presence of Filipino laborers is the direct result of an intensive and extensive labor migration industry. Through Lisa we gain insight into how one individual has negotiated the parameters of this industry.

Lisa understands her global experiences as a pragmatic response to a particular context; she grew up within an impoverished household and saw employment in Japan as a means to improve not only her life but also that of her family. Neither acting out of blind altruism, nor oppressed by patriarchal expectations as a "sacrificial lamb," Lisa acted upon the most viable opportunity available at the time. Through her experiences, we see clearly how migrants' decisions are contingent upon familial, institutional, and structural parameters. We understand also a little bit more of the humanism that is inseparable from processes of globalization.

Beyond the Philippines
Six

> ... the POEA shall be able to contribute significantly to making our shared vision of making the global Filipino worker number one in the world a reality.[1]

Globalization is both "real" and "imagined." It is real, in the sense that millions of migrants leave the Philippines for destinations beyond their country of birth. From Austria to Zambia, Filipino workers actively participate in nearly 200 labor markets. Most significant, however, is that advents in telecommunications systems are revolutionizing patterns and processes of international labor migration. Consider, for example, the recent initiatives of the Philippine Overseas Employment Administration. In 2006 the POEA launched the aptly named Global OFW Mapping and Profiling Program (GOMPP), a system designed to facilitate the monitoring of Overseas Filipino Workers (OFWs) abroad, as well as to identify particular skills that are projected to be in demand in the global market. Concurrently, the POEA has also initiated the e-Services Delivery Infrastructure (e-SDI). Building on recent advances in information technology capabilities, the POEA is making it easier to electronically submit worker contracts, thereby reducing the processing time of employment contracts. Previously, the POEA required 4 hours to process a single worker; under the e-SDI system, the processing time has been reduced to just 5 minutes. And in 2006, over 80 percent of all licensed recruitment agencies deploying land-based workers were using the electronic submission facility.[2] According to Arturo Brion, Secretary of the Department of Labor and Employment, and Chairperson of the Governing Board of the POEA, once the e-SDI is fully implemented, it will provide the POEA's major stakeholders with access to information on overseas employment procedures and processes, including the accreditation of foreign employers and deployment of OFWs.[3] Clearly, the Philippines' global presence is the result of a deliberate strategy on the part of the Philippine state.

However, globalization is also imagined, it is envisioned, in the sense that discourses of globalization are used to justify and legitimate the export of workers. Indeed, Brion explains that "As more and more Filipinos choose to explore work opportunities abroad, globalization has opened up the world's doors to accommodate them more readily." But of course, it was not globalization per se that opened up the world's door to the Philippines. Rather, it was the efforts of myriad individuals working within the Philippine migration industry: The recruiters, the agents, the ambassadors and consular officials and members of the POEA, DOLE, DFA. The very real presence of millions of Filipinos working in nearly 200 countries and territories is the result of specific marketing missions, bilateral negotiations and other multinational arrangements, all couched within the context of globalization. In fact, Brion later explains that "Market-responsive policies shall be developed in order to strengthen the quality of our skills of our OFWs through stronger linkages with our education and training sector." Thus, specific policies "are aimed at generating the right quality and quantity of workers being sought by overseas labor markets."[4]

So pervasive is the discourse of globalization that Rosalinda

Baldoz, currently serving as the POEA's administrator and Vice-Chairperson of the Governing Board, acknowledged that the agency's battle cry in 2006 was "POEA connects to the world." To this end, three words guided the POEA's efforts: Connect, transform, and protect. According to Baldoz, the POEA is

> helping empower the global Filipinos by connecting them to the world through technology and increased employment opportunities; transforming the quality and image of our OFWs through increased deployment of high-skilled workers in high-end/high-value jobs in the global market; and protecting our OFWs by prioritizing their well-being through fast and efficient service, strategic partnerships with the private sector, convergence of service with other government agencies and its proactive stance against illegal recruitment.[5]

Consequently, throughout 2006 Baldoz oversaw a number of marketing missions dispatched around the world, including Guam, Palau, Australia, Taiwan, and Canada; bilateral agreements, likewise, were coordinated between the Philippines and Spain, Canada, and Libya. The POEA also developed a "Memorandum of Understanding" with the Department of Advanced Education and Employment of the Government of the Province of Saskatchewan of Canada and a "Memorandum of Understanding on Cooperation for the Management of the Migratory Flows" with the Ministry of Labor and Social Affairs of the Kingdom of Spain. This latter arrangement facilitated the hiring of Filipino professionals and medical workers. Other conferences and technical discussions were held with representatives from South Korea and Malaysia.

The results of the POEA's 2006 activities are remarkable. Over one million Filipino workers were deployed; this "record-breaking" performance marked the highest deployment in over 30 years. And in return, a staggering US $12.76 billion in total remittances flowed into the Philippines. But what can be drawn from the experiences of the Philippines?

According to Manfred Steger, globalization refers to a set of social processes that are thought to transform our present social condition into one of globality. This latter term, Steger maintains, refers to a social condition characterized by the existence of global economic, political, cultural, and environmental interconnections and flows that make many of the currently existing borders and boundaries irrelevant.[6] Globalization is thus about shifting forms of human contact and, as such, a number of questions follow: How, for example, does globalization occur? What is driving globalization? Is it one cause or a combination of factors? Is globalization a uniform or an uneven process?[7]

Throughout this book I have considered the role of the Philippines. Since before its existence as a colonized state, the Philippines has long been connected to the world economy. Prior to Spanish colonialism, for example, interregional trade connected and integrated—albeit unevenly—the archipelago with the distant empires of East and Southeast Asia, the Indian subcontinent, and places as far as the Middle East. Following its conquest by Spain, and later the United States, the Philippines remained connected to the world economy, but primarily in a subservient and dependent role. Since the 1970s, however, the Philippine state has actively sought to incorporate itself into the world economy and to expand its horizons beyond the US. On the one hand, the Philippine state opened the country to foreign investment through, for example, the establishment of export-processing zones. On the other hand, the Philippine state was instrumental in constructing a global labor market. Through the active promotion of migrant workers, it is possible to see clearly how the Philippine state contributed to one defining characteristic of globalization, namely the movement toward greater interdependence and integration. Other qualities, or characteristics, of globalization are also visible. According to Steger, globalization involves the creation of new and the multiplication of existing social networks and activities that increasingly overcome traditional political, economic, cultural, and geographical boundaries.[8] And in the Philippines we see how the POEA, through market promotion and the simultaneous intensification and diversification of labor markets, has extended the role of the state into all corners of the world. In the process, most Filipinos have some connection to the world economy, either via actual migration or the receipt of remittances from friends and families living abroad. Second, globalization entails the expansion and stretching of social relations, activities, and interdependencies.[9] It is well established, for example, that financial markets stretch around the globe and that electronic trading occurs around the clock. However, we also see, through the Philippines, that labor markets likewise stretch around the world, and that migrant workers may be "traded" around the clock. And with the initiation of e-services and Web-related recruitment systems, these processes will no doubt intensify in the coming years. Concurrently, migrant communities are likewise responding to these changes. Within the Philippine diaspora, for example, there is evidence of a growing pan-Philippine identity, one that recognizes the interconnectedness of the many disparate Filipino communities that stretch across all continents.

Globalization involves also the intensification and acceleration of social changes and activities. Economic geographers, among others, have written extensively of the development of Information and Communication Technologies (ICT) and of the developments in information handling and processing technologies. These developments have dramatically altered the conduct of business in that data networks have allowed the closer integration of geographically dispersed production.[10] And here, in the Philippines, we are witness to the establishment of electronic contract submission systems, and of online testing, licensing, and accreditation procedures. We can see how the POEA has revolutionized the administration of migration, and can better understand their efforts to efficiently (and profitably) manage the volumes of information generated by hundreds of thousands of local labor markets. We see also the POEA's ability to participate in the "just-in-time" production of migrant workers, and of the state's efforts to package, promote, and distribute particular types of migrant workers in response to market-demands.

David Charles explains that through electronic data interchange (EDI), which refers to the replacement of paper transaction documents such as orders and invoices by electronic messages, internal ICT systems can generate orders to replenish stocks or to match the demands of a production line, and instead of printing and posting these orders, with the added delays and errors from re-keying information at the recipient firm, an order can be entered into the ICT system of the supplier within minutes.[11] The example of the Philippines illustrates that this is the future of international labor migration, where one may (anywhere in the world) order a particular "form" of Filipino laborer, for any occupation or duration. Processes, accreditation, licensing procedures are accomplished in a matter of minutes. And if one is not satisfied with the "ordered" worker, the recruitment agency might even offer a money-back guarantee.

The expansion and intensification of social interconnections and interdependencies, according to Steger, do not occur only on a material, objective level, but also on a subjective plane of human consciousness.[12] This "quality" of globalization recognizes that, increasingly, one's identity is often intimately associated to a sense of globality. As indicated, there exists within the Philippine diaspora an intensification, and a deepening, of the emotional connections within and beyond the dispersed segments of the diaspora. This entails a continued reworking, or refashioning, of a globalized national identity. Indeed, Steger writes that "we must not forget that globalization also refers to people becoming increasingly conscious of growing manifestations of social interdependence and the enormous acceleration of social interactions." He continues that "people's awareness of the receding importance of geographical boundaries and distances fosters a keen sense of becoming part of a global whole" and, when "reinforced on a daily basis, these persistent experiences of global interdependence gradually change people's individual and collective identities, and thus dramatically impact the way they act in the world."[13] And so it is with the emergence of a pan-Philippine national identity, one that recognizes that to be a Filipino in the world, one is also *at home* in the world.

What we learn from the Philippines is straightforward, but not simple. Through its promotion of a flexible labor supply, the Philippine state is actively transforming both the Philippines and the world. Most especially under the auspices of the POEA, and the thousands of private recruitment agencies, the Philippine state is significantly transforming labor markets, and thus social relations, throughout the world economy. These actions, however, remain under-appreciated and under-theorized within broader discussions of globalization. The circulation of capital has most often trumped discussions of the circulation of labor. The story of the Philippines provides a counter to this neglect. As detailed in this book, the

POEA is a key contributor to the processes of globalization. The actions of the POEA and the many other state and private institutions have dramatically impacted places near and far, real and virtual. These actions, moreover, have impacted people—real lives with real dreams and real aspirations. For people like Lisa, globalization is neither context nor concept; rather, globalization is the day-to-day happenings of being alive in an increasingly interconnected world.

Notes

ONE

1. Philippine Overseas Employment Administration, *Empowering the Global Filipino: POEA Annual Report 2006* (Mandaluyong City, Philippines: POEA, 2007), 8.
2. See, for example, Philip F. Kelly, "Urbanization and the Politics of Land in the Manila Region," *Annals, American Academy of Political and Social Science* 590 (2003): 170–187; Gavin Shatkin, "Colonial Capital, Modernist Capital, Global Capital: The Changing Political Symbolism of Urban Space in Metro Manila, the Philippines," *Pacific Affairs* 78 (2005–2006): 577–600.
3. Charles L. Choguill, "Urban Policy as Poverty Alleviation: The Experience of the Philippines," *Habitat International* 25 (2001): 1–13; at 2.
4. James A. Tyner, *Made in the Philippines: Gendered Discourses and the Making of Migrants* (London: Routledge, 2004), 1. See also the Philippine Overseas Employment Administration's Web site, www.poea.gov.ph for up-to-date statistics on migrant flows and remittances.
5. Sheila Coronel, ed., *Pork and Other Perks: Corruption and Governance in the Philippines* (Pasig City: Philippine Centre for Investigative Journalism, 1998). Some studies suggest that 30 to 50 percent of the entire Philippine population is dependent on migrant worker remittances. See Grace Chang, *Disposable Domestics: Immigrant Women Workers in the Global Economy* (Cambridge, MA: South End Press, 2000), 130.
6. Philip F. Kelly, *Landscapes of Globalization: Human Geographies of Economic Change in the Philippines* (New York: Routledge, 2000), 43.
7. See, for example, data provided in James A. Tyner, "Migrant Labor and the Politics of Scale: Gendering the Philippine State," *Asia Pacific Viewpoint* 41 (2000): 131–154.

8. Overseas Performing Artists, also known as "entertainers," are defined by the POEA as musicians, dancers, and other performers. The term, however, is often considered a euphemism for "sex workers," in that many of these OPAs find employment in night-clubs, massage parlors, and so on. See, for example, Ma. Rosario P. Ballescas, *Filipino Entertainers in Japan: An Introduction* (Quezon City: the Foundation for Nationalist Studies, 1992); James A. Tyner, "Constructions of Filipina Migrant Entertainers," *Gender, Place and Culture: A Journal of Feminist Geography* 3 (1996): 77–93; James A. Tyner, "Constructing Images, Constructing Policy: The Case of Filipina Migrant Performing Artists," *Gender, Place and Culture: A Journal of Feminist Geography* 4 (1997): 19–35; James A. Tyner, "Scaled Sexuality and the Migration of Filipina Overseas Contract Workers," *Philippine Population Review* 1 (2002): 103–123.
9. Aurora de Dios, "Japayuki-san: Filipinas at Risk," in *Filipino Women Overseas Contract Workers . . . At What Cost?*, edited by Mary R. Palma-Beltran and Aurora Javate de Dios (Manila: Goodwill Trading Co., 1992), 39–58; at 54.
10. Peter Dicken, *Global Shift: The Internationalization of Economic Activity*, 2nd edition (New York: Guilford Press, 1992).
11. John Rennie Short and Yeong-Hyun Kim, *Globalization and the City* (Singapore: Longman, 1999).
12. N. Marshall and P. Wood, *Services and Space: Key Aspects of Urban and Regional Development* (New York: John Wiley & Sons, 1995).
13. Demetrios G. Papademetriou, "Managing Rapid and Deep Change in the Newest Age of Migration," in Sarah Spencer, ed., *The Politics of Migration: Managing Opportunity, Conflict and Change* (Malden, MA: Blackwell, 2003), 39–58; at 39.
14. Victoria P. Cruz, *Seasonal Orphans and Solo Parents: The Impact of Overseas Migration* (Quezon City: Scalabrini Migration Center, 1987); Saskia Sassen, *The Mobility of Labor and Capital: A Study in International Investment and Labor Flow* (Cambridge: Cambridge University Press, 1988); Ronald Skeldon, "International Migration Within and From the East and Southeast Asian Region: A Review Essay," *Asian and Pacific Migration Journal* 1 (1992): 19–63; Stephen Castles and Mark J. Miller, *The Age of Migration: International Population Movements in the Modern World* (New York: Guilford Press, 1993); Aihwa Ong, *Flexible Citizenship: The Cultural Logics of Transnationality* (Durham, NC: Duke University Press, 1999); Rhacel S. Parreñas, "New Household Forms, Old Family Values: The Formation and Reproduction of the Filipino Transnational Family in Los

Angeles," in *Contemporary Asian America: A Multidisciplinary Reader*, edited by Min Zhou and J.V. Gatewood (New York: New York University Press, 2000).

15. There has been a tremendous amount of work conducted on the feminization of international migration in general, and the movement of domestic workers—the so-called "maid trade"—more specifically. Suggested readings include Pierrette Hondagneu-Sotelo, *Gendered Transitions: Mexican Experiences of Immigration* (Berkeley: University of California Press, 1994); Nicole Constable, *Maid to Order in Hong Kong: Stories of Filipina Workers* (Ithaca, NY: Cornell University Press, 1997); Christine B.N. Chin, *In Service and Servitude: Foreign Female Domestic Workers and the Malaysian "Modernity" Project* (New York: Columbia University Press, 1998); Grace Chang, *Disposable Domestics: Immigrant Women Workers in the Global Economy* (Cambridge, MA: South End Press, 2000); Michelle R. Gamburd, *The Kitchen Spoon's Handle: Transnationalism and Sri Lanka's Migrant Housemaids* (Ithaca, NY: Cornell University Press, 2000); Rhacel S. Parreñas, *Servants of Globalization: Women, Migration, and Domestic Work* (Stanford, CA: Stanford University Press, 2001); Nicola Piper and Mina Roces, eds., *Wife or Worker? Asian Women and Migration* (Lanham, MD: Rowman & Littlefield, 2003); Tyner, *Made in the Philippines*; Nana Oishi, *Women in Motion: Globalization, State Policies, and Labor Migration in Asia* (Stanford, CA: Stanford University Press, 2005).
16. See, for example, Neferti Xina M. Tadiar, "Domestic Bodies of the Philippines," *Sojourn* 12 (1997): 153–191; Robyn M. Rodriguez, "Migrant Heroes: Nationalism, Citizenship and the Politics of Filipino Migrant Labor," *Citizenship Studies* 6 (2002): 341–356; Ligaya Lindio-McGovern, "Alienation and Labor Export in the Context of Globalization: Filipino Migrant Domestic Workers in Taiwan and Hong Kong," *Critical Asian Studies* 36 (2004): 217–238.
17. Manolo I. Abella, "Contemporary Labor Migration from Asia: Policies and Perspectives of Sending Countries," in *International Migration Systems: A Global Approach*, edited by Mary M. Kritz, Lin Lean Lim, and Hania Zlotnik (Oxford: Clarendon Press, 1992).
18. Abella, "Contemporary Labor Migration"; Jerrold W. Huguet, "The Future of International Migration Within Asia," *Asian and Pacific Migration Journal* 1 (1992): 250–277.
19. Good starting points on the subject of globalization include John Bryson, Nick Henry, David Keeble, and Ron Martin, eds.,

The Economic Geography Reader: Producing and Consuming Global Capitalism (New York: John Wiley & Sons, 1999); Philip F. Kelly, "The Geographies and Politics of Globalization," *Progress in Human Geography* 23 (1999): 379–400; Manfred B. Steger, *Globalization: A Very Short Introduction* (Oxford: Oxford University Press, 2003); Steven Flusty, *De-Coca-Colonization: Making the Globe from the Inside Out* (New York: Routledge, 2004); Manfred B. Steger, *Globalism: Market Ideology Meets Terrorism*, 2nd edition (Boulder, CO: Westview Press, 2005).

20. Temporary contact workers are deployed usually on 6-month or 2-year contracts, many of which are renewable, depending obviously on the job in question. As such, the POEA distinguishes between "newly-hired" and "re-hired" workers; those classified as "newly-hired" are those who are being deployed for the first time; "re-hires," conversely, are those who have extended their work-contract. Data on the deployment of "new-hires" is frequently used as an indicator of whether labor-markets are growing or declining. Note also that I am talking about those migrant workers who are deployed *legally* through official contracts; this does not consider "undocumented" workers. In the United States, for example, there are many millions of "illegal" or "unauthorized" migrants who enter from Mexico and Central America. These workers, unlike the vast majority who depart the Philippines, are not considered to be government-sponsored contract workers.
21. Domingo C. Salita, *Geography and Natural Resources of the Philippines* (Quezon City: JMC Press, 1997).
22. Over 150 languages are spoken throughout the country. Tagalog, spoken throughout southern Luzon, has become the official language. English is the country's lingua franca.
23. Kelly, *Landscapes of Globalization*, 19.
24. Kelly, *Landscapes of Globalization*, 19–20; see also Elizabeth Uy Eviota, *The Political Economy of Gender: Women and the Sexual Division of Labour in the Philippines* (London: Zed Books, 1992); David J. Steinberg, *The Philippines: A Singular and a Plural Place*, 3rd edition (Boulder, CO: Westview Press, 1994); and Patricio N. Abinales and Donna J. Amoroso, *State and Society in the Philippines* (Lanham, MD: Rowman & Littlefield, 2005).
25. John R. Weeks, *Population Geography: An Introduction to Concepts and Issues*, 9th edition (Belmont, CA: Wadsworth/Thomson Learning, 2005), 73.
26. Knox et al., 127.

27. Abinales and Amoroso, *State and Society*, 53.
28. Abinales and Amoroso, *State and Society*; Eviota, *Political Economy*.
29. Eviota, *Political Economy*, 38.
30. See Abinales and Amoroso, *State and Society*, 55.
31. Steinberg, *The Philippines*, 23.
32. Abinales and Amoroso, *State and Society*, 62.
33. Stanley Karnow, *In Our Image: America's Empire in the Philippines* (New York: Random House, 1989), 50.
34. Lorraine J. Crouchett, *Filipinos in California: From the Days of the Galleons to the Present* (El Cerrito, CA: Downey Place Publishing, 1982), 8.
35. Kelly, *Landscapes of Globalization*, 21.
36. J. Kathirithamby-Wells, "The Age of Transition: The Mid-Eighteenth to the Early Nineteenth Centuries," in *The Cambridge History of Southeast Asia: Volume Two: From c. 1500 to c. 1800*, edited by Nicholas Tarling (Cambridge: Cambridge University Press, 1999), 228–275; at 263.
37. Crouchett, *Filipinos in California*, 7–8. According to Crouchett, the first Filipinos apparently "set foot" in California in 1587.
38. Abinales and Amoroso, *State and Society*, 80.
39. Abinales and Amoroso, *State and Society*, 80–81.
40. See Abinales and Amoroso, *State and Society*; Kelly, *Landscapes of Globalization*.
41. Alfred W. McCoy, "The Social History of an Archipelago: Introduction," in *Philippine Social History: Global Trade and Local Transformations*, edited by Alfred W. McCoy and Ed. C. de Jesus (Quezon City: Ateneo de Manila University Press, 1982), 8.
42. Eviota, *Political Economy*, 56.
43. James A. Tyner, *Iraq, Terror, and the Philippines' Will to War* (Boulder, CO: Rowman & Littlefield, 2005), 10; see also James A. Tyner, *America's Strategy in Southeast Asia: From the Cold War to the Terror War* (Boulder, CO: Rowman & Littlefield, 2007), chapter two.
44. Tyner, *Philippines' Will to War*, 10–11; see also Karnow, *In Our Image*, 10.
45. Richard E. Welch, Jr., *Response to Imperialism: The United States and the Philippine–American War, 1899–1902* (Chapel Hill: University of North Carolina Press, 1979), 10; see also Stuart C. Miller, *"Benevolent Assimilation": The American Conquest of the Philippines, 1899–1903* (New Haven, CT: Yale University Press, 1982); Brian McAllister Linn, *The Philippine War, 1899–1902* (Lawrence: University Press of Kansas, 2000).

46. T. Friend, *Between Two Empires: The Ordeal of the Philippines, 1929–1946* (New Haven, CT: Yale University Press, 1965); David H. Bain, *Sitting in Darkness: Americans in the Philippines* (Boston, MA: Houghton Mifflin, 1984); Glenn A. May, *Social Engineering in the Philippines: The Aims, Execution, and Impact of American Colonial Policy, 1900–1913* (Quezon City: New Day Publishers, 1984); Stephen Rosskamm Shalom, *The United States and the Philippines: A Study of Neocolonialism* (Quezon City: New Day Publishers, 1986); David G. Timberman, *A Changeless Land: Continuity and Change in Philippine Politics* (New York: M.E. Sharpe, 1991); H.W. Brands, *Bound to Empire: The United States and the Philippines* (New York: Oxford University Press, 1992); James Putzel, *A Captive Land: The Politics of Agrarian Reform in the Philippines* (Manila: Ateneo de Manila University Press, 1992); Frank H. Golay, *Face of Empire: United States–Philippine Relations, 1898–1946* (Quezon City: Ateneo de Manila University Press, 1997); Amy Blitz, *The Contested State: American Foreign Policy and Regime Change in the Philippines* (Lanham, MD: Rowman & Littlefield, 2000).
47. Eviota, *Political Economy*, 63; see also May, *Social Engineering*, 30.
48. Benedict J. Kerkvliet, *The Huk Rebellion: A Study of Peasant Revolt in the Philippines* (Lanham, MD: Rowman & Littlefield, 2002 [1977]), 23.
49. Timberman, *Changeless Land*, 10.
50. Kelly, *Landscapes of Globalization*, 26.
51. Putzel, *A Captive Land*, 55.
52. Abinales and Amoroso, *State and Society*.
53. Kerkvliet, *The Huk Rebellion*, 25.
54. Kelly, *Landscapes of Globalization*, 26.
55. Putzel, *A Captive Land*, 55.
56. Sassen, *The Mobility of Labor and Capital*.
57. There exists a sizeable literature on the US–Philippines migration system. Good places to begin include: Carey McWilliams, *Brothers Under the Skin* (Boston: Little, Brown, 1964); Luis V. Teodoro, *Out of This Struggle: The Filipinos in Hawaii* (Honolulu: University of Hawaii Press, 1981); Fred Cordova, *Filipinos: Forgotten Asian Americans, A Pictorial Essay, 1763–circa 1963* (Dubuque, IA: Kendall/Hunt, 1983); Robert N. Anderson with Richard Coller and Rebecca F. Pestano, *Filipinos in Rural Hawaii* (Honolulu: University of Hawaii Press, 1984); E.B. Almirol, "Exclusion and Acceptance of Filipinos in America," *Asian Profile* 13 (1985): 395–408; Antonio J.A. Pido, *The Pilipinos in America: Macro/Micro Dimensions of Immigration and Integration* (New York: Center for

Migration Studies, 1986); Jonathan Y. Okamura, *Imagining the Filipino American Diaspora: Transnational Relations, Identities, and Communities* (New York: Garland Publishing, 1998); Rick Bonus, *Locating Filipino Americans: Ethnicity and the Cultural Politics of Space* (Philadelphia, PA: Temple University Press, 2000); Yen Le Espiritu, *Home Bound: Filipino American Lives Across Cultures, Communities and Countries* (Berkeley: University of California Press, 2003).

58. Kelly, *Landscapes of Globalization*, 29.
59. Espiritu, *Home Bound*, 26. See also Barbara M. Posadas and Roland L. Guyotte, "Unintentional Immigrants: Chicago's Filipino Foreign Students Become Settlers, 1900–1941," *Journal of American Ethnic History* 9 (1990): 26–48.
60. Barbara M. Posadas, "At a Crossroad: Filipino American History and the Old-Timers' Generation," *Amerasia* 13 (1986–87): 85–97; at 86.
61. Espiritu, *Home Bound*, 27–31.
62. Espiritu, *Home Bound*, 28.
63. Espiritu, *Home Bound*, 29. Espiritu explains that before and during World War I Filipinos were allowed to enlist and serve in a range of occupations, including as petty officers, machinists, firemen, and coxswain's mates. However, after the war the Navy issued a new rule restricting Filipinos, even those with a college education, to the ratings of officers' stewards and mess attendants.
64. Tyner, *America's Strategy in Southeast Asia*, 39.
65. Teodoro explains that labor recruitment was not determined by the size of the plantation labor force needed. Instead, planters wanted to ensure the existence of a large reserve of laborers so that wages could be kept at a minimum. Moreover, a large number of reserve laborers would be drawn on as "scab" labor in case of strikes. See Teodoro, *Out of This Struggle*, 10. For other accounts of the conditions on Hawaii's plantations, see Ronald Takaki, *Pau Hana: Plantation Life and Labor in Hawaii, 1835–1920* (Honolulu: University of Hawaii Press, 1983).
66. Eleanor C. Nordyke, *The Peopling of Hawai'i*, 2nd edition (Honolulu: University of Hawaii Press, 1989), 28. Nordyke estimates that from the arrival of the first Westerners in the eighteenth century to the mid-twentieth century, the native population of Hawaii was reduced from 276,000 to only 11,294.
67. Teodoro, *Out of This Struggle*. See also James A. Tyner, *Oriental Bodies: Discourse and Discipline in U.S. Immigration Policy, 1875–1942* (Lanham, MD: Lexington Books, 2006).

68. Initially, sugar planters looked to both India and Russia for labor supplies; these, however, were not successful. See Anderson, *Filipinos in Rural Hawaii*, 1–2.
69. Anderson, *Filipinos in Rural Hawaii*, 4.
70. Teodoro, *Out of This Struggle*, table 2.2.
71. Espiritu, *Home Bound*, 63. See also James A. Tyner, "Filipinos: The Invisible Ethnic Community," in *Contemporary Ethnic Geographies in America*, edited by Ines M. Miyares and Christopher A. Airries (Boulder, CO: Rowman & Littlefield, 2006), 251–270.
72. See Tyner, *Oriental Bodies*, chapter four.
73. Roy Malcolm, "Immigration Problems on the Pacific Coast (part III)," *Current History* 33 (1931): 726–728; at 726.
74. Paul Scharrenberg, "The Philippine Problem: Attitude of American Labor Toward Filipino Immigrants and Philippine Independence," *Pacific Affairs* 2 (1929): 49–54; at 50.
75. Bill Ong Hing, *Making and Remaking Asian America Through Immigration Policy, 1850–1990* (Stanford, CA: Stanford University Press, 1993), 35.
76. Donald Seekins, "Historical Setting," in *Philippines: A Country Study*, edited by Frederica M. Bunge (Washington, DC: US Government Printing Office, 1983), 1–56; at 37.
77. Fred Arnold, U. Minocha, and James T. Fawcett, "The Changing Face of Asian Immigration to the United States," in *Pacific Bridges: The New Immigration from Asia and the Pacific Islands*, edited by James T. Fawcett and Benjamin V. Cariño (Staten Island, NY: Center for Migration Studies, 1987), 105–152; table 6.1. Not surprisingly, American citizens were still allowed unrestricted entry and residence in the Philippines.
78. Seekins, "Historical Setting," 37.
79. Kelly, *Landscapes of Globalization*, 28.
80. Kelly, "Geographies and Politics of Globalization," 380.
81. Kelly, *Landscapes of Globalization*, 11.
82. See, for example, Rob Kitchin, *Cyberspace: The World in the Wires* (New York: John Wiley & Sons, 1998); Mike Crang, Phil Crang, and Jon May, eds., *Virtual Geographies: Bodies, Space and Relations* (New York: Routledge, 1999); Tim Jordan, *Cyberpower: The Culture and Politics of Cyberspace and the Internet* (New York: Routledge, 1999); Marc A. Smith and Peter Kollock, eds., *Communities in Cyberspace* (New York: Routledge, 1999); Jerry Everard, *Virtual States: The Internet and the Boundaries of the Nation-State* (New York: Routledge, 2000).
83. James A. Tyner and Olaf Kuhlke, "Pan-National Identities:

Representations of the Philippine Diaspora on the World Wide Web," *Asia Pacific Viewpoint* 41 (2000): 231–252.

84. Flusty, *De-Coca-Colonization*, 7.

TWO

1. Ricardo R. Casco, *Managing International Labour Migration and the Framework for the Deregulation of the POEA* (Manila: POEA, 1997), 4.
2. Arturo Brion quoted in POEA (2007: 6). Mr. Brion is the Secretary of the Philippines' Department of Labor and Employment and currently serves as Chair of the Philippine Overseas Employment Administration's Governing Board.
3. Filomeno V. Aguilar, Jr., "Beyond Stereotypes: Human Subjectivity in the Structuring of Global Migration," in *Filipinos in Global Migrations: At Home in the World?*, edited by Filomeno V. Aguilar, Jr. (Manila: Philippine Migration Research Network, 2002), 1–36; at 33.
4. The term "diaspora" has been subject to intense scrutiny in recent years. In part, these scholarly exchanges have resulted from an increased attention to the relationship between "globalization" as a process and diasporic community formation. At present, a myriad of exclusive and inclusive definitions has been forwarded. On the one hand, there are scholars who advocate an exclusive usage of the term; this stance stems from work on the catastrophic origin and forcible dispersal of populations. Diasporas therefore characterize populations that were forced to reformulate their sense of identity and belonging as a result of their involuntary displacement. On the other hand, other scholars (myself included) have argued for more inclusive definitions and a broadening of the term "diaspora." N. Van Hear, for example, defines diasporas based on three criteria: Dispersions over two or more territories; an enduring presence, although circulation may exist; and a continued exchange between separated populations. Consequently, diasporas are characterized by transmigrant individuals whose daily lives depend on multiple and constant interconnections across interstate borders and whose public identities are configured and reconfigured in relationship to more than one nation-state. See, for example, Nina Glick Schiller, Linda Basch, and Cristina Szanton Blanc, "From Immigrant to Transmigrant: Theorizing Transnational Migration," *Anthropological Quarterly* 68 (1995): 48–63; at 48. See also N. Van Hear, *New Diasporas: The Mass Exodus,*

Dispersal and Regrouping of Migrant Communities (Seattle: University of Washington Press, 1998), 6; R. Cohen, *Global Diasporas: An Introduction* (Cambridge, MA: Harvard University Press, 1997).

5. Philip F. Kelly, *Landscapes of Globalization: Human Geographies of Economic Change in the Philippines* (New York: Routledge, 2000), 1.
6. The occupational distribution of professionals requires further clarification. Although this sector does include nurses, doctors, and so forth, it also includes those workers classified as "overseas performing artists" (OPAs). Often considered a euphemism for sex workers, OPAs include those women and men deployed overseas as dancers, musicians, and other performers. Of the 51,980 female professionals deployed in 2005, for example, 37,854 (73%) were performing artists. Conversely, of the 11,953 male professional workers, only 18 percent (1,601 workers) were employed in the entertainment sector.
7. In 2006 Japan significantly altered its policy on the importation of OPAs, thereby reducing considerably the deployment of Filipino OPAs.
8. H.W. Brands, *Bound to Empire: The United States and the Philippines* (New York: Oxford University Press, 1992), 209.
9. See, for example, Robert J. McMahon, *The Limits of Empire: The United States and Southeast Asia since World War II* (New York: Columbia University Press, 1999); Roger Buckley, *The United States in the Asia-Pacific since 1945* (New York: Cambridge University Press, 2002); James A. Tyner, *America's Strategy in Southeast Asia: From the Cold War to the Terror War* (Boulder, CO: Rowman & Littlefield, 2007).
10. Stephen R. Shalom, *The United States and the Philippines: A Study of Neocolonialism* (Quezon City: New Day Publishers, 1986).
11. Shalom, *The United States and the Philippines*, 35.
12. Shalom, *The United States and the Philippines*, 36.
13. Shalom, *The United States and the Philippines*, 43.
14. Shalom, *The United States and the Philippines*, 37.
15. Shalom, *The United States and the Philippines*, 43–45.
16. Kelly, *Landscapes of Globalization*, 30.
17. Kelly, *Landscapes of Globalization*, 31. According to Patricio Abinales and Donna Amoroso, Filipino nationalists in the post-war years were increasingly critical of American neocolonial relations as manifest in the presence of the US military in the archipelago, unequal economic treaties, and the "Americanization" of Filipino culture. Abinales and Amoroso, however, also indicate that these nationalist efforts were not uniformly supported by

the Philippine populace. Indeed, conservative forces in the government, coupled with the Church, the universities and the media, worked to suppress many of the efforts of the nationalists. See Patricio N. Abinales and Donna J. Amoroso, *State and Society in the Philippines* (Lanham, MD: Rowman & Littlefield, 2005), especially chapter seven and pp. 186–187.

18. B. Villegas, "The Economic Crisis," in *Crisis in the Philippines: The Marcos Era and Beyond*, edited by J. Bresnan (Princeton, NJ: Princeton University Press, 1986); S.K. Jayasuriya, "The Politics of Economic Policy in the Philippines During the Marcos Era," in *Southeast Asia in the 1980s: The Politics of Economic Crisis*, edited by R. Robison, K. Hewison, and R. Higgot (London: Allen & Unwin, 1987); V.R. Jose, "Philippine External Debt Problems: The Marcos Years," *Journal of Contemporary Asia* 21 (1991): 222–245.
19. Jane Hutchinson, "Pressure on Policy in the Philippines," in *The Political Economy of Southeast Asia: An Introduction*, edited by G. Rodan, K. Hewison, and R. Robison (Oxford: Oxford University Press, 1997), 69–70.
20. Joaquin L. Gonzales, III, *Philippine Labour Migration: Critical Dimensions of Public Policy* (Singapore: Institute of Southeast Asian Studies, 1998), 60.
21. Gonzales, *Philippine Labour Migration*, 60.
22. Kelly, *Landscapes of Globalization*, 33.
23. David G. Timberman, *A Changeless Land: Continuity and Change in Philippine Politics* (New York: M.E. Sharpe, 1991), 86.
24. Villegas, "Economic Crisis," 56.
25. Gary Hawes, *The Philippine State and the Marcos Regime: The Politics of Export* (Ithaca, NY: Cornell University Press, 1987), 45. For more on the declaration of martial law, see Raymond Bonner, *Waltzing with a Dictator: The Marcoses and the Making of American Policy* (New York: Vintage Books, 1988); David Wurfel, *Filipino Politics: Development and Decay* (Ithaca, NY: Cornell University Press, 1988); James K. Boyce, *The Political Economy of Growth and Impoverishment in the Marcos Era* (Quezon City: Ateneo de Manila University Press, 1993).
26. Wurfel, *Filipino Politics*, 135.
27. W.H. Overholt, "Pressures and Policies: Prospects for Cory Aquino's Philippines," in *Rebuilding a Nation: Philippine Challenges and American Policy*, edited by C.H. Lande (Washington, DC: Washington Institute Press, 1987), 91.
28. Kelly, *Landscapes of Globalization*, 33.
29. Villegas, "Economic Crisis," 59.
30. Villegas, "Economic Crisis," 60.

31. Villegas, "Economic Crisis," 61.
32. Villegas, "Economic Crisis," 60–61.
33. Walden Bello, David Kinley, and Elaine Elinson, *Development Debacle: The World Bank in the Philippines* (San Francisco: Institute for Food and Development Policy/Philippine Solidarity Network, 1982).
34. L.Y.C. Lim, "Capitalism, Imperialism, and Patriarchy: The Dilemma of Third-World Women Workers in Multinational Factories," in *Women, Men and the International Division of Labor*, edited by J. Nash and M.P. Fernández-Kelly (Albany: State University of New York Press, 1983); see also Sylvia Chant and Sarah McIlwaine, *Women of a Lesser Cost: Female Labour, Foreign Exchange and Philippine Development* (Quezon City: Ateneo de Manila University Press, 1995).
35. Kelly, *Landscapes of Globalization*, 33.
36. Timberman, *A Changeless Land*, 82.
37. Timberman, *A Changeless Land*, 86.
38. Hutchinson, "Pressure on Policy," 76.
39. Jamie Peck, *Work-Place: The Social Regulation of Labor Markets* (New York: Guilford Press, 1996), 27.
40. J.N. Nolledo, ed., *The Labor Code of the Philippines, with Implementing Regulations, Related Laws, and Other Issuances* (Manila: National Bookstore, 1993).
41. Gonzalez, *Philippine Labour Migration*, 34.
42. For more on the potential political benefits of the Philippines' overseas employment program, see James A. Tyner, "The Politics of Employment: Overseas Job Fairs and Philippine Labor Recruitment," *Applied Geographic Studies* 3 (1999): 1–11.
43. Villegas, "Economic Crisis," 70.
44. Dean T. Alegado, "The Political Economy of International Labor Migration from the Philippines," PhD Dissertation, University of Hawaii at Manoa, 1992.
45. Currently, there are over 2,000 licensed agencies in operation in the Philippines. This number does not include the untold thousands of agencies located through Asia, the Middle East, and the rest of the world, which likewise participate in the circulation of labor, including those from the Philippines.
46. Blas Ople, "The Filipino Diaspora: A Global Tribe?" *Overseas Employment Info Series* 6 (1993): 20–23; at 22.
47. Catholic Institute for International Relations, *The Labour Trade: Filipino Migrant Workers Around the World* (London: CIIR, 1987), 120.
48. Timberman, *A Changeless Land*, 91.

49. S. Kuruvilla, "Economic Development Strategies, Industrial Relations Policies and Workplace IR/HR Practices in Southeast Asia," in *The Comparative Political Economy of Industrial Relations*, edited by K. Wever and L. Turner (Madison: Industrial Relations Association Series, University of Wisconsin-Madison, 1995), 130.
50. David A. Rosenberg, "The Changing Structure of Philippine Government from Marcos to Aquino," in *Rebuilding a Nation: Philippine Challenges and American Policy*, edited by C.H. Lande (Washington, DC: Washington Institute Press, 1987), 329–350; at 331.
51. Villegas, "Economic Crisis," 70.
52. Peck, *Work-Place*, 23.
53. David Harvey, *Spaces of Hope* (Cambridge, MA: Blackwell, 2000), 101–116.
54. For the classical account on the relationship between capital and labor mobility, see Saskia Sassen's *The Mobility of Labor and Capital: A Study in International Investment and Labor Flow* (Cambridge: Cambridge University Press, 1988).
55. After 1997, June 7 was declared "Migrant Workers' Day," in commemoration of the signing of Republic Act 8042 (discussed later). On this day, the POEA conducts free medical services for migrant workers and their families (e.g., x-rays, blood tests, the distribution of free medicine), legal assistance, and the sale of low-priced commodities, such as rice, sugar, soap, and canned goods. On Migrant Workers' Day in 2002 it was announced that the government had developed an "infomercial" on *The Great Filipino Worker* to be shown on international channels, including the Discovery Channel. Other festivals and events, beyond the marking of days, weeks, and months, have also been held. Beginning in 1984 (though stopped between 1986 and 1988), the Bagong Bayani ("New Heroes") Awards have been conferred on overseas Filipino workers who, through outstanding deeds or acts of heroism while employed overseas, have brought recognition and honor to the country. Additionally, every December the POEA sponsors *Pamaskong Handog* ("Christmas Gift"), an event that includes the provision of assorted services for returning overseas workers, such as free medical services, free telephone calls, a trade fair, and entertainment. Finally, in 2000 a commemorative stamp in honor of the country's "modern heroes" was issued to mark the "Year of the OFW." See Philippine Overseas Employment Administration, *POEA Annual Report* 2000 (Manila: POEA, 2001), 17.

56. See Gonzalez, *Philippine Labour Migration*, 6.
57. See James A. Tyner, *Made in the Philippines: Gendered Discourses and the Making of Migrants* (London: Routledge, 2004), chapter four. See also James A. Tyner, "Constructing Images, Constructing Policy: The Case of Filipina Migrant Performing Artists," *Gender, Place and Culture: A Journal of Feminist Geography* 4 (1997): 19–35.
58. Gonzalez, *Philippine Labour Migration*, 6.
59. Manfred B. Steger, *Globalization: A Very Short Introduction* (Oxford: Oxford University Press, 2003), 40; see also David Harvey, *A Brief History of Neoliberalism* (Oxford: Oxford University Press, 2005).
60. Manfred B. Steger, *Globalism: Market Ideology Meets Terrorism*, 2nd edition (Boulder, CO: Westview Press, 2005), 10.
61. Steger, *Globalism*, 8–9.
62. Harvey, *Brief History of Neoliberalism*, 2.
63. www.poea.org.ph
64. Casco, *Managing International Labour Migration*, 4; italics in original.
65. Casco, *Managing International Labour Migration*, 5.
66. Ricardo R. Casco, *Full Disclosure Policy: A Philosophical Orientation* (Manila: POEA, 1995), 1.
67. Casco, *Managing International Labour Migration*, 4.
68. Casco, *Full Disclosure Policy*, 4.
69. Casco, *Full Disclosure Policy*, 6.
70. Casco, *Full Disclosure Policy*, 4.
71. See also Rochelle Ball and Nicola Piper, "Globalisation and Regulation of Citizenship—Filipino Migrant Workers in Japan," *Political Geography* 21 (2002): 1013–1034.
72. National Economic and Development Authority, as quoted in Philip F. Kelly, "Globalization, Power and the Politics of Scale in the Philippines," *Geoforum* 28 (1997): 151–171; at 157.
73. www.poea.org.ph
74. National Economic Development Authority, *The Medium-Term Philippine Development Plan, 2001–2004, with the 2001 State of the Nation Address* (Manila: NEDA, 2001), 270.
75. Office of the President, "PGMA's Speech during the Department of Foreign Affairs Foundation Day 2004," July 23, 2004, www.op.gov.ph/speeches
76. National Economic Development Authority, *Medium-Term Philippine Development Plan*, xiii–xxvi.
77. Office of the President, "PGMA's Speech during the 2nd Annual Philippine Business Outlook Conference," March 1, 2001, www.opnet.ops.gov.ph/speech-2001mar01a.htm

78. National Economic Development Authority, *Medium-Term Philippine Development Plan*, 32.
79. National Economic Development Authority, *Medium-Term Philippine Development Plan*, 37–38.
80. Maruja M.B. Asis, "The Overseas Employment Program Policy," in *Philippine Labour Migration: Impact and Policy*, edited by G. Battistella and A. Paganoni (Quezon City: Scalabrini Migration Center, 1992), 68–112; at 69.
81. For a detailed discussion of the Philippines' anticipated participation in the post-war construction of Iraq, see James A. Tyner, *Iraq, Terror, and the Philippines' Will to War* (Boulder, CO: Rowman & Littlefield, 2005), especially pp. 88–94.

THREE

1. Patricio A. Santo Tomas, Philippine Secretary of Labor, in Philippine Overseas Employment Administration, *Annual Report, 2000* (Manila: POEA, 2001), 2.
2. John Friedmann and Goetz Wolff, "World City Formation: An Agenda for Research and Action," *International Journal of Urban and Regional Research* 6 (1982): 309–344; John Friedmann, "The World City Hypothesis," *Development and Change* 17 (1986): 69–83; Saskia Sassen, *The Global City: New York, London, Tokyo* (Princeton, NJ: Princeton University Press, 1991); David Clark, *Urban World/Global City* (New York: Routledge, 1996); Paul L. Knox and Peter J. Taylor, eds., *World Cities in a World-System* (London: Cambridge University Press, 1995); Barney Warf and R. Erickson, "Introduction: Globalization and the U.S. City System," *Urban Geography* 17 (1996): 1–4; Gavin Shatkin, "Global Cities of the South: Emerging Perspectives on Growth and Inequality," *Cities* 24 (2006): 1–15.
3. Warf and Erickson, "Introduction," 2.
4. Jennifer Robinson, "Global and World Cities: A View from off the Map," *International Journal of Urban and Regional Research* 26 (2002): 531–554; at 549.
5. While I agree in principle with her proposed project, I resist the complete dismissal of the global city concept for the simple reason that this "idea," or nomenclature, is utilized as a political resource among many governments.
6. Paul L. Knox, "World Cities in a World-System," in *World Cities in a World-System*, edited by Paul L. Knox and Peter J. Taylor (London: Cambridge University Press, 1995), 3–20.

7. Saskia Sassen, *Cities in a World Economy* (Thousand Oaks, CA: Pine Forge Press, 1994), xiii.
8. Though see the recent efforts by Michael Samers and Michael Ewers. Michael Samers, "Immigration and the Global City Hypothesis: Towards an Alternative Research Agenda," *International Journal of Urban and Regional Research* 26 (2002): 389–402; at 389. Michael C. Ewers, "Migrants, Markets and Multinationals: Competition Among World Cities for the Highly Skilled," *Geojournal* 68 (2007): 119–130.
9. Kevin Cox, "Globalization and the Politics of Distribution: A Critical Assessment," in *Spaces of Globalization: Reasserting the Power of the Local*, edited by Kevin R. Cox (New York: Guilford Press, 1997), 115–136; at 126.
10. Rochelle Ball and Nicola Piper, "Globalisation and Regulation of Citizenship—Filipino Migrant Workers in Japan," *Political Geography* 21 (2002): 1013–1034; at 1014.
11. Sassen, *Cities in a World Economy*, 10.
12. Sassen, *Cities in a World Economy*, 11–14.
13. Sassen, *Cities in a World Economy*, 19–20.
14. Andrew Herod, "Labor as an Agent of Globalization and as a Global Agent," in *Spaces of Globalization: Reasserting the Power of the Local*, edited by Kevin R. Cox (New York: Guilford Press, 1997), 167–200; at 167.
15. Cox, "Globalization and the Politics of Distribution," 116.
16. Samers, "Immigration and the Global City Hypothesis," 395.
17. Samers, "Immigration and the Global City Hypothesis," 395.
18. Saskia Sassen, "Economic Internationalization: The New Migration in Japan and the United States," *International Migration* 31 (1993): 73–99; at 73.
19. Sassen, *Cities in a World Economy*, 19.
20. John Friedmann, "Where We Stand: A Decade of World City Research," in *World Cities in a World-System*, edited by Paul L. Knox and Peter J. Taylor (London: Cambridge University Press, 1995), 21–47; at 22.
21. Michael J. Dear and Steven Flusty, "The Iron Lotus: Los Angeles and Postmodern Urbanism," *Annals of the American Academy of Political and Social Science* 551 (1997): 151–163; Richard P. Greene, "Chicago's New Immigrants, Indigenous Poor, and Edge Cities," *Annals of the American Academy of Political and Social Science* 551 (1997): 178–190.
22. Carolyn Adams, "The Philadelphia Experience," *Annals of the American Academy of Political and Social Science* 551 (1997): 222–234;

Barney Warf and Brian Holly, "The Rise and Fall and Rise of Cleveland," *Annals of the American Academy of Political and Social Science* 551 (1997): 208–221.

23. Teodoro A. Agoncillo, *A Short History of the Philippines* (New York: Mentor, 1969); Robert R. Reed, *Colonial Manila: The Context of Hispanic Urbanism and Process of Morphogenesis* (Berkeley: University of California Press, 1978).
24. Reed, *Colonial Manila*, 9.
25. Patricio N. Abinales and Donna J. Amoroso, *State and Society in the Philippines* (Lanham, MD: Rowman & Littlefield, 2005), 51.
26. Reed, *Colonial Manila*, 8–10; Abinales and Amoroso, *State and Society*, 50–51.
27. Reed, *Colonial Manila*, 48–49.
28. Reed, *Colonial Manila*, 57–58.
29. Daniel F. Doeppers, *Manila, 1900–1941: Social Change in a Late Colonial Metropolis* (Ithaca, NY: Yale University Southeast Asia Studies, 1984), 9.
30. P.W. Stanley, *A Nation in the Making: The Philippines and the United States, 1899–1921* (Cambridge, MA: Harvard University Press, 1974), 91; see also [Anon.] "Improvements in the City of Manila," *The National Geographic Magazine* 14 (1903): 195–197; [Anon.] "American Development of the Philippines," *The National Geographic Magazine* 14 (1903): 197–203.
31. Gavin Shatkin, "Colonial Capital, Modernist Capital, Global Capital: The Changing Political Symbolism of Urban Space in Metro Manila, the Philippines," *Pacific Affairs* 78 (2005–2006): 577–600; at 581.
32. Manuel A. Caoili, *The Origins of Metropolitan Manila: A Political and Social Analysis* (Quezon City: University of the Philippines Press, 1999), 69.
33. National Economic and Development Authority, *The Medium-Term Philippine Development Plan, 2001–2004* (Manila: NEDA, 2001), 238.
34. Philip F. Kelly, *Landscapes of Globalization: Human Geographies of Economic Change in the Philippines* (London: Routledge, 2000), 64–65.
35. Saskia Sassen, "On Concentration and Centrality in the Global City," in *World Cities in a World-System*, edited by Paul L. Knox and Peter J. Taylor (London: Cambridge, 1995), 63–75; at 63.
36. Kelly, *Landscapes of Globalization*, 33.
37. Kelly, *Landscapes of Globalization*, 64.
38. Sassen, *The Global City*, 3.
39. J.N. Nolledo, ed., *The Labor Code of the Philippines, with Implementing*

Regulations, Related Laws, and Other Issuances (Manila: National Bookstore, 1993).

40. Sassen, *The Global City*, 325.
41. Throughout the 1990s tie-ups between CRA-listed agencies were usually infrequent. The explanation is straightforward, and provides considerable explanatory power to an understanding of exploitation and corruption within the program. Only the most reputable agencies, ostensibly, are allowed to participate in the CRA program; therefore, these agencies adhere to the rules and regulations established by the POEA. Non-reputable agencies, conversely, are able to undermine the CRA-listed agencies by transferring the costs incurred by potential employers onto potential migrant workers. Although illegal, these reduced costs are extremely tempting to foreign employers.
42. This analysis was completed using a special unpublished data set provided by the POEA. A cursory examination of more recent, and still unpublished, data, indicates that the patterns originally identified have only increased in their intensity.
43. During the early 1990s the mayor of Manila shut down many "entertainment" businesses in Ermita, forcing these establishments to relocate to other sectors of the NCR. Consequently, many of the PEAs that specialized in the deployment of overseas performing artists (OPAs) also relocated.
44. Brian J.L. Berry, Edgar C. Conkling, and D. Michael Ray, *The Global Economy in Transition*, 2nd edition (Upper Saddle River, NJ: Prentice Hall, 1997).
45. William McCuskey, "Current Developments in the International Market for Seafarers," *Overseas Employment Info Series* 4 (1991): 13–20; at 20.
46. Robinson, "Global and World Cities," 536.
47. Friedmann, "Where We Stand," 25–26.
48. Robinson, "Global and World Cities," 539.
49. Friedmann, "Where We Stand," 26.
50. Christof Parnreiter, "Mexico: The Making of a Global City," in *Global Networks, Linked Cities*, edited by Saskia Sassen (New York: Routledge, 2002), 145–182; at 147–148.

FOUR

1. Manfred B. Steger, *Globalization: A Very Short Introduction* (Oxford: Oxford University Press, 2003), 17.
2. See, for example, Rob Kitchin, *Cyberspace: The World in the Wires*

(New York: John Wiley & Sons, 1998); Mike Crang, Phil Crang, and Jon May, eds., *Virtual Geographies: Bodies, Space and Relations* (New York: Routledge, 1999); Tim Jordan, *Cyberpower: The Culture and Politics of Cyberspace and the Internet* (London: Routledge, 1999); Marc A. Smith and Peter Kollock, eds., *Communities in Cyberspace* (New York: Routledge, 1999); Jerry Everard, *Virtual States: The Internet and the Boundaries of the Nation-State* (New York: Routledge, 2000).

3. Andrew Stull and Duane Griffen, *Life on the Internet: Geosciences—A Student's Guide* (Englewood Cliffs, NJ: Prentice Hall, 1996); Michael P. Peterson, "Trends in Internet Map Use," in *Proceedings of the 18th ICA/ACI International Cartographic Conference* (1997), 1635–1642.
4. Shaun Ashdowne, William Cartwright, and Liddy Nevile, "A Virtual Atlas on the World Wide Web: Concept, Development and Implementation," in *Proceedings of the 18th ICA/ACI International Cartographic Conference* (1997), 663–672; Lassi Lehto, Jaakko Kähkönen, and Tiina Kilpeläinen, "WWW-technology as a Means of Transfer and Visualization of Geographic Objects," in *Proceedings of the 18th ICA/ACI International Cartographic Conference* (1997), 681–689.
5. While maintaining a focus on the Philippines, in this chapter I broaden my discussion to include other, non-Philippine-based recruitment agencies (i.e., agencies that may physically be present in Singapore or Bangkok). Operating within the cyberworld of labor recruitment, we see quickly how truly interconnected—globalized—the circulation of labor has become. It is not uncommon, for example, to find Manila-based labor recruiters facilitating the movement of Indonesian workers to South Korea, or Singapore-based recruiters coordinating the migration of Thai workers to Germany.
6. Christine B.N. Chin, "Walls of Silence and Late Twentieth Century Representations of the Foreign Female Domestic Worker: The Case of Filipina and Indonesian Female Servants in Malaysia," *International Migration Review* 31 (1996): 353–385.
7. Chin, "Walls of Silence," 372.
8. Pierrette Hondagneu-Sotelo, *Domestic Employment Agencies in Los Angeles* (Los Angeles: University of Southern California, Southern California Studies Center, 1997).
9. Michael Humphrey, "Asian Women Workers in the Middle East: Domestic Servants in Jordan," *Asian Migrant* 4 (1991): 53–60.
10. Peter N. Woodward, *Oil and Labor in the Middle East: Saudi Arabia and the Oil Boom* (New York: Praeger Press, 1988).

11. I have yet to see any man listed as a potential domestic worker on any of these Web sites.
12. Nicole Constable, *Maid to Order in Hong Kong: Stories of Filipina Workers* (Ithaca, NY: Cornell University Press, 1997), 70.
13. Nicole Constable notes that recruitment agency staffs, in both the Philippines and Hong Kong, advise female worker-applicants to apply only after they have lost weight, trimmed their fingernails, and cut their hair.
14. D.J. Elkins, "Globalization, Telecommunication, and Virtual Ethnic Communities," *International Political Science Review* 18 (1997): 139–152; at 148.
15. Nina Glick Schiller, L. Basch and C. Szanton Blanc, "From Immigrant to Transmigrant: Theorizing Transnational Migration," *Anthropological Quarterly* 68 (1995): 48–63; at 52.
16. Yen Le Espiritu, "Filipino Settlements in the United States," in *Filipino American Lives*, edited by Yen Le Espiritu (Philadelphia, PA: Temple University Press, 1995), 1–36; at 26–27.
17 Antonio. J.A. Pido, *The Pilipinos in America: Marco/Micro Dimensions of Immigration and Integration* (New York: Center for Migration Studies, 1986), 114.
18. Peter Kollock and Marc A. Smith, "Communities in Cyberspace," in *Communities in Cyberspace*, edited by Marc A. Smith and Peter Kollock (New York: Routledge, 1999), 3–25; at 19.
19. Elkins, "Globalization," 141.
20. Zeus A. Salazar, "The Outflow of Filipinos to the Bundesrepublik Deutschland since the 1960s," *Philippine Journal of Public Administration* 33 (1987): 463–486.
21. Nicola Piper and Mina Roces, eds., *Wife or Worker? Asian Women and Migration* (Lanham, MD: Rowman & Littlefield, 2003); D. Cahill, *Intermarriages in International Contexts: A Study of Filipina Women Married to Australian, Japanese and Swiss Men* (Quezon City: Scalabrini Migration Center, 1990).

FIVE

1. See, for example, Fe Caces, Fred Arnold, James Fawcett, and Robert Gardner, "Shadow Households and Competing Auspices: Migration Behavior in the Philippines," *Journal of Development Economics* 17 (1985): 5–25; Victoria P. Cruz, *Seasonal Orphans and Solo Parents: The Impact of Overseas Migration* (Quezon City: Scalabrini Migration Center, 1987); Aihwa Ong, *Flexible Citizenship: The*

Cultural Logics of Transnationality (Durham, NC: Duke University Press, 1999).

2. Rachel Silvey, "Transnational Domestication: State Power and Indonesian Migrant Women in Saudi Arabia," *CLARA Working Paper No.* 17 (Amsterdam: IIAS/IISG, 2004), 18.
3. The forwarding of a pan-national Filipino identity, as discussed in Chapter Four, does not constitute an attempt to homogenize the experiences or identities of diasporic Filipinos. Instead, the forward of pan-nationalism is itself a response to the multiple experiences of migrants. It is in effect a "re-territorialization" of the Filipino community.
4. See, for example, Geraldine Pratt, in collaboration with the Philippine Women Centre, "Inscribing Domestic Work on Filipina Bodies," in *Places Through the Body*, edited by Heidi Nast and Steven Pile (London: Routledge, 1998), 283–304; Pauline G. Barber, "Agency in Philippine Women's Labour Migration and Provisional Diaspora," *Women's Studies International Forum* 23 (2000): 399–411; Nobue Suzuki, "Women Imagined, Women Imaging: Re/presentations of Filipinas in Japan since the 1980s," *U.S.-Japan Women's Journal* 19 (2000): 142–175; Nobue Suzuki, "Between Two Shores: Transnational Projects and Filipina Wives In/From Japan," *Women's Studies International Forum* 23 (2000): 431–444; Maruja M.B. Asis, "The Return Migration of Filipino Women Migrants: Home, but Not for Good?" in *Female Labour Migration in South-East Asia: Change and Continuity*, edited by C. Wille and B. Passl (Bangkok: Asian Research Centre for Migration, 2001); Rhacel Parreñas, *Servants of Globalization: Women, Migration and Domestic Work* (Stanford, CA: Stanford University Press, 2001); Ligaya Lindio-McGovern, "Alienation and Labor Export in the Context of Globalization: Filipino Migrant Domestic Workers in Taiwan and Hong Kong," *Critical Asian Studies* 36 (2004): 217–238; Deirdre McKay and Carol Brady, "Practices of Place-Making: Globalisation and Locality in the Philippines," *Asia Pacific Viewpoint* 46 (2005): 89–103; Anna R. Guevarra, "Managing 'Vulnerabilities' and 'Empowering' Migrant Filipina Workers: The Philippines' Overseas Employment Program," *Social Identities* 12 (2006): 523–541.
5. McKay and Brady, "Practices of Place-Making," 90.
6. There is a substantial literature on the migration of Filipina entertainers, and especially those deployed to Japan. See, for example, T. Haruhi, "The Japanese Sex Industry: A Heightening Appetite for Asian Women," *AMPO Japan-Quarterly Review* 18

(1986): 7–76; Randolf S. David, "Filipino Workers in Japan: Vulnerability and Survival," *Kasarinlan* 6 (1991): 8–23; Ma. Rosario P. Ballescas, *Filipina Entertainers in Japan: An Introduction* (Manila: the Foundation for Nationalist Studies, 1992); Aurora de Dios, "Japayuki-san: Filipinas at Risk," in *Filipino Women Overseas Contract Workers . . . At What Cost?*, edited by Mary R. Palma-Beltran and Aurora Javate de Dios (Manila: Goodwill Trading Co., 1992); James A. Tyner, "Constructions of Filipina Migrant Entertainers," *Gender, Place and Culture: A Journal of Feminist Geography* 3 (1996): 77–93; James A. Tyner, "Constructing Images, Constructing Policy: The Case of Filipina Migrant Performing Artists," *Gender, Place and Culture: A Journal of Feminist Geography* 4 (1997): 19–35; James A. Tyner, "Scaled Sexuality and the Migration of Filipina Overseas Contract Workers," *Philippine Population Review* 1 (2002): 103–123; Anne-Marie Hilsdon, "Transnationalism and Agency in East Malaysia: Filipina Migrants in the Nightlife Industries," *The Australian Journal of Anthropology* 18 (2007): 172–193.

7. Suzuki, "Between Two Shores," 432.
8. National Statistics Office, *Philippine Yearbook* (Manila: National Statistics Office, 1989), Table 17.6.
9. B. Wideman, "The Philippines Cashes In," *Far Eastern Economic Review*, 4 October 1974, 36, 38.
10. De Dios, "Japayuki-san: Filipinas at Risk," 42. See also Cynthia Enloe, *Bananas, Beaches & Bases: Making Feminist Sense of International Politics* (Berkeley: University of California Press, 1989), 38–40.
11. C. Nograles-Lumbera, "The Traffic in Japayuki-san," *Education Forum Tap* 7 (1988): 1–10; at 8.
12. The migration of Filipina entertainers to Japan is not restricted to those "legally" entering on labor contracts. Some researchers estimated, at least through the twentieth century, that perhaps as many as 50,000 Filipinas enter under false pretenses (e.g., as tourists or "brides"). See Tyner, "Constructions of Filipina Migrant Entertainers," 84.
13. M. Duenas, "Filipinas as Japayuki-san," *Philippines Free Press*, 29 April 1987, 14–15, 40–42; at 42.
14. Asis, "Return Migration," 45.
15. Y. Matsui, *Women's Asia* (Atlantic Highlands, NJ: Zed Books, 1987); I. Naoki, "The Traffic in Japayuki-san," *Japan Quarterly* 34 (1987): 84–88.
16. David, "Filipino Workers," 13.
17. See, for example, Sallie Yea, "Runaway Brides: Anxieties of Identity Among Trafficked Filipina Entertainers in South Korea,"

Singapore Journal of Tropical Geography 25 (2004): 180–197; Tomoko Nakamatsu, "International Marriage through Introduction Agencies: Social and Legal Realities of 'Asian' Wives of Japanese Men," in *Wife or Worker? Asian Women and Migration*, edited by Nicola Piper and Mina Roces (Lanham, MD: Rowman & Littlefield, 2003), 181–201; Sallie Yea, "Labour of Love: Filipina Entertainer's Narratives of Romance and Relationships with GIs in US Military Camp Towns in Korea," *Women's Studies International Forum* 28 (2005): 456–472.

18. Lisa Law, *Sex Work in Southeast Asia: The Place of Desire in a Time of AIDS* (London: Routledge, 2000), 52.
19. Lucian W. Pye, *Asian Power and Politics: The Cultural Dimensions of Authority* (Cambridge, MA: Harvard University Press, 1985); Jennifer Lauby and Oded Stark, "Individual Migration as a Family Strategy: Young Women in the Philippines," *Population Studies* 42 (1988): 473–486; Lillian Trager, *The City Connection: Migration and Family Interdependence in the Philippines* (Ann Arbor: University of Michigan Press, 1988); Belen Medina, *The Filipino Family* (Manila: University of the Philippines Press, 1991).
20. Victoria P. Cruz and Anthony Paganoni, *Filipinas in Migration: Big Bills and Small Change* (Quezon City: Scalabrini Migration Center, 1989), 100–101.
21. Suzuki, "Between Two Shores," 432–433; Suzuki, "Women Imagined," 142, 167–168; Tyner, "Constructions of Filipina Migrant Entertainers," 85–87.
22. For an interesting discussion on the transformative possibilities of "migrant bodies," see Neferti Xina M. Tadiar, "Domestic Bodies of the Philippines," *Sojourn* 12 (1997): 153–191.
23. Tyner, "Constructing Images," 27–29; see also Philippine Overseas Employment Administration, *Information Primer for the Deployment of Overseas Performing Artists* (Manila: POEA, 1998).
24. Michel Foucault, *Discipline and Punish* (New York: Vintage Press, 1979). For related discussions on the making of workers within multinational corporations and other systems of migration, see Alison Wee Siu Hui, *Assembling Gender: The Making of the Malay Female Labour* (Selangor, Malaysia: Strategic Info Research Development, n.d.); Nicole Constable, *Maid to Order in Hong Kong: Stories of Filipina Workers* (Ithaca, NY: Cornell University Press, 1997); Pun Ngai, *Made in China: Women Factory Workers in a Global Workplace* (Durham, NC: Duke University Press, 2005).
25. Sandra L. Bartky, *Femininity and Domination: Studies in the Phenomenology of Oppression* (London: Routledge, 1990).

26. Bartky, *Femininity and Domination*, 68.
27. Constable finds a similar process of bodily construction among domestic workers in her study of Filipinas in Hong Kong. See Constable, *Maid in Hong Kong*.
28. For a discussion on the perceived differences between clubs, see Saundra Sturdevant and Brenda Stoltzfus, *Let the Good Times Roll: Prostitution and the U.S. Military in Asia* (New York: New Press, 1993); Katherine H.S. Moon, *Sex Among Allies: Military Prostitution in U.S.–Korea Relations* (New York: Columbia University Press, 1997); Yea, "Runaway Brides."
29. Filomeno V. Aguilar, Jr., "Ritual Passage and the Reconstruction of Selfhood in International Labour Migration," *Sojourn* 14 (1999): 98–139; at 106–109.
30. Michel Foucault, *Discipline and Punish* (New York: Vintage Press, 1979), 187.
31. Foucault, *Discipline and Punish*, 180.
32. R. Keyso, *Women of Okinawa: Nine Voices from a Garrison Island* (Ithaca, NY: Cornell University Press, 2000), 138.
33. Saundra Sturdevant, "Okinawa Then and Now," in *Let the Good Times Roll: Prostitution and the U.S. Military in Asia*, edited by Saundra Sturdevant and Brenda Stoltzfus (New York: New Press, 1993), 251.
34. Ballescas, *Filipina Entertainers*; de Dios, "Japayuki-san"; Asis, "Return Migration of Filipino Women Migrants."
35. Bartky, *Femininity and Domination*, 74.
36. See also Ballescas, *Filipina Entertainers*, 99–101.
37. See also Law, *Sex Work in Southeast Asia*.
38. See Ballescas, *Filipina Entertainers*; Yea, "Runaway Brides."
39. De Dios, "Japayuki-san," 47; Medina, *The Filipino Family*, 128.
40. C. Ryan and C.M. Hall, *Sex Tourism: Marginal People and Liminalities* (New York: Routledge, 2001), 92.
41. See Ballescas, *Filipina Entertainers*; de Dios, "Japayuki-san."
42. K. Kempadoo, "Introduction: Globalizing Sex Workers' Rights," in *Global Sex Workers: Rights, Resistance, and Redefinition*, edited by K. Kempadoo and J. Doezema (New York: Routledge, 1998), 3.
43. Law, *Sex Work in Southeast Asia*, 125.
44. Ryan and Hall, *Sex Tourism*, 96.
45. Law, *Sex Work in Southeast Asia*, 63.
46. Yea, "Runaway Brides," 181.
47. Yea, "Runaway Brides," 194.
48. Ballescas, *Filipina Entertainers*, 89.

49. The following discussion is based on James A. Tyner, "Geographics of Identity: The Migrant Experiences of Filipinas in Northeast Ohio," *Asia Pacific Viewpoint* 43 (2002): 311–326.
50. Quoted in Jonathan Y. Okamura, *Imagining the Filipino American Diaspora: Transnational Relations, Identities, and Communities* (New York: Garland Publishing, 1998), 52.
51. Barber, "Agency in Philippine Women's Labour Migration," 406.

SIX

1. Comments of Arturo Brion, in Philippine Overseas Employment Administration, *Empowering the Global Filipino: POEA Annual Report 2006* (Mandaluyong City, Philippines: POEA, 2007), 7.
2. Other innovations include the Seafarer Registration System, designed to automate the assessment of fees, thereby reducing the processing procedures into two stages (evaluation and payment) and thus to cut back the overall processing times and manage the crowds of prospective seafarers who daily gather at the POEA Building. Another initiative, more geographically focused, is the Employment Permit System (EPS) that tracks the progress of worker-applicants destined to South Korea and the establishment of the online Korean Language Test (KLT) Payment System. Overall, these electronic systems are all designed to more efficiently manage the millions of employment contracts and to better gauge the volatility of the global labor market. See POEA, *Empowering the Global Filipino*. Not surprisingly, this report is available on-line, at www.poea.gov.ph
3. POEA, *Empowering the Global Filipino*, 7.
4. POEA, *Empowering the Global Filipino*, 6.
5. POEA, *Empowering the Global Filipino*, 10.
6. Manfred B. Steger, *Globalization: A Very Short Introduction* (Oxford: Oxford University Press, 2003), 6–7. See also Manfred B. Steger, *Globalism: Market Ideology Meets Terrorism*, 2nd edition (Boulder, CO: Westview Press, 2005).
7. Steger, *Globalization*, 8.
8. Steger, *Globalization*, 9.
9. Steger, *Globalization*, 11.
10. David R. Charles, "Information Technology and Production Systems," in *The Global Economy in Transition*, edited by P.W. Daniels and W.F. Lever (Harlow, Essex: Addison Wesley Longman, 1996), 83–102; at 84–85. See also Peter Dicken, *Global Shift:*

The Internationalization of Economic Activity, 2nd edition (New York: Guilford Press, 1992); Ron Martin, ed., *Money and the Space Economy* (New York: John Wiley & Sons, 1999); Paul L. Knox, John Agnew, and Linda McCarthy, *The Geography of the World Economy*, 4th edition (London: Hodder Arnold, 2003); Steven Flusty, *De-Coca-Colonization: Making the Globe from the Inside Out* (New York: Routledge, 2004).

11. Charles, "Information Technology," 94.
12. Steger, *Globalization*, 12.
13. Steger, *Globalization*, 12.

Bibliography

Abella, Manolo I. "Contemporary Labor Migration from Asia: Policies and Perspectives of Sending Countries," in *International Migration Systems: A Global Approach*, edited by Mary M. Kritz, Lin Lean Lim, and Hania Zlotnik (Oxford: Clarendon Press, 1992).

Abinales, Patricio N. and Donna J. Amoroso. *State and Society in the Philippines* (Lanham, MD: Rowman & Littlefield, 2005).

Adams, Carolyn. "The Philadelphia Experience," *Annals of the American Academy of Political and Social Science* 551 (1997): 222–234.

Agoncillo, Teodoro A. *A Short History of the Philippines* (New York: Mentor, 1969).

Aguilar, Jr., Filomeno V. "Beyond Stereotypes: Human Subjectivity in the Structuring of Global Migration," in *Filipinos in Global Migrations: At Home in the World?*, edited by Filomeno V. Aguilar, Jr. (Manila: Philippine Migration Research Network, 2002), 1–36.

Aguilar, Jr., Filomeno V. "Ritual Passage and the Reconstruction of Selfhood in International Labour Migration," *Sojourn* 14 (1999): 98–139.

Alegado, Dean T. "The Political Economy of International Labor Migration from the Philippines," PhD Dissertation, University of Hawaii at Manoa, 1992.

Almirol, E.B. "Exclusion and Acceptance of Filipinos in America," *Asian Profile* 13 (1985): 395–408.

Anderson, Robert N., with Richard Coller and Rebecca F. Pestano. *Filipinos in Rural Hawaii* (Honolulu: University of Hawaii Press, 1984).

Arnold, Fred, U. Minocha, and James T. Fawcett. "The Changing Face of Asian Immigration to the United States," in *Pacific Bridges: The New Immigration from Asia and the Pacific Islands*, edited by James T. Fawcett and Benjamin V. Cariño (Staten Island, NY: Center for Migration Studies, 1987), 105–152.

Ashdowne, Shaun, William Cartwright, and Liddy Nevile. "A Virtual Atlas on the World Wide Web: Concept, Development and Implementation," in *Proceedings of the 18th ICA/ACI International Cartographic Conference* (1997), 663–672.

Asis, Maruja M.B. "The Return Migration of Filipino Women Migrants: Home, but Not for Good?", in *Female Labour Migration in South-East Asia: Change and Continuity*, edited by C. Wille and B. Passl (Bangkok: Asian Research Centre for Migration, 2001).

Asis, Maruja M.B. "The Overseas Employment Program Policy," in *Philippine Labour Migration: Impact and Policy*, edited by G. Battistella and A. Paganoni (Quezon City: Scalabrini Migration Center, 1992), 68–112.

Bain, David H. *Sitting in Darkness: Americans in the Philippines* (Boston, MA: Houghton Mifflin, 1984).

Ball, Rochelle and Nicola Piper. "Globalisation and Regulation of Citizenship—Filipino Migrant Workers in Japan," *Political Geography* 21 (2002): 1013–1034.

Ballescas, Ma. Rosario. *Filipina Entertainers in Japan: An Introduction* (Quezon City: the Foundation for Nationalist Studies, 1992).

Barber, Pauline G. "Agency in Philippine Women's Labour Migration and Provisional Diaspora," *Women's Studies International Forum* 23 (2000): 399–411.

Bartky, Sandra L. *Femininity and Domination: Studies in the Phenomenology of Oppression* (London: Routledge, 1990).

Bello, Walden, David Kinley, and Elaine Elinson. *Development Debacle: The World Bank in the Philippines* (San Francisco: Institute for Food and Development Policy/Philippine Solidarity Network, 1982).

Berry, Brian J.L., Edgar C. Conkling, and D. Michael Ray. *The Global Economy in Transition*, 2nd edition (Upper Saddle River, NJ: Prentice Hall, 1997).

Blitz, Amy. *The Contested State: American Foreign Policy and Regime Change in the Philippines* (Lanham, MD: Rowman & Littlefield, 2000).

Bonner, Raymond. *Waltzing with a Dictator: The Marcoses and the Making of American Policy* (New York: Vintage Books, 1988).

Bonus, Rick. *Locating Filipino Americans: Ethnicity and the Cultural Politics of Space* (Philadelphia, PA: Temple University Press, 2000).

Boyce, James K. *The Political Economy of Growth and Impoverishment in the Marcos Era* (Quezon City: Ateneo de Manila University Press, 1993).

Brands, H.W. *Bound to Empire: The United States and the Philippines* (New York: Oxford University Press, 1992).

Bryson, John, Nick Henry, David Keeble, and Ron Martin (eds.). *The Economic Geography Reader: Producing and Consuming Global Capitalism* (New York: John Wiley & Sons, 1999).

Buckley, Roger. *The United States in the Asia-Pacific since 1945* (New York: Cambridge University Press, 2002).

Caces, Fe, Fred Arnold, James Fawcett, and Robert Gardner. "Shadow Households and Competing Auspices: Migration Behavior in the Philippines," *Journal of Development Economics* 17 (1985): 5–25.

Cahill, D. *Intermarriages in International Contexts: A Study of Filipina Women Married to Australian, Japanese and Swiss Men* (Quezon City: Scalabrini Migration Center, 1990).

Caoili, Manuel A. *The Origins of Metropolitan Manila: A Political and Social Analysis* (Quezon City: University of the Philippines Press, 1999).

Casco, Ricardo R. *Managing International Labour Migration and the Framework for the Deregulation of the POEA* (Manila: POEA, 1997).

Casco, Ricardo R. *Full Disclosure Policy: A Philosophical Orientation* (Manila: POEA, 1995).

Castles, Stephen and Mark J. Miller. *The Age of Migration: International Population Movements in the Modern World* (New York: Guilford Press, 1993).

Catholic Institute for International Relations. *The Labour Trade: Filipino Migrant Workers Around the World* (London: CIIR, 1987).

Chang, Grace. *Disposable Domestics: Immigrant Women Workers in the Global Economy* (Cambridge, MA: South End Press, 2000).

Chant, Sylvia and Sarah McIlwaine. *Women of a Lesser Cost: Female Labour, Foreign Exchange and Philippine Development* (Quezon City: Ateneo de Manila University Press, 1995).

Charles, David R. "Information Technology and Production Systems," in *The Global Economy in Transition*, edited by P.W. Daniels and W.F. Lever (Harlow, Essex: Addison Wesley Longman, 1996), 83–103.

Chin, Christine B.N. *In Service and Servitude: Foreign Female Domestic Workers and the Malaysian "Modernity" Project* (New York: Columbia University Press, 1998).

Chin, Christine B.N. "Walls of Silence and Late Twentieth Century Representations of the Foreign Female Domestic Worker: The Case of Filipina and Indonesian Female Servants in Malaysia," *International Migration Review* 31 (1996): 353–385.

Choguill, Charles L. "Urban Policy as Poverty Alleviation: The Experience of the Philippines," *Habitat International* 25 (2001): 1–13.

Clark, David. *Urban World/Global City* (New York: Routledge, 1996).

Cohen, R. *Global Diasporas: An Introduction* (Cambridge, MA: Harvard University Press, 1997).

Constable, Nicole. *Maid to Order in Hong Kong: Stories of Filipina Workers* (Ithaca, NY: Cornell University Press, 1997).

Cordova, Fred. *Filipinos: Forgotten Asian Americans, A Pictorial Essay, 1763-circa 1963* (Dubuque, IA: Kendall/Hunt, 1983).

Coronel, Sheila (ed.). *Pork and Other Perks: Corruption and Governance in the Philippines* (Pasig City: Philippine Centre for Investigative Journalism, 1998).

Cox, Kevin R. "Globalization and the Politics of Distribution: A Critical Assessment," in *Spaces of Globalization: Reasserting the Power of the Local*, edited by Kevin R. Cox (New York: Guilford Press, 1997), 115–136.

Crang, Mike, Phil Crang, and Jon May (eds.). *Virtual Geographies: Bodies, Space and Relations* (New York: Routledge, 1999).

Crouchett, Lorraine J. *Filipinos in California: From the Days of the Galleons to the Present* (El Cerrito, CA: Downey Place Publishing, 1982).

Cruz, Victoria P. *Seasonal Orphans and Solo Parents: The Impact of Overseas Migration* (Quezon City: Scalabrini Migration Center, 1987).

Cruz, Victoria P. and Anthony Paganoni. *Filipinas in Migration: Big Bills and Small Change* (Quezon City: Scalabrini Migration Center, 1989).

David, Randolf S. "Filipino Workers in Japan: Vulnerability and Survival," *Kasarinlan* 6 (1991): 8–23.

Dear, Michael J. and Steven Flusty. "The Iron Lotus: Los Angeles and Post-modern Urbanism," *Annals of the American Academy of Political and Social Science* 551 (1997): 151–163.

De Dios, Aurora. "Japayuki-san: Filipinas at Risk," in *Filipino Women Overseas Contract Workers . . . At What Cost?*, edited by Mary R. Palma-Beltran and Aurora Javate de Dios (Manila: Goodwill Trading Co., 1992), 39–58.

Dicken, Peter. *Global Shift: The Internationalization of Economic Activity*, 2nd edition (New York: Guilford Press, 1992).

Doeppers, Daniel F. *Manila, 1900–1941: Social Change in a Late Colonial Metropolis* (Ithaca, NY: Yale University Southeast Asian Studies, 1984).

Elkins, D.J. "Globalization, Telecommunication, and Virtual Ethnic Communities," *International Political Science Review* 18 (1997): 139–152.

Enloe, Cynthia. *Bananas, Beaches & Bases: Making Feminist Sense of International Politics* (Berkeley: University of California Press, 1989).

Escobar, Arturo. *Encountering Development: The Making and Unmaking of the Third World* (Princeton, NJ: Princeton University Press, 1995).

Espiritu, Yen Le. *Home Bound: Filipino American Lives Across Cultures, Communities and Countries* (Berkeley: University of California Press, 2003).

Espiritu, Yen Le. "Filipino Settlements in the United States," in *Filipino American Lives*, edited by Yen Le Espiritu (Philadelphia, PA: Temple University Press, 1995), 1–36.

Everard, Jerry. *Virtual States: The Internet and the Boundaries of the Nation-State* (New York: Routledge, 2000).

Eviota, Elizabeth Uy. *The Political Economy of Gender: Women and the Sexual Division of Labour in the Philippines* (London: Zed Books, 1992).

Ewers, Michael C. "Migrants, Markets and Multinationals: Competition Among World Cities for the Highly Skilled," *Geojournal* 68 (2007): 119–130.

Flusty, Steven. *De-Coca-Colonization: Making the Globe from the Inside Out* (New York: Routledge, 2004).

Foucault, Michel. *Discipline and Punish* (New York: Vintage Press, 1979).

Friedmann, John. "Where We Stand: A Decade of World City Research," in

World Cities in a World-System, edited by Paul L. Knox and Peter J. Taylor (London: Cambridge University Press, 1995), 21–47.

Friedmann, John. "The World City Hypothesis," *Development and Change* 17 (1986): 69–83.

Friedmann, John and Goetz Wolff. "World City Formation: An Agenda for Research and Action," *International Journal of Urban and Regional Research* 6 (1982): 309–344.

Friend, T. *Between Two Empires: The Ordeal of the Philippines, 1929–1946* (New Haven, CT: Yale University Press, 1965).

Gamburd, Michelle R. *The Kitchen Spoon's Handle: Transnationalism and Sri Lanka's Migrant Housemaids* (Ithaca, NY: Cornell University Press, 2000).

Golay, Frank H. *Face of Empire: United States–Philippine Relations, 1898–1946* (Quezon City: Ateneo de Manila University Press, 1997).

Gonzalez, III, Joaquin L. *Philippine Labour Migration: Critical Dimensions of Public Policy* (Singapore: Institute of Southeast Asian Studies, 1998).

Greene, Richard P. "Chicago's New Immigrants, Indigenous Poor, and Edge Cities," *Annals of the American Academy of Political and Social Science* 551 (1997): 178–190.

Guevarra, Anna R. "Managing 'Vulnerabilities' and 'Empowering' Migrant Filipina Workers: The Philippines' Overseas Employment Program," *Social Identities* 12 (2006): 523–541.

Haruhi, T. "The Japanese Sex Industry: A Heightening Appetite for Asian Women," *AMPO Japan-Quarterly Review* 18 (1986): 7–76.

Harvey, David. *A Brief History of Neoliberalism* (Oxford: Oxford University Press, 2005).

Harvey, David. *Spaces of Hope* (Cambridge, MA: Blackwell, 2000).

Hawes, Gary. *The Philippine State and the Marcos Regime: The Politics of Export* (Ithaca, NY: Cornell University Press, 1987).

Herod, Andrew. "Labor as an Agent of Globalization and as a Global Agent," in *Spaces of Globalization: Reasserting the Power of the Local*, edited by Kevin R. Cox (New York: Guilford Press, 1997), 167–200.

Hilsdon, Anne-Marie. "Transnationalism and Agency in East Malaysia: Filipina Migrants in the Nightlife Industries," *The Australian Journal of Anthropology* 18 (2007): 172–193.

Hing, Bill Ong. *Making and Remaking Asian America Through Immigration Policy, 1850–1990* (Stanford, CA: Stanford University Press, 1993).

Hondagneu-Sotelo, Pierrette. *Domestic Employment Agencies in Los Angeles* (Los Angeles: University of Southern California, Southern California Studies Center, 1997).

Hondagneu-Sotelo, Pierrette. *Gendered Transitions: Mexican Experiences of Immigration* (Berkeley: University of California Press, 1994).

Huang, Shirlena S. and Brenda S.A. Yeoh. "Ties that Bind: State Policy and

Migrant Female Domestic Workers in Singapore," *Geoforum* 27, 4 (1996): 479–493.

Huguet, Jerrold W. "The Future of International Migration Within Asia," *Asian and Pacific Migration Journal* 1 (1992): 250–277.

Hui, Alison Wee Siu. *Assembling Gender: The Making of the Malay Female Labour* (Selangor, Malaysia: Strategic Info Research Development, n.d.).

Humphrey, Michael. "Asian Women Workers in the Middle East: Domestic Servants in Jordan," *Asian Migrant* 4 (1991): 53–60.

Hutchinson, Jane. "Pressure on Policy in the Philippines," in *The Political Economy of Southeast Asia: An Introduction*, edited by G. Rodan, K. Hewison, and R. Robison (Oxford: Oxford University Press, 1997).

Jayasuriya, S.K. "The Politics of Economic Policy in the Philippines During the Marcos Era," in *Southeast Asia in the 1980s: The Politics of Economic Crisis*, edited by R. Robison, K. Hewison, and R. Higgot (London: Allen & Unwin, 1987).

Jordan, Tim. *Cyberpower: The Culture and Politics of Cyberspace and the Internet* (New York: Routledge, 1999).

Jose, V.R. "Philippine External Debt Problems: The Marcos Years," *Journal of Contemporary Asia* 21 (1991): 222–245.

Karnow, Stanley. *In Our Image: America's Empire in the Philippines* (New York: Random House, 1989).

Kathirithamby-Wells, J. "The Age of Transition: The Mid-Eighteenth to the Early Nineteenth Centuries," in *The Cambridge History of Southeast Asia: Volume Two: From c. 1500 to c. 1800*, edited by Nicholas Tarling (Cambridge: Cambridge University Press, 1999), 228–275.

Kelly, Philip F. "Urbanization and the Politics of Land in the Manila Region," *Annals, American Academy of Political and Social Science* 590 (2003): 170–187.

Kelly, Philip F. *Landscapes of Globalization: Human Geographies of Economic Change in the Philippines* (New York: Routledge, 2000).

Kelly, Philip F. "The Geographies and Politics of Globalization," *Progress in Human Geography* 23 (1999): 379–400.

Kelly, Philip F. "Globalization, Power and the Politics of Scale in the Philippines," *Geoforum* 28 (1997): 151–171.

Kempadoo, K. "Introduction: Globalizing Sex Workers' Rights," in *Global Sex Workers: Rights, Resistance, and Redefinition*, edited by K. Kempadoo and J. Doezema (New York: Routledge, 1998).

Kerkvliet, Benedict J. *The Huk Rebellion: A Study of Peasant Revolt in the Philippines* (Lanham, MD: Rowman & Littlefield, 2002 [1977]).

Keyso, R. *Women of Okinawa: Nine Voices from a Garrison Island* (Ithaca, NY: Cornell University Press, 2000).

Khan, M. *Labour Administration: Profile on the Philippines* (Bangkok: International Labour Organization, Asian and Pacific Regional Centre for Labour Administration, 1988).

Kitchin, Rob. *Cyberspace: The World in the Wires* (New York: John Wiley & Sons, 1998).

Knox, Paul L. "World Cities in a World-System," in *World Cities in a World-System*, edited by Paul L. Knox and Peter J. Taylor (London: Cambridge University Press, 1995), 3–20.

Knox, Paul L., John Agnew, and Linda McCarthy. *The Geography of the World Economy*, 4th edition (London: Hodder Arnold, 2003).

Knox, Paul L. and Peter J. Taylor (eds.). *World Cities in a World-System* (London: Cambridge University Press, 1995).

Kollock, Peter and Marc A. Smith. "Communities in Cyberspace," in *Communities in Cyberspace*, edited by Marc A. Smith and Peter Kollock (New York: Routledge, 1999), 3–25.

Kuruvilla, S. "Economic Development Strategies, Industrial Relations Policies and Workplace IR/HR Practices in Southeast Asia," in *The Comparative Political Economy of Industrial Relations*, edited by K. Wever and L. Turner (Madison: Industrial Relations Association Series, University of Wisconsin -Madison, 1995).

Lauby, Jennifer and Oded Stark. "Individual Migration as a Family Strategy: Young Women in the Philippines," *Population Studies* 42 (1988): 473–486.

Law, Lisa. *Sex Work in Southeast Asia: The Place of Desire in a Time of AIDs* (London: Routledge, 2000).

Lehto, Lassi, Jaakko Kähkönen, and Tiina Kilpeläinen. "WWW-technology as a Means of Transfer and Visualization of Geographic Objects," in *Proceedings of the 18th ICA/ACI International Cartographic Conference* (1997), 681–689.

Lim, L.Y.C. "Capitalism, Imperialism, and Patriarchy: The Dilemma of Third-World Women Workers in Multinational Factories," in *Women, Men and the International Division of Labor*, edited by J. Nash and M.P. Fernández-Kelly (Albany: State University of New York Press, 1983).

Lindio-McGovern, Ligaya. "Alienation and Labor Export in the Context of Globalization: Filipino Migrant Domestic Workers in Taiwan and Hong Kong," *Critical Asian Studies* 36 (2004): 217–238.

Linn, Brian McAllister. *The Philippine War, 1899–1902* (Lawrence: University Press of Kansas, 2000).

Malcolm, Roy. "Immigration Problems on the Pacific Coast (part III)," *Current History* 33 (1931): 726–728.

Marshall, N. and P. Wood. *Services and Space: Key Aspects of Urban and Regional Development* (New York: John Wiley & Sons, 1995).

Martin, Ron (ed.). *Money and the Space Economy* (New York: John Wiley & Sons, 1999).

Matsui, Y. *Women's Asia* (Atlantic Highlands, NJ: Zed Books, 1987).

May, Glenn A. *Social Engineering in the Philippines: The Aims, Execution, and Impact of*

American Colonial Policy, 1900–1913 (Quezon City: New Day Publishers, 1984).

McCoy, Alfred W. "The Social History of an Archipelago: Introduction," in *Philippine Social History: Global Trade and Local Transformations*, edited by Alfred W. McCoy and Ed. C. de Jesus (Quezon City: Ateneo de Manila University Press, 1982).

McCuskey, William. "Current Developments in the International Market for Seafarers," *Overseas Employment Info Series* 4 (1991): 13–20.

McKay, Deirdre and Carol Brady. "Practices of Place-Making: Globalisation and Locality in the Philippines," *Asia Pacific Viewpoint* 46 (2005): 89–103.

McMahon, Robert J. *The Limits to Empire: The United States and Southeast Asia since World War II* (New York: Columbia University Press, 1999).

McWilliams, Carey. *Brothers Under the Skin* (Boston, MA: Little, Brown, 1964).

Medina, Belen. *The Filipino Family* (Manila: University of the Philippines Press, 1991).

Miller, Stuart C. *"Benevolent Assimilation": The American Conquest of the Philippines, 1899–1903* (New Haven, CT: Yale University Press, 1982).

Moon, Katherine H.S. *Sex Among Allies: Military Prostitution in U.S.–Korea Relations* (New York: Columbia University Press, 1997).

Nakamatsu, Tomoko. "International Marriage through Introduction Agencies: Social and Legal Realities of 'Asian' Wives of Japanese Men," in *Wife or Worker? Asian Women and Migration*, edited by Nicola Piper and Mina Roces (Lanham, MD: Rowman & Littlefield, 2003), 181–201.

Naoki, I. "The Traffic in Japayuki-san," *Japan Quarterly* 34 (1987): 84–88.

National Economic Development Authority. *The Medium-Term Philippine Development Plan, 2001–2004, with the 2001 State of the Nation Address* (Manila: NEDA, 2001).

National Statistics Office. *Philippine Yearbook* (Manila: National Statistics Office, 1989).

Ngai, Pun. *Made in China: Women Factory Workers in a Global Workplace* (Durham, NC: Duke University Press, 2005).

Nograles-Lumbera, C. "The Traffic in Japayuki-san," *Education Forum Tap* 7 (1988): 1–10.

Nolledo, J.N. (ed.). *The Labor Code of the Philippines, with Implementing Regulations, Related Laws, and other Issuances* (Manila: National Bookstore, 1993).

Nordyke, Eleanor C. *The Peopling of Hawai'i*, 2nd edition (Honolulu: University of Hawaii Press, 1989).

Oishi, Nana. *Women in Motion: Globalization, State Policies, and Labor Migration in Asia* (Stanford, CA: Stanford University Press, 2005).

Okamura, Jonathan Y. *Imagining the Filipino American Diaspora: Transnational Relations, Identities, and Communities* (New York: Garland Publishing, 1998).

Ong, Aihwa. *Flexible Citizenship: The Cultural Logics of Transnationality* (Durham, NC: Duke University Press, 1999).

Ople, Blas. "The Filipino Diaspora: A Global Tribe?", *Overseas Employment Info Series* 6 (1993): 20–23.

Overholt, W.H. "Pressures and Policies: Prospects for Cory Aquino's Philippines," in *Rebuilding a Nation: Philippine Challenges and American Policy*, edited by C.H. Lande (Washington, DC: Washington Institute Press, 1987).

Papademetriou, Demetrios G. "Managing Rapid and Deep Change in the Newest Age of Migration," in *The Politics of Migration: Managing Opportunity, Conflict and Change*, edited by Sarah Spencer (Malden, MA: Blackwell, 2003), 39–58.

Parnreiter, Christof. "Mexico: The Making of a Global City," in *Global Networks, Linked Cities*, edited by Saskia Sassen (New York: Routledge, 2002), 145–182.

Parreñas, Rhacel. *Servants of Globalization: Women, Migration, and Domestic Work* (Stanford, CA: Stanford University Press, 2001).

Parreñas, Rhacel. "New Household Forms, Old Family Values: The Formation and Reproduction of the Filipino Transnational Family in Los Angeles," in *Contemporary Asian America: A Multidisciplinary Reader*, edited by Min Zhou and J.V. Gatewood (New York: New York University Press, 2000).

Peck, Jamie. *Work-Place: The Social Regulation of Labor Markets* (New York: Guilford Press, 1996).

Peterson, Michael P. "Trends in Internet Map Use," in *Proceedings of the 18th ICA/ACI International Cartographic Conference* (1997), 1635–1642.

Philippine Overseas Employment Administration. *Empowering the Global Filipino: POEA Annual Report 2006* (Mandaluyong City, Philippines: POEA, 2007).

Philippine Overseas Employment Administration. *POEA Annual Report 2000* (Manila: POEA, 2001).

Philippine Overseas Employment Administration. *Information Primer for the Deployment of Overseas Performing Artists* (Manila: POEA, 1998).

Philippine Overseas Employment Administration. *Migrant Workers and Overseas Filipinos Act of 1995: Republic Act 8042 and Its Implementing Rules and Regulations* (Manila: Department of Labour and Employment, 1996).

Philippine Overseas Employment Administration. "Overseas Employment: The Challenge of the Philippines 2000—a Policy Statement and Program of Action." Unpublished mimeograph (Manila: POEA, 1994).

Philippine Overseas Employment Administration. "Market Development: Seeking Purpose and Promise for Filipino Skills," *Overseas Employment Info Series* 1, 1 (1988): 5–9.

Pido, Antonio J.A. *The Pilipinos in America: Macro/Micro Dimensions of Immigration and Integration* (New York: Center for Migration Studies, 1986).

Piper, Nicola and Mina Roces (eds.). *Wife or Worker: Asian Women and Migration* (Lanham, MD: Rowman & Littlefield, 2003).

Posadas, Barbara M. "At a Crossroad: Filipino American History and the Old-Timers' Generation," *Amerasia*, 13 (1986–1987): 85–97.

Posadas, Barbara M. and Roland L. Guyotte. "Unintentional Immigrants: Chicago's Filipino Foreign Students Become Settlers, 1900–1941," *Journal of American Ethnic History* 9 (1990): 26–48.

Pratt, Geraldine, in collaboration with the Philippine Women Centre. "Inscribing Domestic Work on Filipina Bodies," in *Places Through the Body*, edited by Heidi Nast and Steven Pile (London: Routledge, 1998), 283–304.

Putzel, James. *A Captive Land: The Politics of Agrarian Reform in the Philippines* (Manila: Ateneo de Manila University Press, 1992).

Pye, Lucian W. *Asian Power and Politics: The Cultural Dimensions of Authority* (Cambridge, MA: Harvard University Press, 1985).

Ramos, F.V. "Overseas Employment: An Indispensable Program," *Overseas Employment Info Series* 5, 2 (1992): 6–12.

Reed, Robert R. *Colonial Manila: The Context of Hispanic Urbanism and Process of Morphogenesis* (Berkeley: University of California Press, 1978).

Robinson, Jennifer. "Global and World Cities: A View from off the Map," *International Journal of Urban and Regional Research* 26 (2002): 531–554.

Rodriguez, Robyn M. "Migrant Heroes: Nationalism, Citizenship and the Politics of Filipino Migrant Labor," *Citizenship Studies* 6 (2002): 341–356.

Rosenberg, David A. "The Changing Structure of Philippine Government from Marcos to Aquino," in *Rebuilding a Nation: Philippine Challenges and American Policy*, edited by C.H. Lande (Washington, DC: Washington Institute Press, 1987), 329–350.

Ryan, C. and C.M. Hall. *Sex Tourism: Marginal People and Liminalities* (New York: Routledge, 2001).

Salazar, Zeus A. "The Outflow of Filipinos to the Bundesrepublik Deutschland since the 1960s," *Philippine Journal of Public Administration* 33 (1987): 463–486.

Salita, Domingo C. *Geography and Natural Resources of the Philippines* (Quezon City: JMC Press, 1997).

Samers, Michael. "Immigration and the Global City Hypothesis: Towards an Alternative Research Agenda," *International Journal of Urban and Regional Research* 26 (2002): 389–402.

Sassen, Saskia. "On Concentration and Centrality in the Global City," in *World Cities in a World-System*, edited by Paul L. Knox and Peter J. Taylor (London: Cambridge University Press, 1995), 63–75.

Sassen, Saskia. *Cities in a World Economy* (Thousand Oaks, CA: Pine Forge Press, 1994).

Sassen, Saskia. "Economic Internationalization: The New Migration in Japan and the United States," *International Migration* 31 (1993): 73–99.

Sassen, Saskia. *The Global City: New York, London, Tokyo* (Princeton, NJ: Princeton University Press, 1991).

Sassen, Saskia. *The Mobility of Labor and Capital: A Study in International Investment and Labor Flow* (Cambridge: Cambridge University Press, 1988).

Scharrenberg, Paul. "The Philippine Problem: Attitude of American Labor Toward Filipino Immigrants and Philippine Independence," *Pacific Affairs* 2 (1929): 49–54.

Schiller, Nina Glick, Linda Basch, and Cristina Szanton Blanc. "From Immigrant to Transmigrant: Theorizing Transnational Migration," *Anthropological Quarterly* 68 (1995): 48–63.

Seekins, Donald. "Historical Setting," in *Philippines: A Country Study*, edited by Frederica M. Bunge (Washington, DC: US Government Printing Office, 1983), 1–56.

Shalom, Stephen Rosskamm. *The United States and the Philippines: A Study of Neocolonialism* (Quezon City: New Day Publishers, 1986).

Shatkin, Gavin. "Global Cities of the South: Emerging Perspectives on Growth and Inequality," *Cities* 24 (2006): 1–15.

Shatkin, Gavin. "Colonial Capital, Modernist Capital, Global Capital: The Changing Political Symbolism of Urban Space in Metro Manila, the Philippines," *Pacific Affairs* 78 (2005–2006): 577–600.

Short, John Rennie and Yeong-Hyun Kim. *Globalization and the City* (Singapore: Longman, 1999).

Silvey, Rachel. "Transnational Domestication: State Power and Indonesian Migrant Women in Saudi Arabia," *CLARA Working Paper No. 17* (Amsterdam: IIAS/IISG, 2004).

Skeldon, Ronald. "International Migration Within and From the East and Southeast Asian Region: A Review Essay," *Asian and Pacific Migration Journal* 1 (1992): 19–63.

Smith, Marc A. and Peter Kollock (eds.). *Communities in Cyberspace* (New York: Routledge, 1999).

Stanley, P.W. *A Nation in the Making: The Philippines and the United States, 1899–1921* (Cambridge, MA: Harvard University Press, 1974).

Steger, Manfred B. *Globalism: Market Ideology Meets Terrorism*, 2nd edition (Boulder, CO: Westview Press, 2005).

Steger, Manfred B. *Globalization: A Very Short Introduction* (Oxford: Oxford University Press, 2003).

Steinberg, David J. *The Philippines: A Singular and Plural Place*, 3rd edition (Boulder, CO: Westview Press, 1994).

Stull, Andrew and Duane Griffen. *Life on the Internet: Geosciences—A Student's Guide* (Englewood Cliffs, NJ: Prentice Hall, 1996).

Sturdevant, Saundra and Brenda Stoltzfus. *Let the Good Times Roll: Prostitution and the U.S. Military in Asia* (New York: New Press, 1993).

Sturdevant, Saundra. "Okinawa Then and Now," in *Let the Good Times Roll: Prostitution and the U.S. Military in Asia*, edited by Saundra Sturdevant and Brenda Stoltzfus (New York: New Press, 1993).

Suzuki, Nobue. "Women Imagined, Women Imaging: Re/presentations of Filipinas in Japan since the 1980s," *U.S.-Japan Women's Journal* 19 (2000): 142–175.

Suzuki, Nobue. "Between Two Shores: Transnational Projects and Filipina Wives In/From Japan," *Women's Studies International Forum* 23 (2000): 431–444.

Tadiar, Neferti Xina M. "Domestic Bodies of the Philippines," *Sojourn* 12 (1997): 153–191.

Takaki, Ronald. *Pau Hana: Plantation Life and Labor in Hawaii, 1835–1920* (Honolulu: University of Hawaii Press, 1983).

Teodoro, Luis V. *Out of This Struggle: The Filipinos in Hawaii* (Honolulu: University of Hawaii Press, 1981).

Timberman, David G. *A Changeless Land: Continuity and Change in Philippine Politics* (New York: M.E. Sharpe, 1991).

Trager, Lillian. *The City Connection: Migration and Family Interdependence in the Philippines* (Ann Arbor: University of Michigan Press, 1988).

Tyner, James A. *America's Strategy in Southeast Asia: From the Cold War to the Terror War* (Boulder, CO: Rowman & Littlefield, 2007).

Tyner, James A. *Oriental Bodies: Discourse and Discipline in U.S. Immigration Policy, 1875–1942* (Lanham, MD: Lexington Books, 2006).

Tyner, James A. "Filipinos: The Invisible Ethnic Community," in *Contemporary Ethnic Geographies in America*, edited by Ines M. Miyares and Christopher A. Airries (Boulder, CO: Rowman & Littlefield, 2006), 251–270.

Tyner, James A. *Iraq, Terror, and the Philippines' Will to War* (Boulder, CO: Rowman & Littlefield, 2005).

Tyner, James A. *Made in the Philippines: Gendered Discourses and the Making of Migrants* (London: Routledge, 2004).

Tyner, James A. "Scaled Sexuality and the Migration of Filipina Overseas Contract Workers," *Philippine Population Review* 1 (2002): 103–123.

Tyner, James A. "Geographics of Identity: The Migrant Experiences of Filipinas in Northeast Ohio," *Asia Pacific Viewpoint* 43 (2002): 311–326.

Tyner, James A. "Migrant Labor and the Politics of Scale: Gendering the Philippine State," *Asia Pacific Viewpoint* 41 (2000): 131–154.

Tyner, James A. "The Politics of Employment: Overseas Job Fairs and Philippine Labor Recruitment," *Applied Geographic Studies* 3 (1999): 1–11.

Tyner, James A. "Constructing Images, Constructing Policy: The Case of

Filipina Migrant Performing Artists," *Gender, Place and Culture: A Journal of Feminist Geography* 4 (1997): 19–35.

Tyner, James A. "Constructions of Filipina Migrant Entertainers," *Gender, Place and Culture: A Journal of Feminist Geography* 3 (1996): 77–93.

Tyner, James A. and Olaf Kuhlke. "Pan-National Identities: Representations of the Philippine Diaspora on the World Wide Web," *Asia Pacific Viewpoint* 41 (2000): 231–252.

Van Hear, N. *New Diasporas: The Mass Exodus, Dispersal and Regrouping of Migrant Communities* (Seattle: University of Washington Press, 1998).

Villegas, B. "The Economic Crisis," in *Crisis in the Philippines: The Marcos Era and Beyond*, edited by J. Bresnan (Princeton, NJ: Princeton University Press, 1986).

Warf, Barney and R. Erickson. "Introduction: Globalization and the U.S. City System," *Urban Geography* 17 (1996): 1–4.

Warf, Barney and Brian Holly. "The Rise and Fall and Rise of Cleveland," *Annals of the American Academy of Political and Social Science* 551 (1997): 208–221.

Weeks, John R. *Population Geography: An Introduction to Concepts and Issues*, 9th edition (Belmont, CA: Wadsworth/Thomson Learning, 2005).

Welch, Richard E. *Response to Imperialism: The United States and the Philippine-American War, 1899–1902* (Chapel Hill: University of North Carolina Press, 1979).

Woodward, Peter N. *Oil and Labor in the Middle East: Saudi Arabia and the Oil Boom* (New York: Praeger Press, 1988).

Wurfel, David. *Filipino Politics: Development and Decay* (Ithaca, NY: Cornell University Press, 1988).

Yea, Sallie. "Labour of Love: Filipina Entertainer's Narratives of Romance and Relationships with GIs in US Military Camp Towns in Korea," *Women's Studies International Forum* 28 (2005): 456–472.

Yea, Sallie. "Runaway Brides: Anxieties of Identity Among Trafficked Filipina Entertainers in South Korea," *Singapore Journal of Tropical Geography* 25 (2004): 180–197.

Index

For Product Safety Concerns and Information please contact our EU representative GPSR@taylorandfrancis.com
Taylor & Francis Verlag GmbH, Kaufingerstraße 24, 80331 München, Germany

www.ingramcontent.com/pod-product-compliance
Lightning Source LLC
LaVergne TN
LVHW021124300926
849160LV00010B/855
* 9 7 8 0 4 1 5 9 5 8 0 7 3 *